GREAT NAMES FOR GREAT PETS

- ❧ **Snoopy** is the sixth most popular name for a *cat*!
- ❧ A sentry dog named **Chips** was awarded a Silver Star and a Purple Heart during World War II.
- ❧ **Handsome Dan** was the name of Yale's original mascot bulldog.
- ❧ **Figaro** was the name of Gepetto's cat in the Walt Disney animated feature film *Pinocchio* (1940).
- ❧ **Balto** was the name of the dog who led a sled team in Alaska to deliver serum to Eskimos in Nome. (A statue of the dog stands near the zoo in New York City's Central Park.)
- ❧ **Streaky** was Superman's super cat in the comic books.
- ❧ **Grimalkin** was the name of the demon spirit in the form of a cat in Shakespeare's *Macbeth*.
- ❧ **Igloo** was the name of Admiral Byrd's fox terrier, who accompanied Byrd on his explorations in both the Artic and the Antarctic.
- ❧ **Marcus** was the name of James Dean's Siamese cat, a gift from Elizabeth Taylor.

FAMOUS NAMES FOR YOUR PAMPERED PET

Ed Lucaire

HarperPaperbacks
A Division of HarperCollins*Publishers*

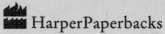
HarperPaperbacks
A Division of HarperCollins*Publishers*
10 East 53rd Street, New York, N.Y. 10022-5299

ISBN 0-06-101056-1

HarperCollins®, ▓®, and HarperPaperbacks™
are trademarks of HarperCollins*Publishers* Inc.

Cover illustrations by Rich Rossiter

First printing: December 1996

Printed in the United States of America

Visit HarperPaperbacks on the World Wide Web at
http://www.harpercollins.com/paperbacks

❖ 10 9 8 7 6 5 4 3 2 1

To the Delta Society*, which recognizes
the importance of cats and
dogs in the lives of many people, especially those
who are disabled and bedridden, some of whom
cannot function without the aid, comfort, and
companionship of their feline
and canine friends.

*The Delta Society
289 Perimeter Road East
Renton, WA 98055-1329
Phone: 206-226-7357
Fax: 206-235-1076

ACKNOWLEDGMENTS

American Kennel Club, Animal Humane Association, the Delta Society, Matthew Margolis of the National Institute of Dog Training, *TV Guide*, Lesly Atlas, Sharon Morey, Alex Hoyt, Kelly Chian, Michele Bonomo, Steven Lindberg, and Scotland by the Yard (Quechee, Vermont).

CONTENTS

The Naming of Cats is a difficult matter,
It isn't just one of your holiday games . . .
. . . But I tell you, a cat needs a name that's particular,
A name that's peculiar, and more dignified, else how
can he keep up his tail perpendicular . . .

T.S. Eliot
"The Naming of Cats"
The Old Possum's Book of Practical Cats

When you meet a cat named Ginger or Puss,
you can be sure that his or her owner has
insufficient respect for his cat. Such plebeian
and unimaginative names are not given cats
by true cat lovers.

Michael Joseph
author, publisher
Charles: The Story of a Friendship

INTRODUCTION

As the author of several books about famous people, I have amassed thousands of facts about the rich and famous of the past and present, including the names and breeds of their pet dogs and cats (and sometimes lions and tigers!)

When HarperCollins asked me to write a book about the naming of cats and dogs, I decided to compile a book of the many names that famous people have given their pampered pets. As a movie and television buff, I also wanted to include the names of cats and dogs that audiences have enjoyed through the years in the movies, Broadway shows, and on television. Such a book, of course, would be incomplete without including the names of cats in literature, cats of accomplishment, cat record setters, and other noteworthy felines.

The fact is that celebrities go about naming their pets just like most other people do. Here are some of the ways:

Coat and Coloration Names

A black cat, considered bad luck by some, is a joy to others, hence the names of writer Doris Lessing's cat (Black Cat) and U.S. president Calvin Coolidge's cat (Blackie). Writer Ernest Hemingway's spaniel was named Blackie and so was one of U.S. president John F. Kennedy's dogs. Similarly U.S. president Lyndon B. Johnson owned a white collie named Blanco, the Spanish word for "white." Many cats receive the name Tiger not for their fierceness but merely for their orange and black stripes.

Breed and Country Specific Names

A Siamese cat, a chow chow dog, a French poodle, German shepherds, etc., often prompt names appropriate to their breed. Names like Ming, Chan, and Yang are used for Oriental breeds of cats and dogs. Beatle drummer Ringo Starr, for example, named his chow chows Ying and Yang. Gigi, Fifi and Bijou are common names for French poodles, although Tennessee Williams named his Boston bulldog Gigi. Schotzie, Wolfgang and Fritzie are good names for German shepherds, Dachshunds and Schnauzers.

Most Common Names and Trendiness

Some people "go with the flow," sometimes unwittingly, and name their cats and dogs what everyone else seems to be naming their pets. Samantha, Ginger, and Max are among the common names given to cats as well as dogs.

Royalty Names

The titles of royalty are always popular names for cats and dogs, perhaps because owners often treat their pets like royalty. King, Lady, Duke, Prince, Princess, Queen, and Queenie are among the top names given to cats and dogs. People such as U.S. presidents Ronald Reagan and George Washington owned dogs named Lady. Actor Rudolph Valentino and writer William Wordsworth are among the notables who owned dogs named Prince.

Famous people

Legendary nurse Florence Nightingale named her dozens of cats after the names of famous statesmen such as Disraeli, Gladstone, and Bismarck. Famous people even name their pets after other famous people. British prime minister Winston Churchill named his cat after the British admiral Horatio Nelson. Country singer Dolly Parton gave one of her dogs the name Mark Spitz after the Olympic swimmer. It helped that Dolly's dog was a spitz.

Movie/TV/Cartoon Pets

Snoopy is probably one of the most recognized names of a dog in the world. Snoopy, of course, is the beagle in the "Peanuts" cartoon strip originated by cartoonist Charles Shulz. It consistently ranks as a popular name for dogs and, would you believe, cats too. Elvis Presley and daughter Lisa Marie once owned a dog that they named Snoopy.

Morris the cat, famous for his 9 Lives cat food commercial, has inspired many cat owners to name their cats Morris, including former M*A*S*H television actor Mike Farrell.

Duos and Trios

When people acquire two cats or dogs at the same time, it is tempting, if not inevitable to give them names of already popularly-known duos. Daytime television talk-show host Regis Philbin has cats named Ashley and Scarlett. Fitness guru Richard Simmons has Dalmatian dogs named Ashley, Scarlett, and a few other Gone With the Wind characters. Actress Tiffani-Amber Thiessen has Golden retrievers named Bonnie and Clyde. U.S. president Ronald Reagan back when he was married to actress Jane Wyman, named their two Scotch terriers Scotch and Soda.

Of course, with trios and triplets, we know there are many Larry, Moe and Curleys, and Grouchos, Chicos and Harpos in the pet world out there.

Role Models

Actors sometimes name their pets after roles with which they are identified. Television actor James Arness named his Bichon frisé dogs Matt and Miss Kitty after his role (and Amanda Blake's) in his long-running television series *Gunsmoke*. Actor William Shatner, widely known as Captain Kirk in the *Star Trek* television series and features, named his Doberman pinscher Kirk. Singer-actor Robert Goulet named his German shepherd Lance, short for Lancelot, his role in the Broadway musical *Camelot*.

Names You Can Drink To

Some celebrities have actually named their pets after alcoholic drinks. Among these notables are sports announcer Frank Gifford and his wife Kathie Lee, who named their Bichon frisés Chablis and Chardonnay, singer-actress Doris Day, who gave one of her many dogs the malt-and-hops name of Heineken, and U.S. senator Daniel Patrick Moynihan, not averse to having a drink or two, named his terrier Whiskey. Of course, there are many reasons why owners give their cats and dogs their names. In this book you will find over 3,000 names, from Abakaaru, Admetus, and Agrippina to Zorro, Zsa Zsa, and Zuzu.

I hope you have a good time pouring through the many names of these pampered felines and canines of the rich and famous as you try to find the best name for *your* cat or dog.

Ed Lucaire
New York City

CATS

A

Admetus • One of the "fancier" named cats mentioned in writer T.S. Eliot's *Old Possum's Book of Practical Cats*.

Adolf • A cat that wandered aboard a U.S. Air Force plane in Australia in February 1945 and was nicknamed Adolf by the crew for its resemblance to Hitler. By the end of the war, it had logged over ninety thousand miles.

Agrippina • A cat owned by essayist Agnes Repplier, named after the mother of the Roman emperor Nero.

Ajax • One of actress Nanette Fabray's cats, not named after the Greek hero of the Trojan War, but after the brand of household cleanser! Also see **Borax**, **Brillo**, and **Spic & Span**.

Aladdin • An Abyssinian cat owned by author Gladys Taber (*The Stillmeadow Album*).

Albert the Good • A Siamese cat owned by movie actor Vincent Price (*House of Wax*).

Alexander • One of many cats owned by movie actress

Sandy Dennis (*Who's Afraid of Virginia Woolf?*), who owned dozens of altered cats at any given time.

Alice • The bewitched cat owned by Beatle John Lennon and Yoko Ono. It slipped off the ledge of one of the windows of their New York apartment and fell to its death.
   • A pet lion of film actress Tippi Hedren (*The Birds*).
   • One of television actor (*Police Woman*) Earl Holliman's cats.

Alley Cat • The name of one of writer Ernest Hemingway's cats when he lived in Key West, Florida.

Allison • A cat owned by Frankie Valli, lead singer of The Four Seasons rock 'n' roll group.

Alonzo • One of the cats mentioned in T.S. Eliot's *Old Possum's Book of Practical Cats* that possessed a "sensible everyday" name.

Am • One of the Siamese cats in the 1955 movie *Lady and the Tramp*.

Amanda • One of many cats owned by movie actress Sandy Dennis (*Who's Afraid of Virginia Woolf?*). Dennis owned dozens of altered cats at any given time.

Amani • A tiger owned and raised by television talk-show host emeritus Jack Paar.

Amber • The name of *New Yorker* cartoonist George Booth's 22 $1/2$-pound cat (also known as Ambrosia and Amslatts).
   • The Patsy-winning cat in the 1978 Disney movie *The Cat from Outer Space*.
   • A cat owned by movie actress Merle Oberon (*Wuthering Heights*).

• The Abyssinian cat in writer Gladys Taber's *Amber: A Very Personal Cat.*

Amy • A white cat with calico spotting owned by *New Yorker* cartoonist Edward Gorey.

Angel or Angela • The sixth most popular name for a female cat in the U.S. A cat owned by comedic actress Victoria Jackson (*Saturday Night Live*).

Angus Silky • A Siamese cat owned by actor James Mason (*Lolita*) and his wife, Pamela.

Anna • A Siamese (as in *Anna and the King of Siam*?) cat of James Mason and his wife, Pamela.

Anta-M-Nekht • A lion that accompanied Pharaoh Rameses II of Egypt in battle.

Anthony • The cat owned by modern painter Robert Delaunay, given to him by heiress and art patron Peggy Guggenheim.

Appollinaris • One of author and humorist Mark Twain's cats.

Archibald Buchanan • One of actress Pamela Mason's many cats.

Arthur • The cat of former U.S. ambassador to the United Nations Jeane Kirkpatrick.

Ashley • A gray cat owned by game-show hostess (*Wheel of Fortune*) Vanna White. See **Rhett Butler**.
• A cat owned by television actress Tara Buckman (Brandy on *Lobo*).
• Television talk-show host Regis Philbin's Himalayan.

Asole • One of actress (*Knot's Landing*) Joan Van Ark's cats. Pronounce the name carefully!

Asparagus • 'Gus, the "Theatre Cat" in writer T.S. Eliot's *Old Possum's Book of Practical Cats*. He was once a "Star of the highest degree" and an audience once gave him seven cat-calls.

Athenaeum • British short-story writer Katherine Mansfield's cat, named after the literary weekly *Athenaeum* which was edited by her husband, John Middleton Murry.

Atossa • The favorite cat of nineteenth-century British Victorian poet Matthew Arnold. He immortalized the Persian "Toss" in many of his writings, including his poem "Poor Mathias":
> Cruel, but composed and bland,
> Dumb, inscrutable and grand,
> So Tiberius might have sat,
> Had Tiberius been a cat.

Augustus • One of the cats mentioned in T.S. Eliot's *Old Possum's Book of Practical Cats* that possessed a "sensible everyday" name.

Autocat • One of Hanna-Barbera's cartoon cats, with its voice provided by comedian Marty Ingels.

B

Baal • The cat of comedic actor Jim Belushi (*K-9*). (Baal was the chief god, the solar deity, of ancient Phoenicians.)

Babas • A female Egyptian Mau owned by Russian princess Natalie Troubetskoy in the mid-1950's. It was the first Egyptian Mau to be exhibited in North America.

• One of television actress (*All in the Family*) Sally Struthers's cats.

Babou • One of many cats owned by French writer Colette (*Gigi*). It was remarkable because it was an extremely long cat.

Baby • One of restaurateur Elaine Kaufman's cats, which she bought after seeing the cat in a pet-shop window every day for two straight weeks.

• The name of the leopard in the 1930 movie *Bringing Up Baby*, starring Katharine Hepburn and Cary Grant. See **Nissa**.

• One of British film actor James Mason's many cats.

Baby Mew • A cat owned by actor Jackie Joseph (Jackie Parker on *The Doris Day Show*; also on the original *Bob Newhart Show*).

Bacchus • A pet lion of film actress Tippi Hedren (*The Birds*), mother of actress Melanie Griffith. (Bacchus was the Greek god of wine.)

Bagheera • The black panther in Rudyard Kipling's *The Jungle Book* that guarded Mowgli and kept him away from the menacing tiger. See **Shere Khan**.

Bali • A Persian cat owned by actor Erik Estrada of television's police series *CHiPS*.

Barnaby • A cat owned by Tony-winning Broadway musical composer Jerry Herman (*Hello Dolly*).

Barney • A cat owned by stage and screen actress Colleen Dewhurst (*A Fine Madness*).

Baron Raticide • One of British poet laureate Robert Southey's cats.

Barre-de-Rouille • French novelist and art critic Joris-Karl Huysmans's red-and-black-striped cat, which liked to catch bats.

Bast • One name for the Egyptian cat-goddess. It is also listed as **Pasht** or **Bastet** in various sources.

Bastet • See **Bast**.

Bathsheba • A cat whose epitaph was written by Massachusetts-born poet and essayist John Greenleaf Whittier:
Bathsheba:
To whom none ever said scat,
No worthier cat
Ever sat on a mat
Or caught a rat:
Requies-cat
(In the Bible, Bathsheba was the mother of Solomon.)

Bear • The Persian cat of television actress Lisa Hartman (*Knot's Landing* and *Tabitha*).

Beauty • The white cat and protagonist of Honoré de Balzac's satirical *Heartaches of an English Cat*. Beauty was married to a black Angora cat named **Puff** but fell in love with a cat named **Brisquet**.

Bedford • The name of a cat owned by actress Tammy Grimes and another cat owned by actor Rex Harrison.

Bee Bee • One of TV's *Charlie's Angels* actress Tanya Roberts's cats.

Beelzebub • One of humorist Mark Twain's cats. (The name refers to the "prince of the devils" in the Bible and is derived from the Hebrew phrase for "lord of the flies," a synonym for Satan.

Belaud • French poet Joachim du Bellay's silver-grey cat.

Bella • One of British actor (*Star Trek: The Next Generation*) Patrick Stewart's cats. (*Bella* means "beautiful" in both Italian and Spanish.)

Benny • Also known as Benny the Ball, the not-so-smart cat on the Hanna-Barbera television cartoon *Top Cat*. The cat's voice was that of actor Maurice Gosfield, who was Doberman on *The Phil Silvers Show*.

Bernie • A black and white cat owned by writer Dan Greenburg (*How to Be a Jewish Mother*).

Berries • A pet lion of movie actress Tippi Hedren (*The Birds*).

Bes Mudi • Movie actor and "swashbuckler" Errol Flynn's Siamese cat.

Betti • A cat owned by *Cabaret* star Joel Grey.

Bianca • A long-haired, white cat that appeared on the television soap operas *Ryan's Hope* and *Santa Barbara*. It also appeared on the Fox television comedy *Women in Prison*.
• A cat owned by Frankie Valli, lead singer of The Four Seasons rock 'n' roll group.

Bijou • A cat owned by French writer Colette (*Le chatte*) in her childhood. Its mother was named Nonoche. The cat is immortalized in *Sido* and *La maison de Claudine*. *Bijou* is French for "jewel."

Bilbo • Television actress Mariette Hartley's cat.

Bill • The cat in Berkeley Breathed's comic strip *Outland*.

Bill Bailey • One of the cats mentioned in T.S. Eliot's *Old Possum's Book of Practical Cats* that possessed a "sensible everyday" name.

Billy • A stray ginger cat adopted by author and illustrator Edward Gorey.
  • A cat owned by television actor Willie Aames (*Eight Is Enough*).
  • A pet lion of actress Tippi Hedren.

Bing Clawsby • A cat owned by cabaret singer and pianist Michael Feinstein.

Binky • The cat owned by Suzy Becker, author of *All I Need to Know I Learned from my Cat.*

Biscuit • The name of the cat in the toy line based on Pillsbury's little "dough boy."
  • A cat owned by actress Gina Gallego (Alicia Sanchez on *Flamingo Road*).

Bismarck • One of many cats owned by British nurse Florence Nightingale, named after the German "Iron Chancellor."

Black and White • A cat owned by television actor Devon Gummersall (*My So-Called Life*).

Black Beau • The unusual cat of former Miss America Lee Meriwether—it is noteworthy for having seven toes on each front paw. See **S.C.**

Black Cat • Writer Doris Lessing's cat, which is described in her *Particularly Cats* as a "steady, obstinate, modest little beast."

Blackberry • The mother cat from which all "munchkin" cats (a new breed) are descended.

Blackie* or *Blacky • A cat that was sent to U.S. president Calvin Coolidge by a citizen, perhaps not a well-wisher. The black cat obviously brought his lackluster administration bad luck.

• The name of one of British prime minister Winston Churchill's cats.

• A black cat owned by comedic actor Lou Costello of the Abbott and Costello movies.

• A former British stray cat that inherited £20,000 in 1975.

• Nineteenth-century British Victorian poet Matthew Arnold had a cat named Blacky, which was missing one leg.

Black Jack • A legendary English cat famous for meandering around the reading room of the British Museum.

Black Kitty • A cat belonging to actor Richard Basehart (*Voyage to the Bottom of the Sea*).

Blatherskite • One of author and humorist Mark Twain's cats. (An archaic term, "blatherskite" referred to someone given to idle chatter and gossip.)

Blaze • One of several cats owned by U.S. president Calvin Coolidge.

Blondie • The name of cats owned by funnyman Red Skelton and by actress Tanya Roberts (*Charlie's Angels*).

Bluegrass • American pioneer Daniel Boone's cat, named for the Bluegrass State—Kentucky—where he did most of his pathfinding. (Boone, by the way, was actually born in Reading, Pennsylvania.)

Bluebell • A South African Persian cat which in 1974 produced fourteen kittens in one litter.

Bob • A cat named after its owner, comedy legend Bob Hope (*Thanks for the Memory*).

Boche • A cat who lived in the warehouse below where Anne Frank lived in Holland during the German occupation in World War II. (*Boche* is derogatory French slang for "German.").

Boise • One of writer Ernest Hemingway's cats, named after the capital of Idaho; it needed Seconal to go to sleep.

Bomba • The ocicat owned by children's author Tomie de Paola, so named because it was spotted like the loincloth worn by "Bomba, the Jungle Boy" of fiction.

Bombalurina • One of the cats with a "peculiar" and "more dignified" name that is mentioned in writer T.S. Eliot's *Old Possum's Book of Practical Cats*.

Bona Marietta • One of English poet laureate Robert Southey's *many* felines. It is Italian for "good little Mary" (as opposed to "Naughty Marietta"?).

Boo Boo • A cat owned by actor Daryl Anderson (Animal on *Lou Grant*).

Boomer • A pet lion of movie actress Tippi Hedren (*The Harrad Experiment*).

Boo-Boo Kitty • Laverne De Fazio's stuffed cat in the television series *Laverne and Shirley*, which ran from 1976 to 1983. The cat was usually located on their sofa.

Boots or *Bootsie* • The tenth most popular name for a male cat in the U.S. and a common name for cats, which originated with the classic Puss in Boots story.

Boots was the name of Bunny Olsen's cat in the television series *Gomer Pile, U.S.M.C.*

• A cat owned by actress-singer Carol Lawrence (*West Side Story*).

• An artistic cat, specifically a Trans-Expressionist, featured in the book *Why Cats Paint: A Theory of Feline Aesthetics* by Heather Busch and Burton Silver.

Bootsy • *Roots* actor Le Var Burton's cat.

Borax • A cat owned by actress Nanette Fabray, another name based on a household cleanser. See **Ajax, Brillo,** and **Spic and Span.**

Bosco • A cat that belonged to television comedian George Gobel.

Bounder • One of U.S. president Calvin Coolidge's cats.

Brain • The nongenius cat in the Hanna-Barbera television cartoon *Top Cat*. Actor Leo De Lyon did the voice-overs for The Brain.

Brando • A cat owned by movie actress Bonnie Bedelia (*Lovers and Other Strangers*), named after actor Marlon Brando who, in the film *The Godfather*, is well remembered for stroking a white cat.

Bridget • A pet lion of movie actress Tippi Hedren.

Brie • A cat owned by television actor Bill Beyers (*Joe and Valerie*), who likes to name his cats after types of cheeses. See **Camembert, Gouda, Muenster,** and **Velveeta.**

Brillo • Another cat owned by actress Nanette Fabray, named after the household cleaning product. See **Ajax, Borax,** and **Spic and Span.**

Brisquet • In Honoré de Balzac's *Heartaches of an English Cat*, the philandering cat, a descendant of Puss in Boots, who is murdered for having one love affair too many. Also see **Beauty** and **Puff**.

Brownie • One of two cats that inherited $415,000 when its owner died in 1961. See **Hellcat**.

Bruce • Television actress Fannie Flagg's Persian cat.
• The name of actress Anne Francis's pet ocelot in the 1965–66 television show *Honey West*.

Bruno • A cat owned by movie director Wes Craven (*Nightmare on Elm Street*).

Brutus • The name of one of the assassins of Roman emperor Julius Caesar, Brutus is a distinctive name for a pet.
• The Holiday family's pet lion in Hanna-Barbera cartoons.
• The last known descendant of English diarist Samuel Pepys's cat. Brutus died in 1933.
• A pet lion of movie actress Tippi Hedren.

Bubber • A cat owned by film actress and dancer Ann-Margret (*Viva Las Vegas*).

Buckwheat • A cat owned by actress Patricia McPherson (Bonnie Barstow on *Knight Rider*).

Bucky • *Charlie's Angels* actress Tanya Roberts's cat.

Buffalo Bill • One of writer Mark Twain's cats.

Buffy • One of many felines owned by science-fiction author Ray Bradbury.

Bull • A male Singapura, it was the most valuable cat in the world, when its owner was offered $10,000 for the cat in 1988.

Buns • The name of a Burmese cat owned by *Dallas* actress Victoria Principal.
   • A seal-point Siamese cat owned by television actress Tanya Roberts (*Charlie's Angels*).

Burbank the Cat • The cat in the 1987 movie *Lethal Weapon*, starring Mel Gibson. See **Sam**.

Buster • A cat that inherited $40,000 when its owner, Boston lawyer Woodbury Rand, died in the early 1940s.
   • One of movie actress Tippi Hedren's pet leopards.
   • A dog owned by broadcasting executive and author Fred Bergendorff.

Bustopher Jones • The fat black "Cat About Town" in writer T.S. Eliot's *Old Possum's Book of Practical Cats*. He belongs to "eight or nine clubs" and wears "well-cut trousers" and white spats.

Butch • In the 1957 movie *The Incredible Shrinking Man*, the cat who tried to kill its owner Scott Carey (played by actor Grant Williams).

Buttercup • A yellow tomcat that in Colorado in the 1930s gave its blood to two other cats, **Skeezix** and **Snicklefritz**, thereby saving them from an otherwise lethal disease.

C

Caboodle • A cat owned by singer Kenny Rogers, which is especially significant because the singer is allergic to cats!

Cactus Jack • A cat owned by author Ray Bradbury.

Cadillac • Cat owned by pro-basketball-player-turned-executive Isiah Thomas.

Cali or *Calico* • The fourth most popular name for a cat in the U.S. and an obvious name for a calico cat—or, in the case of Cali, a cat from Colombia? Movie actress Joan Fontaine (*Suspicion*) owned a gray Persian cat named Calico.

Calvin • A large Maltese owned by author Harriet Beecher Stowe (*Uncle Tom's Cabin*) and later given to writer Charles Dudley Warner.

Camembert • A cat owned by television actor Bill Beyers (*Joe and Valerie*), who likes to name his cats after types of cheeses. See **Brie, Gouda, Muenster,** and **Velveeta.**

Captain Midnight • An American black cat that was sent as a "special envoy" to Germany in 1942 to fly over the headquarters of Adolf Hitler to bring him bad luck.

Carbucketty • A cat in one of T.S. Eliot's writings and a character in the Broadway musical *Cats.*

Carream • *Knot's Landing* actress Joan Van Ark's *creamy*-white cat.

Caruso • The Siamese cat of singer Roberta Flack, who named the cat after Italian tenor Enrico Caruso.
   • A black cat with green eyes that belonged to British writer Edmund Gosse (*Father and Son*).

Casey • The pet lion of movie actress Tippi Hedren (*The Birds*) that bit her daughter Melanie Griffith, who was known to sleep with Hedren's lions.

Cassandra • A cat in one of T.S. Eliot's writings, and a character in the Broadway musical *Cats*. (In Greek mythology, Cassandra was the prophetess who made correct predictions but was condemned by Apollo not to be believed.)

Cat • The name of Audrey Hepburn's cat in the 1961 movie *Breakfast at Tiffany's*. The cat won the Patsy Award for its performance. The cat's real name was Orangey. See **Minerva** and **Rhubarb**.

Cat Ballou • A cat owned by television actress Peggy McKay (Stacy on *The Lazarus Syndrome*).

Cat Fright • The cat mentioned in an old nursery rhyme:
    Poor Cat Fright,
    Ran off with all her might,
    Because the dog was after her,
    Poor Cat Fright.

Catarina • Writer Edgar Allan Poe's large tortoiseshell cat, which kept his wife, Virginia, company when she was bedridden.

Cato • A cat owned by actress Lindsay Wagner (*The Bionic Woman*).

Celestine • An abandoned cat saved by actress Rue McClanahan (*Golden Girls*).

Chan • A Siamese cat owned by U.S. president Gerald R. Ford.

Chang • A cat owned by television actress Cindy Williams (*Laverne and Shirley*).

Chang Mai • A cat owned by television talk-show host Sally Jessy Raphael.

Chanoine • French author (*Les misérables*) Victor Hugo's favorite cat. The word *chanoine* in French means "canon" (a type of clergyman).

Charity • One of many cats owned by movie actress Sandy Dennis (*Who's Afraid of Virginia Woolf?*), who owned dozens of cats.

Charles O'Malley • The Siamese cat owned by Michael Joseph, the author of *Charles: The Story of a Friendship*, who believed that cats should be given distinct names out of "true appreciation of feline character."

Charlie • Author and illustrator Edward Gorey's ginger cat.
   • A Siamese cat of actress Shelley Smith (*The Associates* and *For Love and Honor*).
   • A Siamese cat owned by actress Pamela Mason.

Charlie Brown • One of actress Elizabeth Taylor's cats.

Charlie Chan • One of the world's richest felines, this white cat inherited $250,000 when its owner, Gene Patterson of Joplin, Missouri, died in 1978—back when a quarter of a million dollars was worth a lot of money!

Charo • Yoko Ono's tortoiseshell Persian cat, presumably named after the Latin "coochie-coochie" singer and wife of the late bandleader Xavier Cugat.

Cheeries • A pet lion of film actress Tippi Hedren.

Cheeseler • Late-night television talk-show host Jay Leno's cat.

Cheetah • One of *Police Woman* actor Earl Holliman's cats.

Chelsea • One of actress Tippi Hedren's pet lions.

Cheshire Cat • Author Lewis Carroll's famous feline character is known for its huge grin and gossipy nature. Of course, it was featured in Walt Disney's animated movie *Alice in Wonderland* (1951).

Chessie • The sleeping kitten in the corporate logo of the Chesapeake (hence the kitten's name) and Ohio Railway, familiar to the public in the heyday of railroad travel. See **Peake**.

Childebrand • One of French writer Théophile Gautier's many cats.

Chilla • One of two Ukrainian gray cats owned by writer Paul Gallico. See **Chin**.

Chim • The demonic cat in writer J.W. Meinhold's historical romance *Sidonia the Sorceress*.

Chin • One of writer Paul Gallico's two Ukrainian gray cats. See **Chilla** (as in chinchilla!).

Chocolate Chip • A cat owned by singer Jay Osmond of The Osmond Brothers.

Cho Cho • A cat owned by actor-painter Billy Dee Williams (*Scott Joplin*).

Choo-Choo • The errand-running cat in Hanna-Barbera's television show *Top Cat*, whose voice was that of actor Marvin Kaplan.

Chopin • F. Scott and Zelda Fitzgerald's white Persian cat, named after Polish-born composer-pianist Frédéric Chopin.

Chrissy • Television actress Suzanne Somers's cat, named after her character Chrissy Snow in *Three's Company*, which aired from 1977 to 1984.

Christopher • One of The Four Seasons lead singer Frankie Valli's Persian cats.

Church • In Stephen King's novel *Pet Sematary*, the cat that is buried by its owner in the cemetery, thereby setting the plot in motion. The name is short for Winston Churchill.

Cindi • A pet lion of movie actress Tippi Hedren.

Cinema • A cat owned by actress Peggy McKay (Stacy on *The Lazarus Syndrome*).

Clarence • A cat that belonged to actress Frances Farmer (*Come and Get It*).
   • A cat owned by actor Stephen Dorff (*What a Dummy*).
   • The leonine star of the 1965 movie *Clarence the Cross-Eyed Lion*.

Cleo • A Siamese cat owned by actor Richard Burton and Elizabeth Taylor—named for her role in the movie *Cleopatra* in which they both were acting when they met and fell in love.

Cleopatra • The detective's cat in mystery writer Lawrence Sanders's *The Timothy Files*. The name was based on Sanders's own cat, which looked "vaguely Egyptian."
   • One of actress Tippi Hedren's pet leopards.

Cloth Cap • A cat owned by Pamela Mason.

Clothild the User • The multicolored female cat with whom animal lover and author Roger Caras cohabitates. He describes Clothild as "just a plain opportunist" in the book *A Celebration of Cats*.

CoCo • Television actor Ed Asner's Siamese cat.

Colleen • Film and television actor Michael J. Fox's cat.

Columbine • British writer Thomas Carlyle's black cat.

Consuelo • An albino cat owned by radio personality and animal adoption activist Pegeen Fitzgerald. She and her husband Ed owned as many as thirty-nine cats at any given time.

Coon Dog • A Maine coon cat owned by *10* actress Bo Derek.

Coricopat • One of the cats with a "peculiar" and "more dignified" name that is mentioned in writer T.S. Eliot's *Old Possum's Book of Practical Cats*.

Country • One of the rock 'n' roll cats in the Hanna-Barbera television series *The Cattanooga Cats*.

Crinkle • A grey cat whose likeness was printed on Kellogg's Toasted Corn Flakes boxes in 1914. The cat was held by a child and the slogan read, "For Kiddies, not Kitties."

Crocus • A cat owned by French actress Brigitte Bardot (*And God Created Woman*).

Crumpet • One of actress Meredith MacRae's cats.

Cuba • Writer Ernest Hemingway named this cat after the country where he had his *finca* (farm).

Cuddles • One of singer-writer Kinky Friedman's cats.

Curry • A cat owned by *New York Times* book reviewer Christopher Lehmann-Haupt.

Curtis • A cat owned by actress Amanda Bearse, who plays the character Mary Rhoades D'Arcy on television's *Married . . . with Children*.
  • A cat owned by actress-singer Gloria De Haven (*Best Foot Forward*).

Cuthbert • A black cat owned by mystery writer P.D. James.

D

Daddy Warbucks • The father (sire) of the first rag-doll cat.

Daisy • A legendary cat that made several voyages from upstate New York to New York City on its own. A family adopted it while on vacation and left it in its upstate environs, only to find it on their city doorstep a month later.
  • A cat owned by actress-singer Gloria De Haven.

Dancer • Retired television newscaster Walter Cronkite's cat.

Daphne • A cat owned by actress and former Miss America Lee Meriwether.

David • A Siamese cat owned by British stage actress Gertrude Lawrence (*The King and I*).

D.C. • In the 1965 Disney movie *That Darn Cat*, the Siamese cat who helped the FBI agents find the kidnapped woman. Its code name was "Informant X-14."

Debbie • A pet lion of movie actress Tippi Hedren.

Demeter • One of the "fancier" named cats mentioned in writer T.S. Eliot's *Old Possum's Book of Practical Cats*.

Desdemona • A cat owned by the Archbishop of Taranto, one of many that ate at the dinner table of the prelate. Desdemona was Othello's wife, killed by Othello in William Shakespeare's play *Othello*.

Dick • A cat owned by actress Amanda Bearse (*Married . . . with Children*).
   • A cat owned by English-born author Frances Hodgson Burnett (*Little Lord Fauntleroy*).

Dickens • A cat owned by magician David Copperfield (real name David Kotkin). (David Copperfield is the title character of a Charles Dickens's novel.)

Digger • A cat owned by actress Robin Riker (Bobbi Turner on *Thunder Alley*).

Dinah • In Lewis Carroll's *Alice's Adventures in Wonderland*, the real cat that Alice left behind when she fell down the rabbit hole.

Dingo • One of science-fiction author Ray Bradbury's many cats. (A dingo is a wild, wolflike dog native to Australia.)

Dinky • The name of one of Felix's nephews in the *Felix the Cat* comic strips and cartoons.

Dirty Dick • A fourteen-time champion black Persian cat in the early 1900s.

Disraeli • A Persian cat owned by British nurse Florence Nightingale, named after British statesman and novelist Benjamin Disraeli.

Ditzie • One of science-fiction author Ray Bradbury's many cats.

Dr. Carlton B. Forbes • A tiger-striped cat owned by comedic actor Steve Martin.

Dr. Henry Metzger • In Thomas Perry's comic story *Metzger's Dog*, a wily cat owned by Chinese Gordon.

Dolly • Actress Tallulah Bankhead's Siamese cat.

Domino • A cat eulogized in the poem "In Memory of My Cat," written by Roy Fuller.

Don Pierrot de Navarre • French writer Théophile Gautier's white Angora cat mentioned in his autobiographical *The White and Black Dynasties*.

Dr. Scat • One of singer-author Kinky Friedman's cats.

Dreamer • A cat owned by television actor Willie Aames (*Eight Is Enough*).

Duchess • The Parisian cat in Walt Disney's 1969 animated movie *The Aristocats*, who has a romance with the alley cat O'Malley. The voice of Duchess was that of actress Eva Gabor.

Dudley • Film actress (*Love Story*) Ali McGraw's cat.

Dusty • The name of the most prolific cat on record, according to the *Guinness Book of World Records*. The Texas-born tabby gave birth to 420 kittens during her life. The tomcats of Bonham, Texas, loved to pay her a visit!

Dweezil • A cat given to veejay Katie Wagner, daughter of actor Robert Wagner, by Dweezil and Moon Unit Zappa, children of the late rock composer Frank Zappa.

E

Earl Tomlemange • One of British poet laureate Robert Southey's cats.

Eartha Kat • An abandoned black kitten that *A Celebration of Cats* author Roger Caras rescued.

Eggbag • The mascot cat of the Magic Center magician supply store in New York City. It was named after a classic trick in which an egg mysteriously appears inside of a previously empty purse.

El C. • A black cat owned by *Knott's Landing* actress Joan Van Ark. Also see **Asole** and **Carream**.

Electra • One of the "fancier" named cats mentioned in writer T.S. Eliot's *Old Possum's Book of Practical Cats*. (In Greek mythology, Electra was the daughter of Agamemnon and Clytemnestra.)

Elizabeth • In the 1948 movie *I Remember Mama* the pet tomcat of the daughter Christine.

Elsa • The pet lion of Joy Adamson, author of *Born Free*. The lion portraying Elsa in the 1966 feature movie *Born Free* won the Patsy Award for its performance.

Elvis • A cat owned by Julia Baird, half-sister of Beatles singer and songwriter John Lennon.
• *Cheers* actress Kirstie Alley's cat.

Enjolras • A black cat owned by French writer Théophile Gautier. The name is from a character in Victor Hugo's *Les misérables*. See **Eponine** and **Gavroche**.

Enrique de Lome • An Angora cat owned by U.S.

president William McKinley. It was named after the Spanish ambassador to the U.S. at the time.

Eponine • The name of a black cat owned by French writer Théophile Gautier, taken from a character in Victor Hugo's *Les misérables*. See **Enjolras** and **Gavroche**.

Esme • A Siamese cat owned by author Gladys Taber, who wrote *The Stillmeadow Album*.

Esmeralda • In the comic strip *Mutt and Jeff*, the cat of Augustus Mutt's son Cicero. (It was also in the strip *Cicero's Cat*, which began in 1933.)

Etcetera • A cat in one of T.S. Eliot's writings, and a character in the Broadway musical *Cats*.

F

Face • A cat owned by actress Pamela Mason.

Fagin • A cat owned by actress Jean Arthur (*You Can't Take It with You*), named after the villainous character in Charles Dickens's novel *Oliver Twist*.

Faith • An heroic church cat, a tabby, in England during World War II. During the Blitz, it removed its kitten, named Panda, from the rectory of St. Augustus's church in London. The church received a major hit but the cats survived.

Fancy Fancy • The ladies' man cat in the Hanna-Barbera television cartoon *Top Cat*. Actor John Stephenson did the voice-overs for Fancy Fancy.

Fat Albert • A tomcat and first member of the Pet

Food Institute's "Hall of Fame for Cats." It was a regular feline blood donor in the early 1970s.

Fat-Fat • A cat owned by sculptor Louis Nevelson.

Fatrick • A cat owned by stage actress and dancer Gwen Verdon (*Damn Yankees*).

Feathers • A kitten owned by author Carl Van Vechten (*A Tiger in the House*).

Feets Fosse • A cat owned by actress Gwen Verdon, who dated and worked with director-choreographer Bob Fosse.

Felimare • One of many cats owned by French prelate and statesman Cardinal Richelieu, Louis XIII's chief minister.

Felix • Pat Sullivan's *Felix the Cat* has been a popular syndicated-cartoon character since August 14, 1923.

Ferguson • A cat owned by Nancy Seaver, wife of professional baseball pitcher Tom Seaver. The cat was named after another pitcher—Ferguson Jenkins.

Fiddler • Actress Jacqueline Bisset's cat.

Figaro • The name of Gepetto's cat in the Walt Disney animated feature film *Pinocchio* (1940).
• A Himalayan cat owned by television actress Loni Anderson (*WKRP in Cincinnati*).

Fisher • A cat owned by Russian composer Aleksandr Borodin. See **Rybolov**.

Flash • A cat owned by actress Patricia McPherson (*Knight Rider*).

Flat Nose • The name of a "fat cat" in Chicago that inherited $24,000 in 1959, along with four other cats, from its owner Margaret Montgomery.

Flavia • A cat owned by Irish-born British dramatist and essayist Sir Richard Steele (*Tatler* and *Spectator*).

Flora • A cat owned by actress Tallulah Bankhead (*Little Foxes*).

Florence • A cat owned by singer-songwriter James Taylor "Fire and Rain".

Fluffy • A popular name for a long-haired cat, it was the name of the Brady family's cat in the television series *The Brady Bunch*.
• *Three's Company* television star John Ritter's cat.

Folly • A Siamese cat owned by movie actor James Mason.

Foshay • An Abyssinian owned by children's author Tomie de Paola, named after the Foshay Tower, in Minneapolis, Minnesota.

Foss • Cat-lover and writer Edward Lear's striped, stubby-tailed, well-fed tomcat, for whom he wrote *The Heraldic Blazon of Foss the Cat*.

Found • A Maltese cat owned by theatrical producer and agent Charles Feldman and his wife Jean Howard.

Fourrure • A cat owned by French author André Malraux, from the French word for "fur."

F. Puss • One of writer Ernest Hemingway's cats during his days in Paris.

Frank • A cat owned by Amanda Bearse (*Married . . . with Children*).
• A cat owned by *Today Show* host Katie Couric.

Frankie • One of film actress Tippi Hedren's pet lions.

Fred • A cat owned by film and television actress Candice Bergen (*Murphy Brown*).

Freddie • A cat owned by comedic movie and television actor Red Skelton (*The Fuller Brush Man*).

Frimbo • A cat owned by *New Yorker* cartoonist Charles Addams.

Fritz • A cat owned by television and radio broadcaster Charles Osgood.

Fritz the Cat • An irreverent cartoon cat created by Robert Crumb in 1959. Director-writer Ralph Bakshi produced an X-rated animated movie *Fritz the Cat* in 1972.

Furball • A cat owned by actress Candice Bergen (*The Group*).

Fusto • A cat owned by actress Adrienne Barbeau (*Maude*).

G

Gainsborough • A Russian blue cat owned by Oscar-winning Hollywood costume designer Edith Head. (English artist Thomas Gainsborough's most famous painting was <u>*Blue*</u> *Boy*.)

Gamma • One of actor James Mason's Siamese cats.

Garfield • Cartoonist Jim Davis's comic strip cat, a lazy, cranky, striped ginger cat, but one of the most popular cats in cartoon and book history. He can be seen sticking to the windows of autos with paws that strongly resemble suction cups. Garfield has been seen in American Express commercials—his credit rating is tops.

Gatita • A cat in the George Herriman comic strip *Krazy Kat*. Although *gatita* means "small female cat" in Spanish, the cat was a he.

Gato • A cat owned by television quiz-show host Bob Barker. (*Gato* means cat in Spanish.)

Gavroche • A crafty black cat owned by French writer Théophile Gautier, named after a character in Victor Hugo's novel *Les misérables*. See **Enjolras** and **Eponine**.

Gazette • One of Cardinal Richelieu's many cats.

Gazza • One of science-fiction writer Ray Bradbury's cats.

General Felix • A cat owned by film and stage actor Mickey Rooney (*Boys' Town*).

General Sterling Price • The cat that drank beer in the 1969 John Wayne movie *True Grit* and its 1975 sequel *Rooster Cogburn*. The cat was named after a northern Civil War general.

Gent • *Dynasty* actress Linda Evans's Siamese cat.

Gentleman Caller • A cat owned by playwright Tennessee Williams, named after a character in his play *The Glass Menagerie*.

Geoffrey • One of two cats owned by mystery writer John D. MacDonald, author of Travis McGee novels. MacDonald wrote about the cats in *The House Guests.* See **Roger.**

George • A Siamese cat owned by film and television actress Cybill Shepherd (*Last Picture Show* and *Moonlighting*).
　• A Burmese cat owned by actress Valerie Bertinelli (*One Day at a Time*) and rock singer Eddie Van Halen.
　• One of author and illustrator Edward Gorey's six cats.
　• One of the cats mentioned in T.S. Eliot's *Old Possum's Book of Practical Cats* that possessed a "sensible everyday" name.
　• Yes, *Cats* composer Andrew Lloyd Webber has owned a cat—one named George.

George Pushdragon • One of writer T.S. Eliot's pet cats.

Geraldine • On the radio series *Lum 'n' Abner*, the cat owned by Abner Peabody.

Gilligan • A pet lion owned by movie actress Tippi Hedren (*Marnie*).

Gilly • A Himalayan cat owned by television actress Morgan Fairchild (*Flamingo Road*).

Gin • A Siamese cat owned by writers Richard and Frances Lockridge, who wrote the Mr. and Mrs. North novels made popular as movies. See **Martini** and **Sherry.**

Gina • An ocelot owned by film actress Bo Derek.

Ginger • The seventh most popular name for a female cat in the U.S.
　• A cat owned by actress-singer Jane Powell (*Seven*

Brides for Seven Brothers), which appeared with her on the cover of the September 6, 1946, issue of *Life* magazine.

• One of movie actress Natalie Wood's cats.

Giorgio • A Persian cat owned by heiress Peggy Guggenheim. It was originally owned by Giorgio Joyce, son of writer James Joyce.

Gipsy • In Booth Tarkington's novel *Penrod*, the salt and pepper cat who ran away from its owner to become an "alley cat." According to the book, Gipsy had "the soul of a bravo of fortune, living on his wits and his valor, asking no favors and granting no quarter."

Gladstone • One of British nurse Florence Nightingale's cats.

Godzilla • A cat owned by actress-turned-diplomat Shirley Temple, inspired by the cinema monster.

Goo Goo • A cat owned by comedic actor Dom DeLuise (*The Best Little Whorehouse in Texas*).

Goofy • A Siamese cat owned by actress Christopher Norris (*Trapper John, M.D.*).

Gouda • A Manx owned by television actor Bill Beyers (*Joe and Valerie*), who likes to name his cats after types of cheeses. See **Brie, Camembert, Muenster,** and **Velveeta.**

Gorgeous • A calico cat that appears in the mystery novels of Peter Israel. The cat was owned by the housekeeper, Althea.

Grace • Film actor Christopher Walken's cat.

Grandview • A cat owned by movie and television actor Rick Schroder.

Gray Pearl • One of science-fiction author Ray Bradbury's many cats.

Great Rumpuscat • The fierce and hairy cat that scared away the menacing Pekes and Pollicles in writer T.S. Eliot's *Old Possum's Book of Practical Cats*.

Gregory • A Siberian tiger owned by actress Tippi Hedren.
   • One of several Siamese cats owned by actress Shelley Smith (*The Associates* and *For Love and Honor*).

Grey Cat • A cat mentioned in writer Doris Lessing's *Particularly Cats*.

Griddlebone • A female cat "enraptured by" Growltiger's "manly baritone" in writer T.S. Eliot's *Old Possum's Book of Practical Cats*.

Grimalkin • A popular name for a cat, possibly because it is an Old English word for "grey cat." It was the name of a gray cat owned by Heathcliff in Emily Brontë's novel *Wuthering Heights*, and, in Shakespeare's *Macbeth*, a demon spirit in the form of a cat that was mentioned by the First Witch.

Gris-Gris • A cat owned by France's General Charles de Gaulle. The name means "gray-gray" in French.

Grizabella • A cat in one of T.S. Eliot's writings, and a character in the Broadway musical *Cats*.

Groovy • One of the rock 'n' roll cats (voice-over by Casey Kasem) in the Hanna-Barbera television series *The Cattanooga Cats*.

Growltiger • "The "roughest cat" and "Terror of the Thames" in writer T.S. Eliot's *Old Possum's Book of Practical Cats*. A Siamese cat mauled one of its ears.

Grumbushkin • A "bucko mate" of **Growltiger**, in writer T.S. Eliot's *Old Possum's Book of Practical Cats*.

Gucci • A cat owned by *CHiPS* television actor Erik Estrada.

Gumbie Cat • See **Jennyanydots**.

Guntry • A cat owned by actress Patricia Arquette (*True Romance*).

Gus • Short for Asparagus, a cat in T.S. Eliot's *Old Possum's Book of Practical Cats*. See **Asparagus**.

Gypsy • A cat owned by television personality and producer Dick Clark.
 • A cat owned by English-born singer Olivia Newton-John.
 • *Night Court* actress Markie Post's cat.
 • A Persian cat owned by heiress and art patron Peggy Guggenheim.

H

Hamilcar • The cat of Nobel Prize–winning French novelist and essayist Anatole France, named after Hamilcar Barca, the father of Carthaginian general Hannibal.

Hamlet • A cat (and its namesakes) which has resided royally at the Algonquin Hotel in New York City for many years. The third Hamlet was in the cast of the Broadway play *You Can't Take It with You*.

Hannibal • One of many cats owned by movie actress Sandy Dennis (*Who's Afraid of Virginia Woolf?*).

Harry • The "spokescat" in the 1970s Nine Lives' Square Meals cat food commercial.

Harvey • The incredible smoke-colored Persian cat that survived ten minutes inside a fully loaded and spinning washing machine.

Haskell • Comedienne Paula Poundstone's cat.

Heathcliff • The somewhat ill-tempered marmalade tomcat in George Gately's comic strip *Heathcliff*.

Hecate • Screen vamp-actress Elvira (real name Cassandra Peterson) has been known to own a cat named Hecate (who, in Greek mythology, was goddess of the earth and the underworld).

Hector • One of science-fiction author Ray Bradbury's many cats.

Hel • A German goddess that was portrayed as a black cat and harbinger of bad luck.

Helen • The cat that almost dies in a clothes dryer in Anne Tyler's novel *The Accidental Tourist*, on which the movie was based.

Hellcat • One of two cats that inherited $415,000 after its owner died in 1961. See **Brownie**.

Hershey Bar • A cat owned by television huckster and ex–talk-show sidekick Ed McMahon.

Hillary • A cat owned by movie director Wes Craven (*Nightmare on Elm Street*).

Himmy • The heaviest domestic cat on record—a neutered male tabby weighing 46 pounds, 15 $1/4$ ounces, according to the *Guinness Book of World Records*.

Hinse • A tomcat owned by Scottish author Sir Walter Scott (*Ivanhoe*). Its full name was Hinse of Hinsefield. The cat was killed by Nimrod, Scott's large hound.

Hobo • A cat owned by actress Meredith MacRae (*My Three Sons*) and husband, Greg Mullavey (*Mary Hartman, Mary Hartman*).

Hodge • The oyster-eating cat of lexicographer Dr. Samuel Johnson.

Holly-Go-Lightly • A cat owned by movie actress Frances Farmer (*The Party Crashers*).

Homer • A cat owned by documentary filmmaker Ken Burns, who made a documentary about the history of baseball, hence the name Homer.

Honey • The names of cats owned by actor Earl Holliman and by actor-singer Bobby Sherman.

Hope • Chester and Min Gump's cat in Sidney Smith's comic strip *The Gumps*.

Hoppy • In *The Flintstones* cartoon series, the name of Rubble's sabretooth cat.

Hotdog • Dennis's cat in the comic strip *Dennis the Menace*.

Humphrey • Superkatt's feline sidekick in 1940s comic books.
　• The cat currently living at 10 Downing Street in London—British prime minister John Major's feline.

Hurlyburlybuss • A cat owned by English poet laureate Robert Southey, "Hurly" was primarily an outdoor cat. See **Rumpelstilzchen**.

I

Icarus • A cat owned by boxing great Muhammad Ali. (In mythology Icarus was the son of Daedalus who flew too close to the sun, melted his wax wings, and fell to his death in the sea.)

Ickey • The name of one of Felix's nephews in the *Felix the Cat* comics and cartoons.

Igor • One of actress Tippi Hedren's pet lions.

Ike • A lion owned by actress Tippi Hedren.

Isolde • A cat owned by actress Catherine Oxenberg (*Dynasty*). (Isolde was the wife of Tristan in Wagner's opera and earlier Arthurian lore.)

Ito • One of two cats belonging to former Tennessee governor Lamar Alexander. See **Kato**.

Ivan • The cat in *Peter and the Wolf*.
• A pet tiger owned by actress Tippi Hedren.

J

Jack • One of *Married . . . with Children* television actress Amanda Bearse's cats.

Jackie • The lion in the MGM feature film logo for almost twenty years. It was named after actress Jacqueline Logan, who starred in the 1922 movie *Burning Sands*.

• A lion named Jackie appeared in the 1950 movie *Samson and Delilah*.

Jackson • A cat belonging to the copy editor of this book, named after the American abstract-impressionist painter Jackson Pollock.

Jade • A cat owned by film actress Bo Derek.

James • One of the cats mentioned in T.S. Eliot's *Old Possum's Book of Practical Cats* that possessed a "sensible everyday" name.

Jasper • One of humorist Orson Bean's cats.

Jaws • A cat owned by *West Side Story* movie star Natalie Wood.

Jeepers Creepers • A black cat owned by actress Elizabeth Taylor early in her acting career. It was named after the song "Jeepers Creepers," popular in the 1930s.

Jeffrey • British poet Christopher Smart's cat, mentioned in his poem "Jubilate Agno."

Jekkel • In British poet Walter de la Mare's poem "Five Eyes," one of the three black cats trying to keep rats out of a mill. See **Jessop** and **Jill**.

Jellicle Cats • Black and white "merry and bright" cats in writer T.S. Eliot's *Old Possum's Book of Practical Cats*.

Jellylorum • One of the cats with a "peculiar" and "more dignified" name that is mentioned in writer T.S. Eliot's *Old Possum's Book of Practical Cats*.

Jenny • A pet lion of actress Melanie Griffith's mother—Tippi Hedren.
• One of many cats owned by movie actress Sandy Dennis (*Who's Afraid of Virginia Woolf?*), who owned dozens of altered cats at any given time.

Jennyanydots • The "Gumbie Cat" in writer T.S. Eliot's *Old Possum's Book of Practical Cats*. She has a tabby coat with "tiger stripes and leopard spots" and "sits and sits and sits and sits."

Jenny Baldrin • A tabby in Paul Gallico's *The Abandoned*. The cat teaches a boy, Peter Brown, to be a cat.

Jeremiah • A Himalayan cat owned by actress Donna Mills, who was Abby Cunningham Ewing Sumner on television's *Knot's Landing* from 1980 to 1989.

Jessie • A cat owned by television actress Laurie Burton (Sara Gallagher on *Rituals*).
• One of many cats owned by movie actress Sandy Dennis (*Who's Afraid of Virginia Woolf?*), who owned dozens of altered cats at any given time.

Jessop • In British poet Walter de la Mare's poem "Five Eyes," one of the three black cats trying to keep rats out of a mill. See **Jekkel** and **Jill**.

Jigger • A Persian cat belonging to television actor Willie Aames (*Eight Is Enough*).

Jill • In British poet Walter de la Mare's poem "Five Eyes," one of the three black cats trying to keep rats out of a mill. See **Jekkel** and **Jessop**.
• A cat owned by film star Elizabeth Taylor.

Jimmy • A cat owned by actor René Auberjonois (*Benson*).

Jingles • Model-actress Brooke Shields's cat.

Jock • A marmalade cat given to British prime minister Winston Churchill on his eighty-eighth birthday by Sir John "Jock" Colville. When Jock passed away, another Jock replaced him.

Joan Pawford • A cat cleverly named by television actress Sally Struthers.

Johnny • One of movie actress Tippi Hedren's pet lions.

Joley • A cat owned by George Burns, named after the legendary singer Al Jolson (*The Jazz Singer*).

Jolson • A cat named after singer Al Jolson, owned by comedic actress Victoria Jackson (*Saturday Night Live*).

Jonathan • One of the cats mentioned in T.S. Eliot's *Old Possum's Book of Practical Cats* that possessed a "sensible everyday" name.

Jones • The tomcat living on the ship *Nostromo* in the 1979 movie *Alien*, starring Sigourney Weaver.

Josephine • The white Persian mother (queen) of the first ragdoll cat.
   • A cat owned by film actor Vincent Price.

Junior • Television movie critic Gene Shalit's cat.

K

Kaanaloa • A cat owned by television actress Christina Applegate (*Married . . . with Children*).

Kapok • One of French writer Colette's many cats. (A

Malay word, kapok is used for stuffing pillows and life jackets, and is also known as Java cotton.)

Kashka • A black cat owned by soap-opera actress Deirdre Hall. (*Koshka* is Russian for "cat.")

Katie • Pop artist Andy Warhol's cat.

Kato • One of two cats belonging to former Tennessee governor Lamar Alexander. See **Ito**.

Katrina • A cat owned by Lisa Marie Presley, Elvis's daughter.
  • A pet lion of movie actress Tippi Hedren.

Kawaba • A cat owned by movie actress Lesley Ann Warren (*Victor/Victoria*).

Kemo • A pet lion owned not by actress Tippi Hedren but by Amanda Blake.

Kenya • *Adventures in Paradise* actor Gardner McKay's pet cheetah.

Kiddleywinkempoops • Novelist Thomas Hardy's cat, nicknamed **Trot**.

Kiki • A black and white cat owned by Ford Modeling Agency cofounder Eileen Ford.

Killer • A cat owned by movie actress Janet Leigh, who was "killed" (stabbed in the shower) in the Hitchcock classic movie *Psycho*.

Kisha • One of humorist Orson Bean's cats.

Kissa • A cat owned by television movie critic Pia Lindstrom, daughter of actress Ingrid Bergman.

Kit • A cat owned by singer Kenny Rogers ("Lady").

Kit Kat • The pet lion of the Addams family in the television series *The Addams Family*.

Kitten • A cat owned by President John F. Kennedy's family. See **Tom Kitten**.

Kittens • A cat owned by mail-order executive Roger Horchow.

Kitty • The oldest domestic feline mother on record—thirty years old when she gave birth to two kittens, according to the *Guinness Book of World Records*. She died a year later, having produced 218 kittens in her lifetime.
  • *Dukes of Hazzard* actress Catherine Bach's Persian cat.
  • A cat owned by actor Daniel J. Travanti (*Hill Street Blues*).
  • In Lewis Carroll's *Through the Looking Glass*, the little red kitten who becomes the Red Queen.

Kitty Boo • A cat owned by Lee Meriwether, Miss America of 1955.

Kitty Carlisle • An Abyssinian cat owned by television broadcaster Bill Harris (*Entertainment Tonight* and *At the Movies*), named after the television personality and actress.

Kittycat • The family cat in Bill Keane's comic strip *The Family Circus*.
  • The cat who loved the governor's mansion of New Mexico so much that it kept returning. When its owner Governor David Cargo left office in 1971 and moved, Kittycat left to go back to the governor's mansion and the family of newly elected Bruce King. (King lost the next election but ran again four years later, and Kittycat returned to its rightful place.)

Kitty Dearest • A cat owned by television actress Sally Struthers, who also named one of her cats Joan Pawford. (Actress Joan Crawford's daughter wrote a book about her, entitled *Mommie Dearest*!).

Kitty Jo • One of the rock 'n' roll cats in the Hanna-Barbera television series *The Cattanooga Cats*.

Kitty Kat • A cat owned by *Baywatch* actor David Hasselhoff.

Kliban • A Siamese cat owned by James Gunn, a science-fiction author (*The Immortals*). The name was taken from Ed Kliban, the famous cat cartoonist.

Koko • A cat who fell from a tenth-floor window and inspired its owner, writer Lillian Jackson Braun, to commence the *The Cat Who . . .* mystery series.

Krazy Kat • A comic strip cat in George Herriman's *The Dingbat Family*, which was first published in 1910. The female feline became so popular that it won its own strip.

Kro • One of French writer Colette's cats.

Kut • The ancient Egyptian word for "male cat."

Kutta • The ancient Egyptian word for "female cat."

L

La Chatte • One of French writer Colette's many cats. The name is French for "female cat."

La Dernière Chatte • A cat owned by French writer Colette (*Chéri*). The name is French for "the last female cat."

La Touten • One of French writer Colette's many cats.

Lady • One of writer-composer Kinky Friedman's cats.
• A cat owned by comedian-turned-actor George Burns who was married to a funny lady, Gracie Allen, for many years.

Lady Arabella • A black kitten owned by John Spencer Churchill, nephew of British prime minister Winston Churchill.

Lady Griddlebone • A cat owned by writer T.S. Eliot.

Lady Jane • In Charles Dickens's *Bleak House*, the dyspeptic gray cat owned by Mr. Krook, proprietor of The Rag and Bottle Shop.

Lady Leeds • A cat owned by actor James Mason.

Langbourne, Sir John • British philosopher Jeremy Bentham's favorite cat.

Lee Chan • A cat owned by actor Richard Hatch, who replaced Michael Douglas on the television series *The Streets of San Francisco*.

Leica • One of movie actress Tippi Hedren's pet Siberian tigers.

Lelong • One of many cats owned by Russian composer Aleksandr Borodin.

Lena • A pet lion owned by movie actress Tippi Hedren.

Lenny the Lion • Ventriloquist Terry Hall's lion in a British television show broadcast in the 1960s.

Leo • The official "stage name" of the lion in the logo of MGM movies. Also see **Jackie**, **Slats** and **Tanner**.

• A Himalayan owned by actress Loni Anderson (*WKRP in Cincinnati*).

• A cat owned by actress Gloria De Haven (*Best Foot Forward*).

Leonardo • A cat owned by movie and theater critic Pia Lindstrom, daughter of actress Ingrid Bergman.

• The lion in Adrian Mitchell's children's book *Leonardo the Lion from Nowhere*.

Lilith • A black cat owned by French symbolist poet Stéphane Mallarmé ("Herodias"). (In Jewish literature, Lilith was the first wife of Adam, who later became a demon that attacked children.)

Lillian • According to writer Damon Runyon, a black cat known to drink Scotch with its milk.

• One of movie actress Tippi Hedren's pet lions.

Lilly • One of English lexicographer Samuel Johnson's cats.

Lily • *New Yorker* cartoonist George Booth's gray cat.

Limpy • A barn cat owned by writer Paul Gallico.

Lippy • The bragging lion in Hanna-Barbera cartoons, and sidekick of hyena Hardy Har-Har.

Lisa Douglas • A cat named by actress Eva Gabor, after the character she played in television situation comedy *Green Acres*.

Little Clay • A marmalade-colored cat owned by actress Amanda Blake, who played the role of Miss Kitty on the television series *Gunsmoke*.

Lollipop • *Knot's Landing* actor Stephen Macht's cat.

Lord Nelson • An orange-striped cat owned by English poet laureate Robert Southey who, in *Memoirs of the Cats of Greta Hall*, wrote that he was an "altogether good cat." Southey also addressed the cat alternately as Baron, Viscount, or Earl, depending on its level of behavior.

Louie • A Himalayan cat owned by actress Loni Anderson.

Louis • A cat owned by movie actress Natalie Wood (*Splendor in the Grass*).

Louis XIV • A cat owned by actor James Dean. (King Louis XIV of France was the "Sun King," an absolute monarch who had the longest reign in European history, 1643 to 1715.) See **Dogs—Bonne, Nonne,** and **Ponne**.

Louisa • Indian-born British writer William Makepeace Thackeray's cat.

Luci • A Persian cat owned by television and movie actor Richard Crenna (from *Our Miss Brooks* to the Rambo movies).

Lucifer • A black cat owned by Cardinal Richelieu, named after the rebellious archangel.
  • The name of Cinderella's stepmother's cat in the Disney feature cartoon movie *Cinderella*.

Lucy • *Tess* star Nastassja Kinski's cat.
  • A cat owned by *The New York Times* book reviewer Christopher Lehmann-Haupt.

Ludovic the Cruel • A cat belonging to Cardinal Richelieu that was notorious for menacing rats.

Luisito • One of restaurateur Elaine Kaufman's cats, a "Bowery street" cat.

Luke • An Abyssinian cat that was owned by nationally syndicated gossip columnist Liz Smith.

Lulu • One of several cats owned by humorist Orson Bean.

Lulu II • A seal-point Siamese cat owned by author Paul Gallico. The cat had a tendency to disappear for long periods of time "mooching on an amiable spinster" who called the cat Pitipoo.

Lump • The Abyssinian of Bounty paper towel spokeswoman-actress Nancy Walker.

Lurch • A pet lion of movie actress Tippi Hedren.

Lustre • A cat owned by French writer André Malraux.

M

Ma • The oldest cat on record, according to the *Guinness Book of World Records*. The female tabby died at the age of thirty-four on November 5, 1957.

Macavity • The tall and thin ginger cat and "Napoleon of Crime" in T.S. Eliot's *Old Possum's Book of Practical Cats*. He has "broken every human law" and "breaks the law of gravity." Whenever anything is missing, Macavity is implicated but never around.

Madame Bianchi • A predominantly white cat owned by English poet laureate Robert Southey.

Madame Butterfly • A calico cat owned by abstract-realist artist and educator Will Barnet.

Madame Catalini • Another cat owned by English poet laureate Robert Southey.

Madame Théophile • A reddish cat owned by French poet Théophile Gautier, to which he refers in *The Intimate Menagerie* (*La menagerie intime*).

Mafdet • The Egyptian cat-goddess who kept snakes out of the Pharaoh's house.

Magda • A Siamese cat owned by Hungarian-born actress Eva Gabor, named after one of her sisters.

Maggie • A cat owned by actress Natalie Wood (*Miracle on Thirty-fourth Street*).
 • One of many cats owned by movie actress Sandy Dennis (*Who's Afraid of Virginia Woolf?*), who owned dozens of altered cats at any given time.

Magic • A cat owned by songwriter-poet Rod McKuen.

Mai Tai • A cat owned by television personality Art Linkletter (*People Are Funny*).

Malbrouk • A Siamese cat given to Lady Ottoline Morrell by Gladys, Duchess of Marlborough.

Mama Sophie • One of many cats owned by movie actress Sandy Dennis (*Who's Afraid of Virginia Woolf?*), who owned dozens of altered cats at any given time.

Mamelouk • A black cat in the Margery Sharp book *The Rescuers*, on which the 1977 Disney animated feature movie was based.

Manmalotta • One of science-fiction author Ray Bradbury's many cats.

Marbles • A cat owned by television actor Jonathan Brandis (Lucas Wolenczak on *Seaquest DSV*).

Marcus • The name of actor James Dean's Siamese cat, which was a gift from actress Elizabeth Taylor.

Margate • A black stray cat adopted by British prime minister Winston Churchill in 1953.

Mariah • One of movie actress Tippi Hedren's pet leopards.

Maridadi • A silver-haired tabby owned by author and cat lover Roger Caras. The name is from the Swahili for "beautiful."

Marilyn • A tabby cat owned by singer Whitney Houston, to which her album *Whitney* is dedicated. See **Miste**.

Mark • A cat owned by movie and television actor Robert Wagner (*The Pink Panther*).

Marmalade • A cat owned by actress Anne Bancroft and her husband, Mel Brooks.

Marmelade • One of science-fiction author Ray Bradbury's many cats.

Marquis Macbum • One of British poet laureate Robert Southey's cats.

Martini • A Siamese cat (nickname Teeny) owned by writers Richard and Frances Lockridge, who wrote the Mr. and Mrs. North novels made popular as movies. See **Gin and Sherry**.

Marvin • A cat owned by stage and screen actress Colleen Dewhurst (*Annie Hall*). It was named for Marvin Gardens, "his favorite spot on the Monopoly board."

Masaccio • A cat belonging to the copy editor of this book, named after the Italian Renaissance painter.

Maunz • A cat in the German children's tale *Struwwelpeter*.

Maurice • An orange cat owned by writer Dan Greenburg (*How to Be a Jewish Mother*).

Master's Cat • A deaf cat owned by novelist Charles Dickens.

Max • The fourth most popular name for a male cat in the U.S. It was also the name of the *Daily Planet* editor Perry White's cat in the Superman comic books.
   • The name of cats owned by clothing designer Calvin Klein and by singer-actress Michelle Phillips.
   • A Siamese cat of actress Shelley Smith (*The Associates* and *For Love and Honor*).

Maxwell • A longer and more formal variation of Max and equally popular.

Maybell • A cat owned by *Police Woman* actor Earl Holliman.

Mazel • A cat owned by *Golden Girls* actress Estelle Getty. (The word *mazel* means "luck" or "good luck" in Yiddish.)

Ma-Zul • One of laid-back pop singer James Taylor's cats.

McDermot • A cat owned by Scottish-born pirate Captain Kidd.

McGee • A cat owned by actress Kathleen Turner (*Body Heat*).

Meatball • A cat owned by television personality Jane Pauley.

mehitabel • The name of the feline companion, an alley cat, of archy, a cockroach, in columnist Don Marquis's cartoons and stories, eventually compiled in *archy and mehitabel* (1927), *archy's Life of mehitabel* (1933), and *The Life and Times of archy and mehitabel* (1940). In the play *Shinbone Alley*, mehitabel was played by singer-actress Eartha Kitt.
   • Ballet dancer Mikhail Baryshnikov's cat.

Mei Mei • A cat owned by wine maker Robert Mondavi.

Melancholy • A cat owned by actor Michael Gray (*The Brian Keith Show*).

Melanie • Movie actress Tippi Hedren (*Marnie*) not only named her daughter Melanie (Griffith)—she gave the same name to one of her many pet lions.

Melba • A cat owned by actress Ann-Margret (*Bye Bye Birdie*).

Meno • A black cat owned by television actor Harry Hamlin (*L.A. Law*).

Mephistopheles • In writer Doris Lessing's *Particularly Cats*, a gray cat (real name Billy) and ardent admirer of Lessing's own cat. The name is derived from one of the seven chief devils in medieval demonology.

Merlin • *Love Story* actress and former model Ali MacGraw's magical cat, named after the Arthurian seer Merlin the Magician.

Merrie • One of movie actress Tippi Hedren's pet lions.

Mewsette • The heroine cat of the 1962 feature cartoon *Gay Purr-ee*. (Judy Garland did the voice-over.)

Micetto • A "grey and very gentle" cat owned by Pope Leo XII and later given to author-statesman Chateaubriand.

Michael • A large Maine coon cat, the first cat owned by writer and animal lover Roger Caras in his youth.

Mick • A Himalayan cat owned by actress Morgan Fairchild (*Flamingo Road*).

Mickey • The eighth most popular name for a male cat in the U.S., and the name of the most famous mouse in the world.
  • A champion tabby mouser that worked for Shepherd & Sons in Burschough, England. It killed about 22,000 mice in twenty-three years.

Midnight • The black cat (with the diamond-studded collar) at the beginning of the television series *Mannix*. It also appeared on the *Barnaby Jones* show, and was the winner of a 1974 TV Patsy Award.
  • The name of a cat offered to Chelsea Clinton, daughter of U.S. president Bill Clinton, by her piano teacher but she picked another cat. See **Socks**.
  • A puppet black cat featured on the television show *Andy's Gang* in the 1950s.

Mike • A pet lion owned by movie actress Tippi Hedren (*The Countess from Hong Kong*).

Mike the Magicat • A cat owned by U.S. president Harry S Truman.

Millie • A Persian cat owned by actress Shirley Jones and husband, Marty Ingels.

Miltie • One of actress Pamela Mason's many cats.

Mimie Paillou • One of French minister Cardinal Richelieu's four cats.

Minerva • In the television series *Our Miss Brooks*, the cat owned by Eve Arden's landlady Mrs. Maggie Davis. Its real name was Orangey. (Minerva was the ancient Roman goddess of wisdom.) See **Cat** and **Rhubarb**.

Minet • A kitten that was found in a mailbag in a London post office just before World War II and subsequently traced to a French post office where it had been employed to reduce the rodent population.

Minette • A cat owned by Hungarian artist Gottfried Mind, who was known as the "Raphael of cats" because of his proclivity to draw cats.

Ming • The cat featured in writer Patricia Highsmith's story *Ming's Biggest Prey*.

Mini-Mini • A cat owned by French writer Colette.

Minioone • Another cat owned by French writer Colette.

Minna Minna Mowbray • A tortoiseshell tabby owned by Michael Joseph, the author of *Charles: The Story of a Friendship*, who believed that cats should be given distinct names out of "true appreciation of feline character." Also see **Charles O'Malley**.

Minnaloushe • The dancing black cat praised in poet William Butler Yeats's "The Cat and the Moon."

Minnie • A name commonly used for ship's cats.

Minnie Esso • The paid mouser cat of the Standard Oil (Ess + O) Development Co. in Bayonne, New Jersey from 1933 to 1946. See **Timmie Esso.**

Minou • A cat owned by actress Betsy von Furstenberg.

Minouche • A fictional cat in Émile Zola's story "La joie de vivre."

Minz • A cat featured in the German children's story *Struwwelpeter.*

Misha • A black Persian cat owned by John Lennon's widow Yoko Ono.

Miss Abigail • *Mary Tyler Moore Show* actor Ed Asner's cat.

Miss Chief • Television actress (*Eight Is Enough*) Susan Richardson's cat.

Miss Hit • A feline owned by actress and felinophile Pamela Mason.

Miss Lucy • One of actress Doris Day's cats.

Miss Mais Oui • Model-actress Lauren Hutton's cat. *Mais oui* means "but yes" or "of course" in French.

Miss Pitty • A cat owned by actress Julie Parrish (*Good Morning World*).

Miss Puss Puss • One of Hungarian-born actress Eva Gabor's cats.

Miss Pussy • A Siamese kitten given to "Lemonade" Lucy, wife of U.S. president Rutherford B. Hayes, by David B. Sickels, a diplomat from Siam. The cat was immediately renamed Siam.

Miste • An Angora cat owned by singer Whitney Houston, to which her album *Whitney* is dedicated. See **Marilyn.**

Misteblu • Singer Whitney Houston's Persian cat.

Mister • A gentlemanly cat owned by television actor (*Police Woman*) Earl Holliman.

Mr. Bigelow • The resident cat at C.O. Bigelow Chemists in New York City at 414 Avenue of the Americas for over fifteen years. When Mr. Bigelow died at eighteen years of age (and eighteen pounds) in mid-1995, many customers mourned the death of the beloved feline.

Mr. Blue • The cat of English-born actor Roddy McDowall (*How Green Was My Valley*).

Mr. Essex • A cat owned by actor Ed Asner (*The Mary Tyler Moore Show*).

Mr. Feather Puss • A kitten given to writer Ernest Hemingway at a time when he called his wife, Hadley, "Feather Cat." He wrote about the cat in the story "Cat in the Rain."

Mr. Jinks • The cat in the cartoons who menaced two mice named Pixie and Dixie, proclaiming "I'll get you meeses!"

Mr. Lucky • One of actress Doris Day's cats.

Mr. Meeyowl • A cat in George Herriman's comic strip *Krazy Kat* and father of Gatita.

Mr. Mistoffelees • "The Original Conjuring Cat" in T.S. Eliot's *Old Possum's Book of Practical Cats* who "produced seven kittens right out of a hat!" He is a small, black cat who can "creep through the tiniest crack."

Mr. Peepers • A cat belonging to actress Edith Fellows, who was a child star in the 1930s and has been in such movies as *Huckleberry Finn* and *Jane Eyre*. (Mr. Peepers was the name of the nerdy science teacher, played by actor Wally Cox, in the 1952–55 television series of the same name.)

Mr. Peter Wells • A cat owned by writer H.G. Wells (*The War of the Worlds*).

Mr. Roots • Television actress Fannie Flagg's cat.

Mr. Ships • A cat that spent some time (like two ships in the night?) at gossip columnist Liz Smith's New York apartment.

Mr. Toby • A black cat owned by Scottish folklore and fairy-tale writer Andrew Lang.

Mrs. Poodles • The name of the first Siamese cat exhibited at an 1871 English cat show.

Mistigris • The cat of Madame Vauquer in Honoré de Balzac's *Old Goriot* (*Père Goriot*).

Mistoffelees • See **Mr. Mistoffelees.**

Misty • The second most popular female cat name in the U.S.

• The full name of presidential daughter Amy Carter's Siamese cat was Misty Malarkey Ying Yang.

Misty Grey • Film actress Mariel Hemingway's cat.

Mitsou • A white Persian cat owned by actress Marilyn Monroe during her marriage to playwright Arthur Miller.

Mittens • In Beatrix Potter's *The Tale of Tom Kitten*, the kitten who laughed so hard she fell off the wall.

Mittons • Comedic television and movie actor Billy Crystal's cat.

Mo • The Maine coon cat owned by science-fiction author James Gunn (*The Immortals*). It weighed twenty-two pounds!

Momcat • A cat owned by actor Michael Callan (*Cat Ballou*) and wife, K Callan (Martha on *Lois and Clark*).

Monroe • The name of cats owned by actor Chris Lemmon (son of Jack) and television actor Earl Holliman (*Police Woman*).

Monsieur Tibault • In Stephen Vincent Benet's *The King of the Cats*, published in 1929, the cat that conducted a symphony orchestra with its tail.

Monstrello • British screen actress (*The Deep*) Jacqueline Bisset's cat.

Monty • Television personality Ed McMahon's cat.

Moon • One of *Hart to Hart* star Robert Wagner's cats.

Moortje • The cat owned by Anne Frank, immortalized in *The Diary of Anne Frank*.

Moppet • One of two kittens that "trod upon their pinafores and fell on their noses" in Beatrix Potter's *The Tale of Tom Kitten*.

Morgan • The ex-pirate cat with a "kind 'art" in writer T.S. Eliot's *Old Possum's Book of Practical Cats*.

Morris • The seventh most popular name for a male cat in the U.S., mostly because it is the name of the finicky feline star of the Nine Lives' cat food commercials that have run on television since the early 1970s. He appeared in the movie *Shamus* (1972) and received the first Patsy Award for an animal in television commercials. The famous tomcat's authorized biography was published by Mary Daniels in 1974.
   • Morris is also the name of cats owned by television actor Mike Farrell (*M*A*S*H*) and writer Paul Gallico (*The Abandoned*).
   • A cat owned by television actress Ruta Lee (*Coming of Age*).

Moshie Cat • The protagonists of the book *Moshie Cat* by Helen Griffith about the "true adventures of a Majorcan kitten."

Mother Tabbyskins • A cat featured in a poem by Elizabeth Anna Hart, described as a "very old, crumplety and lame" cat.

Mouche • The gray cat with green eyes owned by French writer Joris-Karl Huysmans, who mentioned the cat in several of his stories. The name means "fly" in French.
   • Writer Victor Hugo also owned a cat named Mouche.

Moumou • The black cat mentioned in French writer Émile Zola's story "The Sin of Father Mouret" ("La faute de l'abbé Mouret").

Moumoutte Blanche • A white cat owned by French writer Pierre Loti.

Moumoutte Chinoise • A cat owned by French writer Pierre Loti.

Mourka • A cat "spy" in World War II, which was a factor in the battle at Stalingrad. It carried messages back and forth about enemy positions.
• Russian-born ballet master George Balanchine's cat, whom it taught various leaps.

Mouschi • The cat that Anne Frank mentioned in her diary, published posthumously as *The Diary of a Young Girl*. The cat was owned by Peter van Daan whose family was in hiding with the Frank family.

Mouse • A cat owned by singer-songwriter James Taylor ("Fire and Rain").

Muenster • A cat owned by television actor Bill Beyers (*Joe and Valerie*), who likes to name his cats after types of cheeses. See **Brie, Camembert, Gouda,** and **Velveeta.**

Muezza • Muslim prophet Mohammed's favorite cat. The name means "prayer" in Arabic. The cat was bestowed three times three lives by the prophet, hence the "nine lives of a cat" myth.

Muffin • A cat owned by television actress Kate Vernon (*Falcon Crest* and *Who's the Boss?*).

Mungojerrie • Along with Rumpelteazer, "quick-change comedians" and "highly efficient cat-burglars" in writer T.S. Eliot's *Old Possum's Book of Practical Cats*.

Munkustrap • One of the cats with a "peculiar" and "more dignified" name that is mentioned in writer T.S. Eliot's *Old Possum's Book of Practical Cats*.

Munson • A cat belonging to actress Joan Van Ark (*Knot's Landing*).

Murr • A cat owned by writer E.T.A. Hoffmann, who wrote a novel called *Life-Views of the Tomcat Murr*. Murr is mentioned in Honoré de Balzac's *A Daughter of Eve*.

Muscat • One of French writer Colette's many cats.

Mush • Actress Pamela Mason's cat.

Mysouff • A clairvoyant cat owned by French author Alexander Dumas (*The Three Musketeers*).

N

Nancy • One of movie actress Tippi Hedren's many pet lions.

Napoleon • The country cat in the 1970 Disney movie *The Aristocats*.

Natasha • A pet tiger of movie actress Tippi Hedren (*Tiger by the Tail*).

Needra • One of actress Tippi Hedren's pet lions.

Neil • A lion in the Patsy Award Hall of Fame.
   • A pet lion owned by actress Tippi Hedren.

Nellie Bly • The Siamese cat of actress Kim Cattrall, named after the peripatetic American journalist who wrote *Around the World in Seventy-two Days*.

Nelson • A large, black cat owned by British prime minister Winston Churchill during World War II, and named after the famous British admiral Horatio Nelson.

Nemo • British prime minister Harold Wilson's Siamese cat.

Nero • A pet lion owned by Tippi Hedren (*The Birds*).

Nerone • A cat owned by English-born American poet W.H. Auden.

New • One of actress Vivien Leigh's and actor Laurence Olivier's cats.

Nichols • Another cat owned by movie actress Vivien Leigh.

Nickie • The cat of author James Cain (*The Postman Always Rings Twice*).

Nicole • A cat owned by child-actress-turned-diplomat Shirley Temple.

Nikki • A Siberian tiger owned by movie actress Tippi Hedren (*Satan's Harvest*).

Ninja • One of singer Mariah Carey's Persian cats.

Ninety • A "mouser" cat that led a parade across a bridge over the Connecticut River in Old Lyme, Connecticut, as a reward and honor for killing various rodents in the office of engineers.

Nissa • The real name of the baby leopard in the 1930 movie *Bringing Up Baby*, starring Katharine Hepburn and Cary Grant.

Nitchevo • A stray cat in playwright and writer Tennessee Williams's short story "The Malediction." The name comes from the Russian word for "nothing."

Noel • A cat owned by film and television actor Richard Basehart (*Voyage to the Bottom of the Sea*).

Noelle • One of movie actress Tippi Hedren's pet lions.

Noname • The cat of writer-producer Noel Behn, who won an Obie for producing the 1958 Off-Broadway Samuel Beckett play *Endgame*.

Nonoche • One of French writer Colette's cats in her youth, and the mother of **Bijou**.

Norton • The name of the gray striped Scottish Fold cat in Peter Gethers's book *The Cat Who Went to Paris* and its sequel. He was named after Norton, the sewer worker (played by actor Art Carney), in television's *The Honeymooners* series.

Nutty • One of science-fiction author Ray Bradbury's many cats.

O

Octavia • One of many cats owned by movie actress Sandy Dennis (*Who's Afraid of Virginia Woolf?*).

Oedipus Bruiser • A cat owned by actor Brendan Fraser (*The Scout* and *Airheads*).

Old Deuteronomy • A very old cat in writer T.S. Eliot's *Old Possum's Book of Practical Cats*. He's "lived many lives" and "buried many wives."

Olga • One of actress Cybill Shepherd's Siamese cats.

Oliver • The name of the kitten in the 1996 animated Disney feature *Oliver & Company*, a feline and canine variation of Charles Dickens's *Oliver Twist*.
   • The names of cats owned by television actor Daniel J. Travanti (*Hill Street Blues*) and science-fiction author Ray Bradbury.

Ollie • Another black and white cat owned by writer Dan Greenburg (*How to Be a Jewish Mother*).

Oltman • The name of a cat that was elected to the student senate at Southern Illinois University in 1971. (Its owner, Diane E. Oltman, entered the feline in the election to prove that students don't pay attention to student elections!)

O'Malley • The alley cat that rescued and was befriended by Duchess in Walt Disney's 1969 movie *The Aristocats*. Also see **Charles O'Malley**.

One and Only, The • One of French writer Colette's cats.

Orange Cat • Avuncular movie critic Roger Ebert's cat.

Orange Oliver • *Dallas* actress Linda Gray's cat.

Orangey • See **Cat**.

Oscar • A cat eulogized ("Nine lives in one disaster" swallowed "with Sabazian rage") by writer H.P. Lovecraft (*The Dunwich Horror*).

Othello • A black kitten owned by writer and English poet laureate Robert Southey.

Otis • One of British actress Miranda Richardson's two Siamese cats.

Ovid • Another cat owned by writer and English poet laureate Robert Southey, named after the Roman poet.

P

Pammy • A gray and white cat owned by Richard and Francis Lockridge, authors of the Mr. and Mrs. North mystery books.

Panda • See Faith.

Pandora • The Persian cat of actor Clayton Moore, who starred in *The Lone Ranger* during the early years of television.

Pangur Bán • The name of a cat alluded to by a ninth-century Irish scholar, one of the earliest references to the domestic cat in literature.

Pansy • A black cat owned by writer P.D. James.

Panther • *Golden Girls* actress Rue McClanahan's cat.
   • A cat that survived twenty-seven days in a packing box without food and water. In a move from Florida to Oregon, the cat was accidentally shipped in a box. It survived because it was overweight (fourteen pounds) and lost five pounds during the trip.

Partner • A pet lion of actress Melanie Griffith (*Body Double*).

Pascal • A stray cat given to writer Anatole France by his cook, who named the cat after French philosopher and mathematician Blaise Pascal (*Pensées*).

Pasht • Another name for the Egyptian cat-goddess. It is also listed as **Bast** or **Bastet** in various sources.

Patches • A cat owned by actor Stephen Dorff (*What a Dummy*).

Patrina • The Patsy-winning tiger in the Disney movie *A Tiger Walks*, starring Sabu.

Patsy • The name of the kitten photographed with aviator Charles Lindbergh in the cockpit of the Spirit of St. Louis.

Paws • A cat owned by actor Michael Callan and wife K Callan (Martha on *Lois and Clark*).

Peach, The • A cat owned by actress Tammy Grimes (*The Unsinkable Molly Brown*).

Peaches • Singer Barbara Mandrell's cat.
• One of many cats owned by movie actress Sandy Dennis (*Who's Afraid of Virginia Woolf?*), who owned dozens of altered cats at any given time.

Peake • The "husband" of **Chessie**, the feline mascot of the Chesapeake and Ohio Railway.

Penguin • One of actress (*10*) Bo Derek's cats and many pets.

Penny • A pet lion of film actress Tippi Hedren (*The Man with the Albatross*).

Pepe • *Hart to Hart* actor Robert Wagner's cat.

Pepper • The third most popular name for a male cat in the U.S. It was also the name of the alley cat that appeared in Mack Sennett's movies.

• One of movie actress Tippi Hedren's pet leopards.

Pepperpot • A cat owned by English poet and humorist Thomas Hood. It was one of three kittens born to Hood's cat **Tabitha Longclaws Tiddleywink**. See **Scratchaway** and **Sootikins**.

Percy • A cat owned by Czech writer Karel Capek, author of the play *R.U.R.* See **Philip**.

Perruque • A cat owned by French Cardinal Richelieu. The name comes from the French word for "wig" because the cat was rumored to have been born in the Marquis de Racan's wig. See **Racan**.

Persian • Actress Marilyn Monroe's cat.

Persian Snow • A cat owned by naturalist Erasmus Darwin, grandfather of Charles Darwin, the pioneer in evolutionary theory.

Petepeetoo • Pop artist Robert Indiana's cat.

Peter • The legendary Whitehall "mouser" at England's Home Office from 1948 to the late 1950s. It killed hundreds of mice and rats, earning its owner about fifty cents a week.

• One of the cats that possessed a "sensible everyday" name in T.S. Eliot's *Old Possum's Book of Practical Cats*.

• A black cat that resided at London's Savoy Hotel for many years.

Peter Grimm • A "cynical and temperamental" gray cat in Albert Payson Terhune's book *Lad: A Dog*.

Petey • One of actress Pamela Mason's cats.

Petiteu • One of French writer Colette's many cats.

Pettipaws • One of writer T.S. Eliot's pet cats. Also see **George Pushdragon** and **Wiscus**.

Pharaoh • A pet cheetah of movie actress Tippi Hedren (*The Harrad Experiment*).

Philip • A "disheveled and carroty" Angora cat owned by Czech writer Karel Capek, author of the play *R.U.R.* The cat was also known as **Percy**, **Scamp**, or **Rogue**.

Philippe • One of screen actress Jean Arthur's cats.

Phoebe • A cat of television actor Earl Holliman (*Police Woman*).

Phyllis • The name of Felix's girlfriend in the *Felix the Cat* syndicated newspaper cartoons.

Pichinette • A cat owned by French writer Colette.

Picklepuss • A cat belonging to writer Margaret Cooper Gay (*How to Live with a Cat*).

Pierrot • See **Don Pierrot de Navarre**.

Pilar • The name of one of writer Ernest Hemingway's cats—which was also the name of his boat.

Ping • *Trapper John, M.D.* actress Christopher Norris's cat.

Pinkle • Another artistic cat (which rearranged refrigerator magnets) that was featured in the book *Why Cats Paint: A Theory of Feline Aesthetics* by Heather Busch and Burton Silver.

Pinky • A cat owned by television actress Ruta Lee (*Coming of Age*).

Pippers • A grey and white cat owned by *New Yorker* cartoonist George Booth. Originally named Philippa, it was nicknamed Pips.

Pissed Off • A Persian cat of actress Bo Derek (*Tarzan the Ape Man*).

Pitipoo • The name given to writer Paul Gallico's seal-point Siamese cat when it strayed from home to visit a woman in the neighborhood. See **Lulu II**.

Pitti-Sing • One of the "detective" cats in Lilian Jackson Braun's *The Cat Who . . .* mystery novel series. See **Poo-Bah**.

Pixel • The name of a cat owned by science-fiction author Robert Heilein (*Stranger in a Strange Land*).

Plato • One of the "fancier" named cats mentioned in writer T.S. Eliot's *Old Possum's Book of Practical Cats*, obviously inspired by the Greek philosopher and student of Socrates.

Pluto • The storyteller's black cat in Edgar Allan Poe's short story "The Black Cat."

Polar Bear • The name of the white cat in Cleveland Amory's best-seller *The Cat Who Came for Christmas* and its sequel *The Cat and the Curmudgeon*.

Pong • A cat belonging to actor Christopher Norris (*Trapper John, M.D.*).

Poo-Bah • One of the "detective" cats in Lilian Jackson Braun's *The Cat Who . . .* mystery novel series. See **Pitti-Sing**.

Poo Jones • A Siamese cat owned by British actress Vivien Leigh (*A Streetcar Named Desire*).

Poppaea • A stray cat featured in French writer Jean-Paul Sartre's novel *The Age of Reason*. (Poppaea was Roman emperor Nero's wife.)

Poppet • A cat owned by pro football quarterback Joe Namath.

Pouncival • A cat in one of T.S. Eliot's writings, and a character in the Broadway musical *Cats*.

Powderpuff • One of *Charlie's Angels* actress Tanya Roberts's cats.

Pretty White • A pretty, white cat owned by comedic actor and humorist Orson Bean.

Prince Igor • A cat owned by television actress Kate Vernon (*Falcon Crest* and *Who's the Boss?*).

Princess • Another royal and ninth most popular name for a female cat. Artist John Spencer Churchill owned a long-haired tabby named Princess Sophie Louise of Sweden. Princess Vivrakanarda was a cat featured in writer Stephen Vincent Benét's "The King of the Cats."
• The name of one of Ernest Hemingway's many cats.

Princess Squaddle • One of actress Pamela Mason's many cats.

Prudence • A black cat owned by French statesman Georges Clemenceau.

Puddy • The name of cats owned by entertainer-entrepreneur Merv Griffin and actress-dancer Juliet Prowse.

Pudlenka • A stray cat owned by Czech writer Karel Capek. She eventually gave birth to twenty-six kittens.

Puff • The name of the cat in the Dick and Jane reading books for beginning readers. See **Spot**.
• A black Angora cat in Honoré de Balzac's *Heartaches of an English Cat* (*Peines de cœur d'une chatte anglaise*).

Puffing • One of singer-songwriter James Taylor's cats.

Puffins • U.S. president Woodrow Wilson's white cat.

Pulcheria • A cat owned by English poet laureate Robert Southey. (*Pulcher*, as in pulchritude, means "beauty" in Latin.)

Pumpkin • The tenth most popular name for a female cat in the U.S., and a popular name for orange-colored cats in general.

Punkin Puss • A cat featured in Hanna-Barbera cartoons.

Purcy • A cat owned by actor Jackie Joseph (Jackie Parker on *The Doris Day Show*).

Purdoe • A cat that English novelist (*Erewhon*), essayist and satirist Samuel Butler gave to a friend. (Purdoe was one of Butler's pseudonyms.)

Pushdragon • See **George Pushdragon**.

Puss in Boots • In children's stories, a cat, inherited by a poor boy, who challenged an enemy to turn into a mouse and then ate him. He and his master subsequently took over the dead man's castle.

Pussm • A cat owned by television actor Jonathan Brandis (Lucas Wolenczak on *Seaquest DSV*).

PussyCat • The cat of screenwriter Edward Anhalt, who won an Oscar for the 1964 movie *Becket*.

Pussy Galore • A tomcat owned by comedic actor and humorist Orson Bean, named, tongue-in-cheek, after one of James Bond's love interests.

Pussy Gato • The name of Gordo's cat in the comic *Gordo* by Gus Arriola. (*Gato* means "cat" in Spanish.)

Pyewacket • The lavender Siamese cat in the 1950 John Van Druten play *Bell, Book and Candle* and subsequent 1958 movie starring Kim Novak and James Stewart. The cat was the winner of the 1959 Patsy Award.

Q

Quartz • See Tom Quartz.

Quaxo • One of the cats with a "peculiar" and "more dignified" name that is mentioned in writer T.S. Eliot's *Old Possum's Book of Practical Cats*.

Queen • The most royal of names to bestow upon a female cat, and much less popular (#192) than Princess (#9).

Queen Di • One of actress Pamela Mason's cats.

Queen Tut • Television personality and talk-show sidekick Ed McMahon's cat.

Queenie • A much more popular variation of Queen and the twentieth most popular cat name.

Quentin • A cat owned by former child actor Rick Schroder (*Champ* and *Silver Spoons*).

R

Ra • The Egyptian sun-god, which is occasionally portrayed as a cat.

Raggedy Ann • A tabby cat owned by artist Louise Nevelson.

Ralph • A "therapy cat" and cowinner of the Delta Society's Lifetime Achievement Award in 1995 for frequent visits to nursing homes to make patients smile, talk, and, in general, feel better.

Ramaahipati IV • The Siamese cat of Irish-born film actress Greer Garson (*Mrs. Miniver*).

Rascal • A cat owned by actress Leigh Lawson (*Tess*).

Ratzo • Actress Shelley Taylor's cat, named after Dustin Hoffman's character in the film *Midnight Cowboy*.

Raul • A talkative cat featured in Howard Chaykin's comic strip *American Flagg!*

Ready • A cat in the *Ruff and Ready* comic series.

Rebel • Actress Shirley Jones and comedian-husband Marty Ingels's cat.

Reddy • The ginger cat in Hanna-Barbera's 1957 animated television series *The Ruff and Reddy Show*, their first television series.

Renfield • A cat owned by actor Jay Johnson (Chuck/Bob Campbell on *Soap*), named after the real-estate agent in the movie *Dracula*, based on the Bram Stoker novel.

Renfield Dracu • One of screen vamp Elvira's cats.

Reno • The cat of actress Barbara Bach (*The Spy Who Loved Me*).

Rhadame • A cat owned by English-born American poet W.H. Auden.

Rhett Butler • One of movie actress Tippi Hedren's pet cheetahs. See **Scarlett O'Hara**.
• A cat owned by game-show hostess Vanna White. See **Ashley**. Both names come from the classic Margaret Mitchell novel *Gone with the Wind*.

Rhubarb • The name of the cat who inherits a baseball team in H. Allen Smith's story "Rhubarb," made into a movie in 1951 starring Ray Milland, Jan Sterling, and Gene Lockhart, for which the striped cat, whose real name is Orangey, won a Patsy Award. The film feline went on to play Minerva in the *Our Miss Brooks* television series. Orangey also costarred with Jackie Gleason in the 1961 film *Gigot* and appeared as Audrey Hepburn's **Cat** in the movie *Breakfast at Tiffany's* (1961), and was awarded another Patsy.

Ringo • A cat owned by television actor Dennis Weaver (*Gunsmoke* and *McCloud*).

Riff-Raff • The yellow ginger cat star of the British television cartoon series *Cats & Co*. Riff Raff was an American alley cat that wore a cap and scarf and was a gang leader.

Roadie • A cat of television actress Jennie Garth (Kelly Taylor on *Beverly Hills 90210*).

Robbie, Jr. • One of movie actress Tippi Hedren's many pet lions.

Rocky • The name of the bobcat in the Mercury Bobcat television commercials.
• A cat owned by humorist Wil Shriner, son of humorist Herb Shriner.

Roger • One of two tiger cats owned by mystery writer John D. MacDonald, author of Travis McGee novels, and featured in *The House Guests*. See **Geoffrey**.

Rogue • One of Czech playwright Karel Capek's cats.

Roma • One of many cats owned by movie actress Sandy Dennis (*Who's Afraid of Virginia Woolf?*), who owned dozens of altered cats at any given time.

Romeo • A Persian cat owned by heiress Peggy Guggenheim.
• A cat owned by Mary Frances Crosby, widow of Bing Crosby.

Ruff • The cat in the comic book series and television series *Ruff and Ready*.

Rumpelstilzchen • A cat owned by English poet laureate Robert Southey, "Rumpel" or "Rumples" McBum was primarily an indoor cat. See **Hurlyburlybuss**.

Rumpler • The Abyssinian cat who starred in the 1978 Disney movie *The Cat from Outer Space*.

Rumpleteazer • Along with Mungojerrie, "quick-change comedians" and "highly efficient cat-burglars" in writer T.S. Eliot's *Old Possum's Book of Practical Cats*.

Rumpuscat • See **Great Rumpuscat**.

Rum Tum Tugger • One of the cats, billed as a "Curious Cat" but really a contrary cat, in T.S. Eliot's *Old Possum's Book of Practical Cats*.

Rusty or ***Rusti*** • The ninth most popular name for a male cat in the U.S.
   • The name of cats owned by actor Bruce Boxleitner (ex-wife named Kitty!) and baseball pro Ozzie Smith.
   • The cat of Elly May Clampett (Donna Douglas) in television's *The Beverly Hillbillies*.

Ruth • One of actress Pamela Mason's cats.

Rybolov • The name of a cat owned by Russian composer Aleksandr Borodin. The name means "fisher" in Russian, and the cat was named because it was able to catch fish in a stream near Borodin's house.

S

S.C. • The remarkable cat of "Peekaboo" hairdo actress Veronica Lake. It made Robert Ripley's *Believe It or Not* column for having six toes on each of its front paws. The S.C. stood for "Solid Citizen." See **Black Beau**.

Sabo • A cat owned by actress Stella Stevens (*The Poseidon Adventure*).

Sadie • The name of cats owned by comedic actor Dudley Moore, actress Eva Gabor, and actor James Mason.

Saha • A cat in French writer Colette's novel *The Cat* (*La chatte*).

Saki • Actress Joanne Woodward and husband Paul Newman's cat.

Salem • The cat of teenage witch Sabrina in television cartoons.
   • A cat owned by British-born actress Kim Cattrall (*Star Trek VI*).

Salome • One of *Charlie's Angels* actress Tanya Roberts's cats.

Sam • A green-eyed black cat in writer Walter de La Mare's story "Broomsticks."
   • The name of cats owned by actress Adrienne Barbeau and by actress Jean Arthur.

Samantha • The most popular name for a female cat in the U.S., Samantha has been the name of cats owned by *Cosmopolitan* magazine editor Helen Gurley Brown, and by actress Shirley Jones and her husband, Marty Ingels.
   • The name of the Persian cat of actor Jonathan Taylor Thomas (*Home Improvement*).

Sans Lendemain • A Persian cat owned by heiress Peggy Guggenheim, given to her by writer James Joyce's son, Giorgio. The name means "without the next day" in French.

Sara • The Siamese cat of actress Jamie Lyn Bauer (*Bare Essence*).

Sascha • A large white cat owned by television talk-show host Regis Philbin.
   • A Persian cat owned by Yoko Ono, John Lennon's widow.

Sassy • One of actress Linda Evans's cats.

• The prima donna Himalayan cat (voice-over by Sally Field) in the 1996 Disney movie *Homeward Bound 2: Lost in San Francisco*.

Satan • A white-spotted cat whose owner, Agnes Waterhouse (with her daughter Joan), was executed in 1566 in the first witchcraft trial in England.

Satin • A tiger in the 1954 movie *Demetrius and the Gladiator*, starring Victor Mature and Susan Hayward.

Sausage • British actor (*Star Trek: The Next Generation*) Patrick Stewart's cat.

Savortooth • One of cartoonist George Booth's cats.

Scamp • Czech playwright Karel Capek's cat.

Scamper • A cat owned by actress Brooke Adams (*Days of Heaven*).

Scarface • A pet lion owned by movie actress Tippi Hedren.

Scarlet • One of television talk-show host Regis Philbin's Himalayan cats.

Scarlett O'Hara • Another pet cheetah of film actress Tippi Hedren.

Scheherazade • A cat owned by writer Carl van Vechten, named after the Sultan's wife in *The Arabian Nights*. Van Vechten wrote *The Tiger in the House*, generally considered a classic book about cats.

Schnitz • A cat of actor Bruce Boxleitner (*How the West Was Won*).

Scooter • Television actress Priscilla Presley's cat.

Scootz • One of the rock 'n' roll cats in the Hanna-Barbera television series *The Cattanooga Cats*.

Scotty • One of actress Sally Struthers's cats.

Scratch • *Weird Science* actress Kelly LeBrock's cat.

Scratchaway • A cat owned by English writer Thomas Hood. It was one of three kittens born to Hood's cat **Tabitha Longclaws Tiddleywink**. See **Pepperpot** and **Sootikins**.

Sebastian • A pet cat in the *Josie and the Pussycats* animated television series.

Sekmet • An Egyptian goddess in the form of a cat. In contrast to **Bast**, it is a destructive force.

Selima • British writer Horace Walpole's tabby cat which drowned in a goldfish bowl while trying to catch a fish—and the subject of a poem by Thomas Gray—"Ode on the Death of a Favourite Cat Drowned in a Tub of Gold Fishes."

Señor • A blind cat owned by actress Stefanie Powers (*Hart to Hart*). (It was featured on a cat food calendar as Mr. July.)

Séraphîta • A white female Angora in French writer Théophile Gautier's novel *The White and Black Dynasties*. (The name is from a character in an Honoré de Balzac novel.)

Serpolet • One of Cardinal Richelieu's cats.

17 • The name of the cat in the mid-1970s movie *Dr. Shrinker*.

Seymour • A cat owned by mystery writer Lawrence Sanders (*The First Deadly Sin*).

Sharky • Comedic actor Dom DeLuise's cat.

Shayna • A cat owned by Estelle Getty (*Golden Girls*).

She • The name of a Persian cat owned by actress Bo Derek and a Siamese cat owned by actress Linda Evans—both of whom, by the way, have been married to actor-director John Derek.

Sheba • A queenly cat owned by television talk-show host Sally Jessy Raphael.

Shelia • One of movie actress Tippi Hedren's pet lions.

Shelly • *Memphis Belle* actor Sean Astin's cat.

Shere Khan • The lame tiger in Rudyard Kipling's *The Jungle Book* that kept threatening Mowgli. See **Bagheera**.

Sherry • A Siamese female cat that traveled 225,000 miles in thirty-three days when it left its cage in the cargo section of a Pan Am jet.
   • A Siamese cat owned by the writing couple Richard and Frances Lockridge, who wrote the Mr. and Mrs. North series. See **Gin** and **Martini**.

Shimbleshanks • One of the cats in T.S. Eliot's *Old Possum's Book of Practical Cats*.

Si • The name of one of the Siamese cats in the 1955 Disney feature *Lady and the Tramp*. (The other Siamese cat was named Am—as in Siam!)

Siafu • A "runty" cat owned by author and animal lover Roger Caras. The name is Swahili for "small biting ant."

Sillabub • A cat in one of T.S. Eliot's writings, and a character in the Broadway musical *Cats*.

Simba • A cat owned by actress Gretchen Wyler (*On Our Own*).
   • Singer Michael Jackson's pet lion.

Sillabub • A cat in one of T.S. Eliot's writings, and a character in the Broadway musical *Cats*.

Simon • The fifth most popular name for a male cat in the U.S.
   • A British black and white neutered male that won a medal for "meritorious and distinguished service." It was the mascot of the *H.M.S. Amethyst*, which was attacked by the Chinese at the Yangtse River in 1949. Although wounded, Simon killed large numbers of rats, which prevented the spread of disease on the frigate.

Simpkin • The tailor's cat in Beatrix Potter's *The Tailor of Gloucester* (1903).

Singh Singh • A pet tiger of movie actress Tippi Hedren (*Roar*).

Sir Green-Eyes Grimalkin de Tabby de Sly • The focus of writer Laura E. Richard's book *The Dandy Cat*.

Sir John Langbourne • A cat owned by English jurist and philosopher Jeremy Bentham, who fed it pasta at the dinner table.

Sir John Rumpalo • A cat owned by cartoonist George Booth. Its nickname was Rumples.

Sir Thomas Dido • One of British poet laureate Robert Southey's cats.

Sir Tom • A mountain lion befriended by a young boy in the 1966 movie *The Cat*.

Sizi • A cat owned by Albert Schweitzer while doing missionary work in Africa.

Skaratch • One of the many cats owned by British poet laureate Robert Southey.

Skeezix • A cat owned by television newscaster Bree Walker. (The name is from a character in Frank King's comic strip *Gasoline Alley*. It was a baby found on the doorstep of a bachelor on Valentine's Day, 1921.)
 • One of two cats that received a blood transfusion in the 1930s from **Buttercup**, a yellow tomcat from Colorado, thereby saving its life. See **Snicklefritz**.

Skimbleshanks • The "Railway Cat" in writer T.S. Eliot's *Old Possum's Book of Practical Cats*. Skimble is always "fresh and bright," even in the middle of the night.

Skipper • A cat owned by actress Jean Arthur (*Diamond Jim*).

Skittles • Ice skater Kristi Yamaguchi's cat.

Skunk • The unusually marked black and white cat owned by writer Ernest Hemingway.

Slats • The first lion featured in the MGM movie studio logo.

Sleator • A cat owned by actress Kathleen Beller (Kirby in *Dynasty*.)

Slippers • A six-toed gray cat owned by U.S. president Theodore Roosevelt.

Smirky • Phileas' cat in the Hanna-Barbera cartoon *Around the World in Seventy-nine Days*.

Smokey • A good name for a gray cat. Actress Shirley Jones and singer husband Jack Cassidy owned a Smokey.
  • Actor Rick Schroder also named one of his cats Smokey.

Smoky • U.S. president Calvin Coolidge was once given a bobcat named Smoky.
  • A cat owned by television actress Ruta Lee (*Coming of Age*).

Smudge • A white cat with a black "smudge" on its forehead, the childhood cat of writer John Gardner.

Snagglepuss • A cat in a Hanna-Barbera cartoons.

Sneakers • The protagonist in Margaret Wise Brown's *Seven Stories about a Cat Named Sneakers*.
  • A cat owned by actress-singer Doris Day.

Snicklefritz • One of two cats that received a life-saving blood transfusion from a yellow tomcat named **Buttercup** in Colorado in the 1930s. See **Skeezix**.

Snooper • A cat featured in Hanna-Barbera cartoons.

Snoopy • The famous name of cartoonist Charles Schulz's beagle, Snoopy, is actually a good name for a curious cat, but there are many! It is the sixth most popular name for a male cat in the U.S.

Snowdove • One of English writer Thomas Hardy's many cats.

Snowdrop • The White Queen cat in Lewis Carroll's *Through the Looking Glass*.

Snowy • A white cat featured in the advertising of the Utica and Mohawk Cotton Mills many years ago.

Snug Harbor • A cat owned by Joan Van Ark (*Knot's Landing*).

Socks • The white-footed cat of Chelsea Clinton, daughter of U.S. president Bill Clinton. It was given to her by her piano teacher. Chelsea chose the cat over its sibling **Midnight** because the white toes looked like socks, hence the name.

Solomon • The white long-haired cat owned by the villain Bloefeld in two James Bond films, *You Only Live Twice* and *Diamonds Are Forever*.
• A cat that worked with a customs inspector on the Texas border in 1949, famous for its ability to detect illegal items in luggage.

Sonja • The female Persian cat friend of Heathcliff, the cartoon cat created by George Gatley.

Sonny • A cat owned by television actress Mary Jo Catlett (Pearl Gallagher on *Diff'rent Strokes*).

Sootikins • The third of three kittens born to writer Thomas Hood's cat **Tabitha Longclaws Tiddleywink**. See **Pepperpot** and **Scratchaway**.

Soriana • A white cat mentioned by Italian short story writer Giovanni Strapola in his version of the Puss in Boots story.

Soumise • One of Cardinal Richelieu's many cats.

Sour Mash • One of Mark Twain's many cats, named after the starter from which bourbon is made.

Souris • A cat owned by stage and screen actress Colleen Dewhurst (*Annie Hall*). About the cat, she noted, "We found him in the town of Souris on Prince Edward Island. *Souris* means 'mouse,' and if you stick a T at the beginning, it's Yiddish for trouble."

Spic & Span • Another cat of actress Nanette Fabray, named after a household cleanser. See **Ajax, Borax,** and **Brillo.**

Spice • A forty-three pound ginger and white tomcat, one of the heaviest on record, from Ridgefield, Connecticut. It died in 1977.

Spider • One of actor James Mason's many cats.

Spithead • English mathematician and philosopher Sir Isaac Newton's cat.

Spook • The hip cat in the Hanna-Barbera television cartoon *Top Cat*. Its voice was that of actor Leo De Lyon.

Spooky • The name of Fenwick Flooky's black and white cat in the comic strip *Smokey Stover*, later the "star" of its own strip *Spooky*. It always wore a red bandage (or ribbon?) on the end of its tail.

Sports Fan • A cat owned by movie critic Roger Ebert (the avuncular one!).

Spot • The *feline* companion of the dog Hong Kong Phooey in Hanna-Barbera cartoons.

Spunky • A "therapy cat" and cowinner of the Delta Society's Lifetime Achievement Award in 1995 for frequent visits to nursing homes to make patients smile, talk, and in general, feel better.

Steve • *Flamingo Road* actor Mark Harmon's cat.

Stink • One of James Mason's cats.

Stinky • Actress Morgan Fairchild's Persian cat.

Streaky • Superman's super cat in the comic books.

Stripes • A cat owned by Lorraine Bracco (*Goodfellas*).

Sucker • A cat of actor Stephen Macht (*Knot's Landing*).

Sugar • A sweet feline owned by actor Jack Nicholson (*One Flew over the Cuckoo's Nest*).

Suki • A fairly common name for a Siamese cat even though the name is of Japanese origin.

Sukie • A Maltese gray cat owned by author and illustrator Edward Gorey.

Sumfun Abigail • A Siamese cat owned by writer Roger Caras when he was living in London.

Sunny • A cat owned by actress Jill St. John (*Diamonds Are Forever*).

Super Cat • A cat owned by Oscar-winning actress Janet Gaynor (*Seventh Heaven*).

Superboy • One of actress Eva Gabor's cats.

Superkatt • A feline comic book hero from the 1940s. See Dogs—**Humphrey**.

Susie • The first Scottish fold kitten. It was born in 1961 on the McRae's Tayside farm in Perthshire, Scotland.

Suzanne • A cat of gossip columnist Liz Smith.

Suzie • Actress Stella Stevens's cat.

Sweet White • A cat owned by comedic actor and humorist Orson Bean.

Sybil • A cat owned by television's Mr. Rogers.
  • A cat owned by *Night Court* actress Markie Post.

Sylvester • The lisping ("Thuffering Thuckatash!") black and white Warner Brothers cartoon cat (full name: Sylvester P. Pussycat) that is always chasing Tweety Pie, the canary fond of saying "I tawt I taw a puddytat."
  • Actress Melissa Gilbert's cat.

Sylvia • A cat of television actress Laurie Burton (*Rituals*).

Syn Cat • The Patsy Award–winning Siamese cat that helps FBI agents thwart kidnappers in the Disney movie *That Darn Cat.*

T

Tabasco • A cat owned by political commentator Cokie Roberts.

Tabby • Tad Lincoln's cat when his father Abraham was president of the United States.

Tabitha • Tabby for short, the Siamese cat in Bianco Bradbury's *One Kitten Too Many.*
  • A cat owned by ballerina Cynthia Harvey.

Tabitha Longclaws Tiddleywink • Poet Thomas

Hood's female cat and mother of **Pepperpot**, **Scratchaway**, and **Sootikins**.

Tabitha Twitchit • The mother of Tom Kitten, a shrewd "businesswoman" in Beatrix Potter's *The Tale of Tom Kitten*.

Taffy • A "topaz-coloured cat" in writer Christopher Morley's poem "In Honor of Taffy Topaz."

Tailspin • In Ruthven Todd's "Space Cat," a cat that was born on the moon.

Taki • Detective novelist Raymond Chandler's black Persian cat.

Tallulah • The name of cats owned by actress Fannie Flagg ("Mike" Preston on *The New Dick Van Dyke Show*) and by actress Lorna Patterson (*Private Benjamin* and the feature *Airplane*).

Tama • A tortoiseshell cat owned by British author Lafcadio Hearn, who often wrote about things Japanese (*Tama* is Japanese for "jewel.").

Tammany • A cat of humorist Mark Twain, it was named after Tammany Hall, the headquarters of the Tammany Society, a Democratic political organization in New York City in the late nineteenth and early twentieth centuries, the symbol of which was a tiger.

Tango • A marmalade (or tangerine?) colored cat owned by British prime minister Winston Churchill and painted by artist William Nicholson.

Tanner • The first lion to be used in the Technicolor versions of MGM feature films. See **Jackie**, **Leo**, and **Slats**.

Tante Hedwig • Writer Paul Gallico's farm cat. *Tante* is German for "aunt."

Tantomile • A cat in one of T.S. Eliot's writings, and a character in the Broadway musical *Cats*.

Tao • The male Siamese cat in Sheila Burnford's 1961 novel *The Incredible Journey*.

T.C. • Short for Top Cat, a Hanna-Barbera cartoon character. See **Top Cat**.

Tara • A Siamese cat owned by actor Jack Albertson (*The Subject Was Roses*).

Tater • One of science-fiction author Ray Bradbury's many cats.

Taylor • The Persian cat of soap-opera star Tony Geary.

Teddy Bear • Television's *Lou Grant* star Ed Asner's Persian cat.

Teegy • The cat of actress Tammy Grimes (Broadway's *The Unsinkable Molly Brown*).

Teeney • One of author-trendsetter Martha Stewart's cats. See **Weeney**.

Terra Catta • The cat of Victoria Principal, a play on the words "terra cotta," a type of unglazed earthenware of a brownish-orange color.

Thomas • A cat owned by television game-show host Bob Barker.

Thompkins • See **Tomkins**.

Thrum • A cat taken from Seminole, Oklahoma, to St. Louis, Missouri. On its own, Thrum returned to Seminole six weeks later—a 450-mile trip.

Thunder • Singer Olivia Newton-John's cat.

Tidbits • Stage and screen actress Gwen Verdon's cat.

Tiffany • A cat owned by Dom DeLuise—it likes *dog* food. Actress Bo Derek also named one of her cats Tiffany.

Tiger • The most popular name for a male cat and eighth most popular name for a female cat in the U.S. It was the name of one of U.S. president Calvin "Silent Cal" Coolidge's cats—it had tigerlike striping, and also the name of one of the Brontë sisters' pet cats.
 • A male cat that was lost while on vacation in Wausau, Wisconsin, with its owners, Tim and Susan Fromelt, during the summer of 1977—but returned to the Frommelt's home in Dubuque, Iowa, in February 1978—250 miles away.
 • Singer Aaron Neville's half-Persian, half-alley cat.
 • Another artistic cat (its "crude and indifferent smears ... suggest greed and destruction") that was featured in the book *Why Cats Paint: A Theory of Feline Aesthetics* by Heather Busch and Burton Silver.

Tiger Ann • A cat that accidentally appeared on a Republican fund-raising mailing list.

Tigger • A variation of Tiger and a popular name for both male and female cats. It is also the name of the boundless tiger in A.A. Milne's *The House at Pooh Corner* (1928), later appearing in animated television movies.
 • Writer Gladys Taber owned a Manx named Tigger.
 • A cat owned by actor Stephen Dorff (*What a Dummy*).

Tiggy • Comedic actor (*Sayonara*) Red Buttons's cat.

Timmie Esso • The second-generation, paid mouser cat at the Standard Oil Development Co. in Bayonne, New Jersey, after its mother, **Minnie Esso**, died in 1946.

Timmy's Kitty • One of *Golden Girls* actress Betty White's cats.

Tinker • The name of a black cat owned by ballerina Dame Alicia Markova, and a cat owned by actress Juliet Prowse.

Tinker Bell • Singer Waylon Jennings's cat.

Tinker Toy • The smallest cat on record, according to the *Guinness Book of World Records*—a $2^3/_4$-inch-tall by $7^1/_2$-inch-long male blue-point Himalayan-Persian cat.

Tipperary • A Persian cat that appeared in Albert Payson Terhune's *Lad: A Dog*.

Tippi • A female British tabby cat that produced 343 kittens in its lifetime.
 • One of singer-actor Bobby Sherman's cats.

T. K. • A black cat owned by comedic actress Betty White.

Tobermory • A highly intelligent cat that Saki (H.H. Munro) wrote about in one of his stories ("Beyond Cat").

Togar • One of actress Tippi Hedren's many pet lions.

Tom • A popular name for a cat, if ever there was one.
 • The name of the cat in the Tom and Jerry comedy team in MGM and Hanna-Barbera cartoon produc-

tions. (Tom made his movie debut as Jasper in *Puss Gets the Boot* in 1940.) They soon became cartoon and comic book favorites.

• The name of cats owned by humorist Orson Bean and television actor Earl Holliman (*Police Woman*).

• One of newsman-author Roger Caras's cats—a black one—that came and went as it wished.

Tom Cat • An orange cat owned by television personality Katie Kelly.

Tom, Jr. • A cat owned by writer Harriet Beecher Stowe. According to Stowe's sister Catherine, the cat "had a fit and acted queer" and was "shot with a gun."

Tom Kitten • In Beatrix Potter's *The Tale of Tom Kitten*, the fat kitten who burst out of his clothes, later worn by some ducks. The family of President John F. Kennedy owned a cat named Tom Kitten. JFK was allergic to it and it was given to Jacqueline Kennedy's secretary, Mary Gallagher, who renamed it Tom Terrific.

Tom Quartz • A fictional cat that Mark Twain wrote about in *Roughing It* (1872).

• President Theodore Roosevelt owned a feisty and fluffy cat named Tom Quartz, named after Twain's cat.

Tomkins • One of singer Mariah Carey's Persian cats. (Sometimes spelled as *Thompkins*.)

Tommy • A cat owned by comedic actor Harvey Korman (*The Carol Burnett Show*).

Tomorrow • *Roman Holiday* actress Audrey Hepburn's cat.

Tonga • The name of the first Ocicat, named by the daughter of a breeder who thought it looked like an ocelot.

Tongaru • A pet lion owned by actress Melanie Griffith's mother, Tippi Hedren.

Tonto • Actor Art Carney's orange tabby costar in the movie *Harry and Tonto*.

Tony • The tiger featured on the package and in the advertising of Kellogg's Frosted Flakes cereal. His sales line was, "They're gr-r-reat!"

Toonses • A cat owned by actress Melissa Gilbert (*Little House on the Prairie*).

Topaz • A cat owned by playwright Tennessee Williams (*Cat on a Hot Tin Roof*).

Top Boy • One of actor James Mason's many cats.

Top Cat • A smart-aleck cat in the Hanna-Barbera television cartoon *Top Cat*, also known as T.C. The voice of Top Cat was that of actor Arnold Stang.

Toss • The nickname (short for Atossa) for the Persian cat of nineteenth-century British Victorian poet Matthew Arnold.

Tough Charlie • The tough cat that challenged Tough Tom in Paul Gallico's "The Ballad of Tough Tom."

Tough Tom • The victorious cat in Paul Gallico's "The Ballad of Tough Tom."

Toune • One of French writer Colette's many cats.

Trans • A pet lion owned by actress Tippi Hedren.

Travis • Bandleader Doc Severinsen's cat.

Tree • One of actor James Mason's cats.

Tristan • Actress Catherine Oxenberg's cat and house-mate of cat **Isolde**.

Trot • The nickname of English author and poet Thomas Hardy's cat, **Kiddleywinkempoops**.

Tuffy • A Persian cat of actress Loni Anderson (*WKRP in Cincinnati*).

Tula • The cat of film actress Barbara Baxley (*East of Eden* and *Norma Rae*).

Tugger • Another variation of **Tiger** and **Tigger**.

Tumblebrutus • Growltiger's "bosun" cat in writer T.S. Eliot's *Old Possum's Book of Practical Cats*.

Turkey • Movie actress (*Psycho*) Janet Leigh's cat.

Tut-Azam • A Siamese cat owned by actor Jack Albertson (*Chico and the Man*).

Twinkles • A part Siamese, part tomcat owned by restaurateur Vincent Sardi.

Two Face • A calico cat belonging to *Dynasty* actress Linda Evans.

Tzing-Mao • One of singer-composer James Taylor's cats, no doubt a bit of wordplay on the Chinese beer Tsing-Tao.

Tyg • A baby tiger in the Hanna-Barbera cartoon *Pound Puppies*.

V

Valeriano Weyler • An Angora cat owned by U.S. president William McKinley. It was named after the governor of Cuba.

Vance • An Egyptian cat owned by stage and screen actress Colleen Dewhurst (*Annie Hall*). See **Vivian**.

Vashka • The Russian blue cat of Czar Nicholas I.

Velveeta • A cat owned by television actor Bill Beyers (*Joe and Valerie*), who likes to name his cats after types of cheeses. See **Brie, Camembert, Gouda,** and **Muenster.**

Vic Vic • One of science-fiction author Ray Bradbury's many cats.

Victor • One of the cats mentioned in T.S. Eliot's *Old Possum's Book of Practical Cats* that possessed a "sensible everyday" name.

Victoria • A cat not mentioned in writer T.S. Eliot's *The Possum's Book of Practical Cats* but in the Broadway play *Cats.*

Vincent • A cat owned by a movie actor named Price—Vincent, of course.
  • It is also the name of cat owned by actress Elizabeth Taylor.

Vincentius • One of the oldest cat names on record. A depiction of Vincentius wearing a red collar was found in Morocco and was dated back to Roman times.

Virgil • A cat named after a Roman poet (*The Aeneid*) and owned by English poet laureate Robert Southey.

Vivian • Another Egyptian cat owned by stage and screen actress Colleen Dewhurst (*Annie Hall*). See **Vance.**

Victor • A cat mentioned in T.S. Eliot's *Old Possum's Book of Practical Cats*, referred to as Victoria in the Broadway musical *Cats*.

Voodoo • A champion black Persian cat from England in the late 1950s.

W

W.C. Fields • A cat owned by Ed McMahon, who has always been an admirer of comedic actor and juggler W.C. Fields.

Waldo • One of British actress Miranda Richardson's two Siamese cats.

Wallace • A twenty-pound Russian blue cat owned by composer Ned Rorem.

Wally • English actress Gertrude Lawrence's Siamese cat. (The actress starred in the original Broadway production of *The King and I*).

Waowhler • One of British poet laureate Robert Southey's cats.

Warlord • A cat owned by humorist Orson Bean.

Weasel • Rock singer Cyndi Lauper's cat.

Webster • A large, black cat in P.G. Wodehouse's "The Story of Webster."

Weedon • A white and gray tiger cat owned by author and illustrator Edward Gorey.

Weeney • A cat of author-trendsetter Martha Stewart and companion to a cat named **Teeney**.

Wendy • Another cat owned by humorist Orson Bean.

Whisper • Comedic actor John Belushi's cat.

Whistle • A cat owned by television actress Marcia Rodd (*Trapper John, M.D.*).

White Heather • A blue Persian cat of Queen Victoria, inherited by her son Edward VII.

Whitehead • One of writer Ernest Hemingway's cats, a black and white tomcat, named after the name of the street in Key West, Florida, on which he lived.

Whitey • A white cat owned by actor James Mason and his wife, Pamela.

Wilberforce • A cat cited by British cat psychologist Peter Neville (*Do Cats Need Shrinks? Cat Behavior Explained*) as having an insatiable lust for condoms! When the rubber-loving feline attacked a newly adorned condom, the pouncing irritated its owner *in flagrante delicto* enough to warrant exile to the nearest animal shelter.

William • The name of English novelist Charles Dickens's white cat, later changed to Williamina when its true sex was manifest.

   • It is also the name of the egotistical cat in James Thurber's "The Cat in the Lifeboat" from his *Further Fables for Our Time* (1956).

Williamina • See William.

Willie • The name of cats owned by comic George Burns and producer David Wolper.

Willy Fog • A gentlemanly lion in the animated cartoon *Around the World with Willy Fog*, a spoof of the movie *Around the World in Eighty Days*.

Win Win • One of science-fiction author Ray Bradbury's many cats.

Wingley • A cat owned by New Zealand–born writer Katherine Mansfield and her husband, editor John Middleton Murry.

Winston • In the movie *The Late Show* (1977), the name of Lily (Margo) Tomlin's lost cat. (She hired Art Carney, playing a detective, to track down the cat.)

Winston Churchill • The name of eccentric actress Tallulah Bankhead's pet lion.

Wiscus • A real cat (not just a "literary" one) owned by writer T.S. Eliot.

Wolf • The Abyssinian cat of actor Christopher Walken (*The Deer Hunter*).

Wong Mau • A brown, female, hybrid-Siamese cat that was bred to help establish the Burmese breed.

Wuzzy • One of writer Paul Gallico's cats.

Y

Yankee • Heart surgeon Dr. William De Vries's cat.

Yaz • A cat owned by documentary filmmaker Ken Burns (*Baseball*). Yaz is short for Yazstremski, a Hall of Fame baseball player famous for his slugging.

Z

Zamba • The lion in the movie *Lion*. Zamba also won a Patsy Award for appearances in the Dreyfus Fund television commercials.

Zap • One of basketball great Wilt Chamberlain's cats. See **Zip**.

Zara • A cat owned by English writer Horace Walpole.

Zaza • A gray female cat featured in the 1965 animated television show *Hector's House*.

Zazu • Movie actress Tippi Hedren's pet Bengal tiger.

Zeke • One of actor James Mason's cats.

Ziggy • Television weatherman Willard Scott's cat.

Zip • Another one of basketball great Wilt Chamberlain's cats. See **Zap**.

Zizi • A silver-gray Angora cat owned by French writer Théophile Gautier.

Zizou • A kitten that liked mountain climbing. It was owned by Mont Blanc shelter keepers and could climb 2,000 feet per day.

Zobeide • Another cat owned by French writer Théophile Gautier.

Zoë • The black and white cat owned by British poet and painter Dante Gabriel Rossetti. Zoë is from the Greek word for "life."

Zombi, The • A cat owned by English poet laureate Robert Southey.

Zoroaster • A cat owned by humorist Mark Twain, named after a Persian religious philosopher who believed that life was a continuous struggle between good and evil forces.

Zsa Zsa • Actress Eva Gabor's cat named after sister Zsa Zsa.

Zuleika • A cat owned by French writer Théophile Gautier.

Zulema • A cat owned by French writer Théophile Gautier.

Zula • A cat of singer-songwriter James Taylor.

Zuru • Alphabetically, the last of actress Tippi Hedren's many pet lions.

<u>DOGS</u>

A

Abakaru • The dog of Cheops, the king of Egypt (circa 2650 B.C.) and builder of the Great Pyramid.

Abel • An Alaskan malamute of actress Cheryl Ladd (*Charlie's Angels*).

Abner • A basset hound of political commentator Cokie Roberts.

Abraxas Aaran • See **Willie**.

Ace • In comics, the name of Bruce Wayne's dog, which became Bat Hound.

Adjutant • One of the longest-lived dogs on record, the Labrador retriever lived in England from 1936 to 1963—twenty-seven years!

Adolph • The bulldog featured in Harold Knerr's comic strip *Dinglehoofer und His Dog Adolph*, which was popular in the late 1920s and early 1930s.

Adonis • An English setter, handsome to be sure, he was the first dog to be registered in the U.S., back in 1878.

Aello • In Greek mythology, one of the many hounds of Actaeon, the hunter whom the goddess Artemis turned into a stag. Aello was a "whirlwind," according to *Room's Classical Dictionary*.

Agamemnon • The German shepherd owned by children's book author and illustrator Maurice Sendak (*Where the Wild Things Are*). The dog was named after the Greek Mycenaean king during the Trojan war.

Agatha • The cocker spaniel of singer Lesley Gore ("It's My Party").

Agre • In Greek mythology, one of the many hounds of Actaeon, the hunter whom the goddess Artemis turned into a stag. Agre was the "hunter," according to *Room's Classical Dictionary*.

Aicama Zorba • The heaviest dog on record, an Old English mastiff—an amazing 343 pounds, according to the *Guinness Book of World Records*.

Aileen Mavourneen • The main character in Mark Twain's short story "A Dog's Tale." The mutt (part collie, part Saint Bernard) rescues her master's child in a fire.

Aiwa • A German shepherd owned by actress Bo Derek (*10*).

Ajax • The silver-haired Alsatian dog owned by Prince Edward of England (later King Edward VIII and the Duke of Windsor), named after the Greek warrior.

Aladdin • See **Alidoro**.

Albert • One of actress Jaclyn Smith's poodles.

Alce • In Greek mythology, one of the many hounds of Actaeon, the hunter whom the goddess Artemis turned into a stag. Alce was "powerful," according to *Room's Classical Dictionary*.

Alex • A borzoi, or Russian wolfhound, owned by Princess Alexandra of Wales at the turn of the century.

Alice • The name of dogs owned by television personality and producer Dick Clark and by actress Linda Blair (*The Exorcist*).

Alidoro • In Carlo Collodi's *Pinocchio*, published in 1883, the mastiff that Pinocchio saved from drowning. Alidoro later saved Pinocchio's life. (Alidoro is the Italian name for Aladdin, who in *The Arabian Nights* possessed a magic lamp and a ring.)

Alfie • The sheepdog in the 1973 Al Pacino movie *Serpico*.

Allspice • A dog owned by singer Della Reese, who has a preference for "spicy" names.
   • A dog owned by dancer-singer Fred Astaire (*Top Hat*).

Aloma • One of many King Charles spaniels owned by Gladys, Duchess of Marlborough (née Gladys Deacon), a turn-of-the-century British socialite and friend of writer Marcel Proust and sculptor Auguste Rodin.

Amanda • A dachshund owned by movie director George Cukor (*Camille*).

Amber • A greyhound of movie actress Bo Derek.
   • A Lhasa apso of Hollywood dress designer Bob Mackie.

Ambriget • A dog owned by actor Jonathan Prince (*Alice* and *Throb*).

Amos • One of pop artist Andy Warhol's dachshunds.

Amy • A dog owned by Richard Nixon aide H.R. Haldeman.

Andy • A dog owned by *Peanuts* cartoonist Charles Schulz.
   • The loyal Saint Bernard owned by comic book hero and conservationist Mark Trail.

Angel • One of comic actor and movie director Jerry Lewis' Shih Tzus.
   • The white bull terrier of author John Steinbeck.
   • A poodle owned by television producer Aaron Spelling.

Angie • A dog owned by swimming actress Esther Williams (*Bathing Beauty*).

Annabelle • An English bulldog of cartoonist, editor, and Marvel Comics publisher Stan Lee.

Annie • A poodle owned by *I Dream of Jeannie* actress Barbara Eden.
   • A dog of actor John Glover (*Robocop 2*).

Anubis • The dog-headed god of tombs and embalming in ancient Egypt. The dog was most likely a jackal, a wild dog found in Africa and Asia.

Apollo • In comics, the Great Dane given to Nita van Sloan by her boyfriend Richard Wentworth (*The Spider*). Apollo is the name of a Greek god or beautiful man.
   • One of the Doberman pinschers in the television series *Magnum P.I.*
   • A mastiff owned by television actor Sherman Hemsley (*The Jeffersons*).

Apollon • In T.H. White's *The Sword in the Stone*, one of King Arthur's many dogs.

Archie • A dachshund owned by pop artist Andy Warhol.
• A dog owned by British comedic actor Terry Thomas.
• Television actress Valerie Harper's dog.
• The mixed-breed (German shepherd and golden retriever) that lived in New York mayor Ed Koch's Gracie Mansion, named for Archibald Gracie, the house's first occupant. The dog was removed from the site after biting a sanitation worker.

Arf • The name of Little Orphan Annie's dog **Sandy**'s stand-in in the Broadway play *Annie*. It was named after the cartoon strip's ballooned dialogue for the dog.

Argo • The name of the Wentworth family dog in the 1978 television movie *The Grass Is Always Greener over the Septic Tank* (based on Erma Bombeck's book).

Argos • The name of Odysseus's blind hound dog in Homer's *The Odyssey*.

Argus • Writer Albert Payson Terhune's first collie. He is the author of *Lad: A Dog* and *Bruce*.
• Argus was also the name of actress Gene Tierney's dog as a child.
• In Greek mythology, one of the many hounds of Actaeon, the hunter whom the goddess Artemis turned into a stag. Argus was "bright" or "swift," according to *Room's Classical Dictionary*.

Arizona • One of television talk-show host Oprah Winfrey's golden retrievers.

Arlo • An Irish setter owned by humorist Erma Bombeck (*The Grass Is Always Greener over the Septic Tank*).

Arno • Film star Errol Flynn's schnauzer. After the dog fell off Flynn's boat and drowned, columnist Jimmy Fidler chided Flynn for failing to save the dog. (Flynn later socked Fidler at a Hollywood nightspot in retaliation.)

Arrow • The dog owned by Oblio in the 1971 animated feature movie *The Point*. The major song of the movie, "Me and My Arrow," was sung by Harry Nilsson and became a hit.
  • The name of kidnap victim and publishing heiress Patty Hearst's dog.

Arthur "Drago" Pendragon • A German shepherd owned and named by actor Charlton Heston, for a "medieval" ring. According to Heston, the dog was "a noble animal and we loved him." (Pendragon was a term for "chief leader" in ancient Britain).

Asbolus • In Greek mythology, one of the many hounds of Actaeon, the hunter whom the goddess Artemis turned into a stag. Asbolus was "sooty," according to *Room's Classical Dictionary*.

Ashley • One of physical fitness guru Richard Simmons's many Dalmatians, most of whom are named after characters in Margaret Mitchell's classic novel *Gone with the Wind*. (In the movie, Ashley Wilkes was played by actor Leslie Howard.)
  • One of Los Angeles Lakers' announcer Chick Hearn's Bichon frisés.

Asta • The schnauzer in Dashiell Hammett's novel *The Thin Man*, named after the dog owned by Hammett's mistress, Laura Perelman. Asta was played by a wire-haired fox terrier named **Skippy** in *The Thin Man* movie series from 1934 to 1947, starring William Powell and Myrna Loy. (Several different dogs played the movie role.) Later in the television version, starring Peter Lawford and Phyllis Kirk, the dog won two Patsy awards.

Astor • A dog owned by television and movie actor Burt Reynolds (*Deliverance*).

Astro • The Jetson's dog in the television cartoon series *The Jetsons*. Astro had its own treadmill.
   • Tennis star Monica Seles's Yorkshire terrier.

Astronaut • A dog owned by Luci Baines Johnson, daughter of U.S. president Lyndon B. Johnson.

Atmo • A pet German shepherd of Princess Stephanie of Monaco.

Atticus • Former South Dakota U.S. senator George McGovern's dog when he was a presidential candidate.

Augie-Doggy • In the Hanna-Barbera television cartoon series *Huckleberry Hound*, the puppy son of **Doggie Daddy**.

Autie Murphy • One of actress Doris Day's dogs, and wordplay on the name of war hero-turned-actor Audie Murphy (*To Hell and Back*).

Austin • Los Angeles Dodgers manager Tommy Lasorda's miniature schnauzer.

Autumn • One of actress Doris Day's many dogs.

B

Babil • A basset hound of Queen Alexandra of England.

Baby • A Yorkshire terrier owned by *Green Acres* actress Eva Gabor.

Baby Boy • A favorite French poodle of entertainer Liberace. The pianist picked the puppy because it was the sickest of the litter. The dog ate at the dining room table, owned a very bejeweled collar, and lived eighteen years.

Baby Dauphine • The toy poodle of actress Karen Kelly (*Rituals*).

Baby Doll • A bulldog of playwright Tennessee Williams, who wrote the screenplay to the 1956 movie *Baby Doll* starring Carroll Baker.

Baby Lion • A Lhasa apso owned by actress Eva Gabor.

Babylas • One of many King Charles spaniels owned by Gladys, Duchess of Marlborough.

Bacchus • One of many King Charles spaniels owned by Gladys, Duchess of Marlborough. (Bacchus was the Roman god of wine and revelry.)

Bagel • The name of Barry Manilow's dog, a great name for a beagle owned by a Brooklyn-born singer.

Baghera • A dog that French writer Colette owned during her service as a nurse in World War I.

Balle • One of the first two basset hounds brought to England by Lord Galway in 1866.

Balthasar • The white and brown dog owned by Jolyon Forsyte in John Galsworthy's novel *The Forsyte Saga*.

Balto • The name of the black malamute dog that led a sled team in Alaska to deliver serum to Eskimos in Nome during the diphtheria epidemic of 1925. A statue of the dog stands near the zoo in the southeastern corner of New York City's Central Park. Steven Spielberg produced an animated film of Balto's story in 1995, starring Kevin Bacon and Bridget Fonda. Some sources indicate that the dog was half-wolf, half-husky.

Bambi • A sheltie of Hollywood dancer-singer-actor-choreographer-director Gene Kelly.

Bambina • One of movie and opera director Franco Zeffirelli's dogs.

Banco • A fox terrier owned by French writer Françoise Sagan (*Bonjour tristesse*). She named it after the gambling game baccarat in which one has the option of betting the bank.

Bandit • The Ingalls family dog in the television series *Little House on the Prairie*.
  • The name of the black-eyed bulldog in the Hanna-Barbera television cartoon series *The Adventures of Jonny Quest*.
  • A Pekingese dog owned by comedic actress Betty White of television's *Golden Girls*. The dog, nicknamed Bandy, was given its name because the markings around its eyes resembled a black mask. (Ms. White and her husband Allen Ludden named their production company Bandy Productions.)
  • *Diary of a Mad Housewife* actress Carrie Snodgress's Rottweiler.

Bandy • An English bulldog featured in early American silent movies.
  • A dog owned by Betty White.

Bang • A reddish-haired Chow Chow dog owned by British prime minister David Lloyd George.

• The name of the greyhound that set the record for the longest jump—thirty feet—according to the *Guinness Book of World Records*.

Banquo • The name of writer Anaïs Nin's dog, named after the character in William Shakespeare's *Macbeth*.

Banushka • The dog in popular author Judy Blume's novel *Wifey*.

Barclay • A Jack Russell terrier of actress Amanda Bearse (*Married . . . with Children*).

Barco • A U.S. border patrol dog (a Belgian Malinois) that has had excellent success sniffing out drugs at the Texas-Mexico border. The name is a combination of the words "bark" and "narco."

Barfy • The family dog in Bill Keane's *The Family Circus* comic strip.

Barge • A watchdog from Columbus, Ohio, who was burglarized and jumped out of a window and killed himself—in James Thurber's *The Fireside Book of Dog Stories* published in 1943. Barge, so the story goes, had a drinking problem.

Bark • A golden retriever of comedic actor Bill Murray (*Ghostbusters*).

Barnaby • The real name of the sheep dog Alfie in the 1973 Al Pacino movie *Serpico*.

• A Labrador retriever of clothing designer Bill Blass.

Barney • In the television series *Lou Grant*, the pet Yorkshire terrier of Margaret Pynchon (played by actress Nancy Marchand), owner of the *Los Angeles Tribune*. It was killed by a pit bull in one of the episodes.

• Screen actor Christian Slater's dog.

• A Wheaton terrier owned by television actor Thom Bray (*Breaking Away* and *Riptide*).

Baron • A dachshund featured in Dr. Louis J. Camuti's book *Park Avenue Vet*.

• British actor (*A Man Called Peter*) Richard Todd's dog.

• The dog in the movie *Back to God's Country*.

Barron • A golden retriever of poet-actor James Stewart (*It's a Wonderful Life*).

Barry • Comedic actor Bert Lahr's black Scottish terrier. The dog was named after the Broadway play *Du Barry Was a Lady*, in which Lahr starred with Betty Grable. Rumors were that Lahr, the Cowardly Lion in the movie *The Wizard of Oz*, was not particularly fond of Barry. See **Merlin**.

Bascom • A dog in the 1956 Dean Martin and Jerry Lewis movie *Hollywood or Bust*.

Basher • *Renegade* television actor Lorenzo Lamas's dog.

Baskerville • A great name for a hound—from Sir Arthur Conan Doyle's classic story "The Hound of the Baskervilles." The eponymous black hound haunted moors of Dartmoor and terrorized the Baskerville family.

Basket • One of writer Gertrude Stein's two poodles of the same name. Her friend and lover Alice B. Toklas thought "he looked as if he should carry a basket of flowers in his mouth." After the first one died, they bought another poodle and gave it the same name.

Basset • One of the first two basset hounds brought to England by Lord Galway in 1866.

Bathsheba • The only dog of actress and cat-lover Sandy Dennis (*Who's Afraid of Virginia Woolf?*). In the Bible, Bathsheba was the wife of David and the mother of Solomon.

Beagle • One of large-eared U.S. president Lyndon Baines Johnson's beagles (which have large ears!).

Beans • A poodle owned by actor Robert Vaughn. See **Boston Beans**.

Bear • A mixed-breed German shepherd owned by actress and animal activist Stefanie Powers.
• A Samoyed owned by lyricist-composer Martin Charnin (*Annie*).

Bearface • A Chow Chow of designer and store owner Bijan.

Beaty • A Pomeranian of King Edward VII of England.

Beau • A spaniel owned by eighteenth-century English poet William Cowper. He immortalized the dog in his "On a Spaniel Called Beau Killing a Young Bird" and "The Dog and the Water Lily."
• U.S. general Omar Bradley's poodle.
• A basset hound owned by actor Anson Williams (whose production company is named Basset Productions).

Beau Brummel • The Labrador retriever of writer Armand Deutsch (*Me and Bogie*). (Beau Brummel was a famous English fashion trendsetter in the early nine-teenth century).

Beau Jangles • Comedic television actress Carol Burnett's poodle.

Beauregard • The bloodhound in the comic strip *Pogo*.

Beauregard, Jr. • The snoozing hound dog in the tele-vision show *Hee Haw*.

Beauty • The black Chow Chow owned by British prime minister David Lloyd George.
• A dog of movie actor Corey Feldman (*Goonies*).

Beegle Beagle • A carnival hustler dog in Hanna-Barbera cartoons. Its voice is that of comedian Marty Ingels.

Bela • A Rottweiler owned by screen vampire Elvira, obviously taken from Dracula actor Bela Lugosi.

Belka • Russian for "Squirrel," a Samoyed, one of two Russian dogs put in orbit in August 1960 on the Sputnik V. Also see **Pushinka** and **Strelka**.

Bella • *Night Court* actor John Larroquette's boxer. (*Bella* is the word for "pretty" in both Spanish and Italian.)

Belle • In the comic strip *Peanuts*, Snoopy's sister.
• The Yorkshire terrier of British character actor Arthur Treacher, former talk-show sidekick of Merv Griffin. (*Belle* is the French word for "beautiful.")

Belle Aude • A Belgian sheepdog owned by French writer Colette.

Belshazzar • Rev. Billy Graham's dog, named after a king in the Bible who was known to feed thousands of people.

Belva • Actress Theda Bara's Russian wolfhound.

Ben • Ben was the name of Mack Sennett's comedy dog in early movie shorts.
• The name of a fox terrier owned by Herbert Hoover.
• Also a dog mentioned in Maxwell Knight's *My Pet Friends*.
• German tennis pro Steffi Graf's boxer.

Benita • One of many King Charles spaniels owned by the Gladys, Duchess of Marlborough.

Benji • The name of the heroic dog in the 1974 feature film *Benji*. In the movie, he (played by a dog named **Higgins**) thwarts the kidnappers of two children. Several sequels followed, including *For the Love of Benji* (1977) and *Oh Heavenly Dog* (1980) and others. It is #78 on the list of most popular dog names in the U.S. The dog made its acting debut on television's *Petticoat Junction*.

Beppo • Writer E.B. White's family dog, an Irish setter, when he was a child.
• Also the name of one of Queen Victoria's Pomeranians. See **Fluffy, Gilda, Lulu, Mino,** and **Nino**.

Berganza • In Spanish writer Miguel de Cervantes's satirical *The Dogs' Colloquy*, one of two dogs who are able to speak—Spanish, of course. The other dog was named **Scipio**.

Bernardo • Television personality and producer Dick Clark's dog.

Bert • One of actor-producer Michael Landon's many dogs.

Berthe • A dog owned by composer Cole Porter ("Night and Day").

Bess • In a country in which queens are named Elizabeth, it is noteworthy that Bess, a nickname for Elizabeth, is the third most popular name for female dogs in England.
  • The name of one of fictional detective Bulldog Drummond's three dogs—a cocker spaniel. See **Jerry** and **Jock**.

Bessie • A yellow collie owned by U.S. president Calvin Coolidge.
  • The cockapoo of actress Jennifer Jason Leigh (*Single White Female*).

Betty • A dog owned by actress-turned-film-director Penny Marshall (*Big* and *A League of Their Own*).

Bettysan • One of many King Charles spaniels owned by Gladys, Duchess of Marlborough.

Beverly • A German shepherd of Betsy Bloomingdale, socialite friend of U.S. president and Mrs. Ronald W. Reagan.

Bevis • A mastiff in Sir Walter Scott's *Woodstock*, published in 1826. The dog was believed to be patterned on Scott's real life dog, Maida.

Bianca • Tennis pro Jennifer Capriati's dog.

Bib • The pet dog of Gary Gulliver in the television cartoon series *The Adventures of Gulliver*.

Big Ben • A fox terrier owned by U.S. president Herbert Hoover.

Big Boy • See Fala.

Big Red • In Jim Kjelgaard's book *Big Red*, published in 1945, the Irish setter who injured himself in a fight with a bear and a wolverine to save his master Danny Pickett. The dog in the 1962 film *Big Red* won the Patsy Award in 1963.

Big Spike • A bulldog character in comic books.

Biggest • One of actress Doris Day's dogs.

Bijou • One of the Apple family dogs in the television series *Apple's Way*.
• A basset hound owned by Queen Alexandra of England. (The name means "jewel" in French.)

Bijoux • Actor John Ritter's Jack Russell terrier in the television series *Hooperman*, which ran from 1987 to 1989. He inherited the little terrier from his landlady, who was murdered. The dog's real name was Britches. (The French word *bijoux* means "jewels.")

Bill • The name of the collie in the 1946 movie *The Courage of Lassie*, in which the name Lassie is not mentioned, and in which Elizabeth Taylor starred.
• Also the name of actress Frances Day's brindle bulldog, after whom the song "Blue-Blooded Bill the Autocrat" was written into the play *How D'You Do?* and he appeared every night in a red velvet and ermine costume. (An American actress who moved to England, she was more widely known on the London stage and screen. Her most memorable role was as Poppea in the 1944 film *Fiddlers Three*.)

• A dog owned by actress Cloris Leachman (*The Last Picture Show*).

Billy the Kid • Television actress Valerie Harper's dog.

Bimbo • Betty Boop's pet dog in cartoons and comic strips.

Bingley • An Airedale owned by children's book author Tome de Paola. Bingley is the name of the town in Scotland where Airedales were first bred.

Bingo • The name of the dog on the Cracker Jack box since 1919. The black and white dog was actually the name of the dog owned by the grandson (named *Jack*!) of the company's founder.

• The name of mystery writer Agatha Christie's Manchester terrier.

Binky • Television actress Betty White's Pekingese.

Bird • *Princess Bride* star Robin Wright's Shar-pei, which lost a leg in an auto accident.

Biscuit • The beagle that replaced singer Barry Manilow's beagle named Bagel.

• A dog owned by actor Patrick Wayne, son of Hollywood legend John Wayne.

Bismarck • A Rottweiler owned by actress Shannen Doherty (*Beverly Hills 90210*).

• A boyhood mongrel owned by David Lloyd George, future prime minister of Great Britain. George tended to name pets after world leaders.

Biter of Enemies • The dog owned by Assyrian emperor Ashurbanipal in the seventh century B.C.

Black Jack • The name of one of President Theodore Roosevelt's dogs.

• The Great Dane owned by Nancy Blansky (played by actress Nancy Walker) in the short-lived 1977 television series *Blansky's Beauties*.

Black Tooth • One of comic Soupy Sales's canine puppets on *The Soupy Sales Show*.

Black Watch Moonstruck • A dog owned by comedic actor, raconteur and producer Bill Cosby.

Blackberry • One of two Chow Chows owned by U.S. president Calvin Coolidge.

Blackie • Writer Ernest Hemingway's black spaniel of twelve years.

• A German shepherd owned by *Green Acres* actress Eva Gabor.

• One of U.S. president John F. Kennedy's dogs.

• Swedish-born movie actress (*A Shot in the Dark*) Elke Sommer's dog.

• One of *True Grit* movie actor John Wayne's dogs.

Blanch • One of three dogs mentioned in Shakespeare's play *King Lear* (Act III, Scene 6). Lear thinks that his dogs, as well as his daughters, are turning against him ("The little dogs, and all . . . see, they bark at me."). See **Sweetheart** and **Tray**.

Blanco • A white collie owned by U.S. president Lyndon B. Johnson. *Blanco* is the Spanish word for "white" and is also the name of the county in which Johnson was born.

Blaze • The bullmastiff owned by Elliott Roosevelt, son of U.S. president Franklin D. Roosevelt. It made the newspaper headlines when a U.S. serviceman was bumped off a flight in order for the dog to get on the plane. The dog retired at Hyde Park and after a fight with **Fala** had to be put to sleep.

Blean • The name of one of the earlier members of the basenji breed, also known as a Congo terrier.

Blemie • Playwright Eugene O'Neill's Dalmatian. The name is short for Emblem and the dog's full name was Silverdeen's Emblem O'Neill. The dog had its own four-poster bed and was treated, by most accounts, like a member of the family, perhaps more so.

Bleu • French King Louis IX's dog. (*Bleu* is the French word for "blue.")

Blix • The Airedale owned by A.J. Cronin, author of *The Citadel.*

Blondi • The name of Adolf Hitler's Alsatian dog. It was killed the day on which Hitler and wife Eva Braun committed suicide.

Blondie • One of (*Police Woman*) television actor Earl Holliman's many dogs.

Blood • The dog in the 1976 science fiction movie *A Boy and His Dog,* based on a Harlan Ellison novella. (Don Johnson starred in the movie and the dog was played by Tiger of television's *The Brady Bunch*.)

Blucher • A staghound owned by General George Armstrong Custer. It was killed by an arrow at the Battle of Washita. (Blücher was the surname of a famous Prussian field marshal, after whom the leather shoe was named.)

Blue • The hound dog in the movie *Cool Hand Luke*

(1967), which dies while tracking down the prisoner Lucas.

• The dog of actress Katharine Ross (*Butch Cassidy and the Sundance Kid*).

• The dog kept by Airman Will Stockdale (actor Sammy Jackson) in the television series *No Time for Sergeants*.

Blue Bandit • One of several Siberian huskies owned by actor Eddie Velez (*Extremities*). He hopes to have enough to run his own dog sled in Alaska.

Bluey • The oldest dog on record—twenty-nine years and five months, according to the *Guinness Book of World Records*. It was an Australian cattle dog that was put to sleep in 1939.

Bo • A part German shepherd, part husky that costarred in the movie *Summer School* (1987) with actor Mark Harmon.

• A golden retriever of actor James Stewart (*Rear Window*) and subject of one of the actor's folksy poems.

• Bo was also the name of the white poodle owned by Eleanor "Cissy" Patterson, publisher of the *Washington Times-Herald*.

Boatswain • The name of Lord Byron's Newfoundland dog buried at Newstead Abbey, where the dog's monument is larger than Byron's. Byron praised the dog at its death as one who "possessed Beauty with Vanity, Strength without Insolence, Courage without Ferocity, and all the virtues of Man, without his vices."

• The dog on the whaling ship *Dolly* in Herman Melville's novel *Typee*.

Bob • The loyal cairn terrier owned by England's King George V.

• The bulldog in Hugh Lofting's *The Voyages of Doctor Doolittle*.

• Television talk-show host David Letterman has named one of his canines Bob.

• The collie of movie actor Randolph Scott (*Last of the Mohicans*).

Bob Dylan • A dog owned by rock singer Courtney Love of Hole, named after the great folk-rock singer.

Bobby • A brave spaniel wounded during the Afghan Campaign of 1879–80 and decorated by the Queen of England in 1881. The dog was stuffed and mounted.

• A dog owned by movie star Clark Gable (*Gone with the Wind*).

• A legendary Skye terrier famous for its devotion to an old Scottish shepherd named **Auld Jock**. When Jock died in 1858, Bobby sat by Jock's grave for fourteen years, leaving only to obtain food at a nearby inn. It died in 1872 and was buried next to Auld Jock.

• A cocker spaniel owned by silent-screen comic actor Harold Lloyd.

• In the Ray Milland movie *The Uninvited* (1944), a cairn terrier named Bobby leads Milland and Ruth Hussey to their "dream house," which is later found out to be haunted.

• Author Albert Payson Terhune owned a dog named Bobby.

Bobo • The name of movie actor Bruce Lee's Great Dane and one of actress Doris Day's dogs.

Bodger • The bull terrier in Sheila Burnford's 1961 novel *The Incredible Journey*.

Bodie • Author James Herriot's border terrier. It was named after a character on the British television series *The Professionals*.

Bodri • A German shepherd of movie actor Bela Lugosi (*Dracula*).

Bogie • A Welsh corgi owned by British actor Dirk Bogarde (*Darling*).
• A Labrador retriever of movie actor Bo Hopkins (*The Wild Bunch*) and one of television actor (*Police Woman*) Earl Holliman's dogs.

Bojangles • A toy poodle owned by entertainer Sammy Davis, Jr., named after the famous black entertainer on whom the song "Mr. Bojangles" is based.

Bokoto • The name of one of the earlier members of the Basenji breed, also known as a Congo terrier.

Bolero • A greyhound owned by actress Bo Derek. (Ravel's *Bolero* was the theme music of her big movie *10*.)

Bones • U.S. general George C. Marshall's dog.

Bongo • One of the earlier members of the Basenji breed, also known as a Congo terrier.

Bonne • A favorite hunting dog of King Louis XIV of France.

Bonnie • A golden retriever of television actress Tiffani-Amber Thiessen (*Beverly Hills 90210*).
• U.S. vice-president Walter Mondale's collie when he was in office.
• British actress Diana Rigg's black Labrador retriever, which was a gift from her husband.
• A mixed-breed dog owned by actress Tallulah Bankhead (*Lifeboat*).

Bonso • A dog owned by television actor Tom Brown (Ed O'Connor on *Gunsmoke*).

Boo • One of pro basketball player Karl Malone's Labrador retrievers.

Boojum • A dog owned by movie actress Bette Davis (*Jezebel*). (It is a name mentioned in Lewis Carroll's *Hunting of the Snark*.)

Boomer • A Labrador retriever owned by singer Barbara Mandrell.
• The mutt star in the movie *Here's Boomer*.

Boone • Pop singer Glen Campbell's dog.

Bootie • A Pekingese owned by actress Betty White (*Golden Girls*).

Boots • The name of the station house dog in the television series *Emergency*.
• Also the canine narrator of Rudyard Kipling's *Thy Servant, A Dog*.
• The name of dogs owned by movie legend Charlie Chaplin and British actor Jonathan Pryce (*Glengarry Glen Ross*).

Bootsie • A poodle of actress June Havoc and sister, stripper Gypsy Rose Lee, in their early days.

Bootsy • See Jet.

Bordeaux • A dog owned by movie actress Anne Archer (*Fatal Attraction*), named after a region in southwestern France that produces excellent wines.

Borotra • A Sealyham terrier of heiress and art patron Peggy Guggenheim.

Bosco • Actor Michael J. Fox's Dalmatian.

• A bulldog owned by Queen Victoria's son-in-law, Prince Henry of Battenberg.

Boston Beans • A brown collie owned by U.S. president Calvin Coolidge. (Some sources say that it was a Boston bulldog.)

Bouboule • A bulldog of movie actress Olivia de Havilland (*The Heiress*).

Bouillabaisse • A mutt (named after a French fish and shellfish stew) owned by writer F. Scott Fitzgerald and his wife, Zelda.

Boulder • An Old English sheepdog of actress Joan Van Ark (*Knot's Landing*).

Bounce • A Great Dane owned by English poet Alexander Pope.
• In T.H. White's *The Sword in the Stone*, one of King Arthur's many dogs.

Bourbon • The dog in *Call of the Wild*.

Bowser • The name of Mr. Magoo's dog in cartoons.

Bowzer • The name of the Hanks' family "dog" (it was supposed to be a wolf!) in the CBS television series *Pistols 'n' Petticoats*, which ran from 1966 to 1967.

Boxcar Willie • A mixed-breed dog of Maureen Reagan, daughter of U.S. president Ronald W. Reagan.

Boxey • A dog of movie actress Anne Archer (*Body of Evidence*).

Boy • The Bradley family's dog in the television series *Petticoat Junction*.

• Boy was also the name of Pete's mongrel in C.D. Russell's comic strip *Pete the Tramp*. Boy soon was given his own strip, *Pete's Pup*.

• The hero of Peter Mayle's *A Dog's Life*—a stray dog that Mayle and his wife adopted while in the south of France.

• In T.H. White's *The Sword in the Stone*, one of King Arthur's many dogs.

• An Irish Setter owned by baseball pro Catfish Hunter.

• A dog of Prince Rupert of the Rhine, son of Frederick V.

Bozo • The name of one of U.S. president Jimmy Carter's dogs in his youth.

• One of author-animal lover Roger Caras's dogs.

Brahm • One of screen vamp Elvira's Rottweilers.

Bran • In T.H. White's *The Sword in the Stone*, one of King Arthur's many dogs.

Brandy • A miniature poodle of comedic actor Don Adams (*Get Smart*).

Break • One of author Albert Payson Terhune's many collies.

Brentwood • A cocker spaniel owned by actress Brenda Vaccaro (*Midnight Cowboy*), named after a section of Los Angeles in which many actors live.

Briar • A dog of television actress Susan Dey (*The Partridge Family* and *Love and War*).

Bridget • See O'Casey.

Brin • The sled dog of Canadian-born physician and missionary Sir Wilfred Grenfel.

Brindle • A Belgian sheepdog owned by actress Brenda Vaccaro (Jacqueline Susann's *Once Is Not Enough*).

Bristol • A dog owned by comedian Dick Martin (of Rowan and Martin).

Bristol Hound • An English sheepdog in Hanna-Barbera cartoons. Its signature line is "Bristol Hound's my name, and saving sheep's my game."

Britches • The real name of John Ritter's terrier **Bijoux** in the 1987–89 television series *Hooperman*.

Brother • A Labrador retriever of comedian and comic actor Richard Pryor (*Stir Crazy*).

Brown • The large mongrel dog owned by Dave Blasingame, played by actor Brian Keith, in the 1960 NBC television series *The Westerner*. The dog also was featured in the Disney movie *Old Yeller*.

Brown Wolf • Author Jack London's favorite dog.

Brownie • The female Irish setter of T.H. White, who wrote the book *The Once and Future King*, published in 1958. Many years after the dog died, White wrote, "Dear Brownie, you were and still are the most loved thing in my life."
   • A dog of movie actor Vincent Price (*The Fall of the House of Usher*).

Bruce • The collie protagonist in Albert Payson Terhune's novel *Bruce*. Based on the story of a real dog named Sunnybank Goldsmith, its epitaph read, "The Dog Without a Fault."
   • The name of a dog in Joyce Harrington's story "Dispatching Bootsie."

Bruiser • A dog owned by *Deliverance* actor Burt Reynolds.

Bruno • Augustus Mutt's dog in the comic strip *Mutt and Jeff*.
• Also the name of Cinderella's dog in the 1950 Disney cartoon feature.
• The name of dogs owned by basketball great Kareem Abdul-Jabbar and by Olympic diver Greg Louganis.

Brut • A dog of actor Hugh O'Brian, who played the role of Wyatt Earp on television from 1955 to 1961. (In French *brut* means "rough" or "gross" and is a word to describe a very dry and, therefore, high-quality champagne.)

Brutus • Brutus was one of the assassins of Roman emperor Julius Caesar, and has inspired the names of many a pet:.
• The Great Dane in the 1966 Disney movie *The Ugly Dachshund* who thinks he's a dachshund.
• The name of the invisible German shepherd in the 1940 movie *The Invisible Man Returns*.
• A dog of actor Charlton Heston (who has played the role of Antony, not Brutus, several times in feature films).
• A dog owned by rock legend Elvis Presley and his daughter, Lisa Marie Presley.
• A golden retriever owned by clothing designer Bill Blass.
• Hollywood agent Charles Feldman's dog. Its claim to fame was that it was kidnapped in Capri and discovered in Naples.

Bubbles • One of actress Doris Day's poodles and a dog owned by comedienne Totie Fields.

Bucephalus • A Doberman pinscher owned by Joanne Carson, former wife of talk-show veteran Johnny Carson. (Bucephalus was the name of Alexander the Great's horse.)

Buck • The briard dog on the television situation comedy *Married . . . with Children*.

• The name of the large, mixed-breed dog (part St. Bernard, part Scottish shepherd—son of Elmo and Shep) in Jack London's novel *The Call of the Wild*. Kidnapped from California and sent to Alaska as a sled dog, Buck was "beaten but not broken" and gained acceptance by a pack of wolves. (London's canine hero was based on a real life dog, one owned by Judge Marshall Bond. His son took the real-life dog to the Klondike.)

• Buck was also the name of the dog in the Bob Hope and Bing Crosby "Road" movies.

• *Marcus Welby, M.D.* actor James Brolin's large harlequin, white spotted Great Dane.

• The name of a dog owned by singer Janet Jackson.

• Buck was also the name of the pet dog of the Gump family in the comic strip *The Gumps*.

Also see **Neil**.

Bucky • One of actress Doris Day's many dogs.

Buddy • The world's first Seeing Eye dog, a German shepherd originally named Kiss. Owned by Morris Frank, a blind man from Tennessee, the dog and owner were trained by Dorothy Eustis in Switzerland. Frank changed the dog's name because he thought Kiss was "a hell of a name for a dog." See **Gala**.

• A mixed-breed dog owned by actress-writer Carrie Fisher (*Star Wars*).

• A dog of U.S. president John F. Kennedy.

• *Little House on the Prairie* actor-producer Michael Landon's dog.

Buddy Mozart • *Carol Burnett Show* comedic actor Harvey Korman's dog.

Budgy • U.S. president Franklin D. Roosevelt's first dog, a spitz.

Buffo • A bulldog of playwright Tennessee Williams (*The Glass Menagerie*).

Bugle Ann • A fox-hunting hound and star of the movie *The Voice of Bugle Ann* (1936).

Bull • A dog owned by stage actress and animal lover Sarah Bernhardt.

Bull's-eye • Bill Sikes's white dog in the Charles Dickens's novel *Oliver Twist*. The dog ran away from Sikes when he was about to drown the dog. Bull's-eye later leapt to its death.
  • Also the name of Jimmy Dugan's dog in the comic strip *Reg'lar Fellers*.

Buller • A part bull terrier, part sheepdog owned by aviatrix and writer Beryl Markham as a teenager.

Bullet • Movie cowboy Roy Rogers's German shepherd, which debuted in *Spoilers of the Plains* (1951) and made appearances on Rogers's television show. Bullet is preserved and on display, with Trigger, at the Roy Rogers–Dale Evans Museum in California.

Bullwinkle • A dog owned by television actor Richard Paul (Mayor Sam Booth on *Murder, She Wrote*), named after the cartoon character moose.

Bully • A fawn-colored pug given to Queen Victoria by Prince Albert.
  • A French bulldog owned by Wallis Warfield

Simpson (later the Duchess of Windsor) when she was a child in Baltimore.

Bumper • A Maltese owned by actress Halle Berry (*Boomerang*).

Bumpy • A Cardigan corgi owned by opera diva Beverly Sills. When Sills hit high notes during practice, the dog would "twang like a banjo," according to Sills in her autobiography *Beverly*.

Bunchie • In author Henry James's *Portrait of a Lady*, the terrier owned by Ralph Touchett.

Bunga • An Alsatian (with an enormous appetite for neighbors' food supplies) owned by actor Raymond Massey.

Bungey • In T.H. White's *The Sword in the Stone*, one of King Arthur's many dogs.

Bunk • Writer Dorothy Parker's part Boston terrier, part French bulldog when she was a child.

Bunker • The Sealyham terrier owned by writer A.J. Cronin, author of *The Citadel*.

Bunty • A dog owned by film character actor Pat O'Brien (*Angels with Dirty Faces*).

Burnaby • A pit bull terrier owned by actor Michael J. Fox (*Back to the Future*).

Buster • The name of Edith Ann's dog in Lily Tomlin's comedy routines.
   • A mastiff owned by *Cheers* star Kirstie Alley.
   • A Jack Russell terrier of television actress Amanda Bearse (*Married . . . with Children*).

• The dog of 1930s movie character actor Sir Guy Standing (*The Lives of a Bengal Lancer*).

Butch • The ninth most popular name for a male dog in England.

• The name of the bulldog in the *Tom and Jerry* cartoons.

• The name of Fred and Ethel Mertz's dog in the first season of the classic television series *I Love Lucy*.

• It was also the name of a gray poodle owned by *Washington Times-Herald* publisher Eleanor "Cissy" Patterson. According to a Christmas card send out one year, Butch was "gentle when stroked" and "fierce when provoked."

• A poodle owned by actor Michael Gray (*The Brian Keith Show*).

Butkus • Sylvester "Rocky Balboa" Stallone's bullmastiff in the 1976 movie *Rocky*. The dog, whose name was inspired by pro football player Dick Butkus, was actually owned by Stallone.

Butterfly • One of U.S. president John F. Kennedy's dogs.

Button • A French poodle owned by actress Katharine Hepburn.

Buttons • Once a more popular name for a dog, it is now fiftieth on the most popular name list in the U.S. It was the name of Bing Crosby's dog in the 1948 movie *The Emperor Waltz*.

• The name of *Roots* author Alex Haley's Yorkshire terrier.

• A poodle owned by John Mitchell, Richard M. Nixon's attorney general.

Buzzy • A wirehaired fox terrier owned by actor Michael Gray (*The Brian Keith Show*).

Byron • General George Armstrong Custer's greyhound, one of his several dogs. It was "a lordly dog," according to Custer's wife, Elizabeth, but its "heart could be put into a thimble." Also see **Blucher, Cardigan, Ginnie,** and **Maida.**

• A Siberian husky owned by actor Sean Astin.

C

C.D. • The dog of *Dynasty* and *Models Inc.* television actress Emma Samms.

C. Fred Bush • The cocker spaniel owned by U.S. president George Bush. It published a book, *C. Fred Bush: A Dog's Life* before Millie published hers. Also see **Millie.**

Caacie • One of two Scotties that Dwight D. Eisenhower owned in World War II.

Cabal • One of King Arthur's many hounds.

Cadpig • In author Dodie Smith's *The Hundred and One Dalmatians*, published in 1956, one of Pongo's fifteen puppies. It was the smallest and prettiest and was an avid television viewer.

Caesar • Actor-director-producer Orson Welles's dog, named after a salad or a Roman emperor, probably the latter.

• The watchdog in the 1966 movie *Our Man Flint*.

• The dog in the 1970s television movie *Trapped*.

• On the radio series *Lum and Abner*, Cedric Wehunt's hound dog.

• The long-haired fox terrier belonging to Edward VII. Its collar had the imprint: "I am Caesar, the king's dog." On Edward's tomb at St. George's Chapel, Windsor, the image of the dog lies at the feet of the king.

• Aviatrix and writer Beryl Markham's bulldog, her favorite dog. Also see **Cesare**.

Cajun • A dog owned by singer Della Reese, who has a preference for "spicy" names. (Cajun is short for Arcadian, a term for a French settler who, via Canada, moved to Louisiana.) See **Allspice**.

Calaban • A German shepherd of singer Maureen McGovern.

Calamity Jane • A Shetland sheepdog given to U.S. president Calvin Coolidge and wife by his children, named after the nineteenth-century U.S. frontierswoman. The dog's original name was Diana of Wildwood.

Caliban • The dog owned by television actress Julia Campbell. The name is from the character in Shakespeare's play *The Tempest*—the beastlike slave of Prospero.

Calvin • *Uncle Tom's Cabin* author Harriet Beecher Stowe's Maltese.

Calypso • A dachshund once owned by nationally syndicated gossip columnist Liz Smith. (Calypso was a mythological nymph who detained Odysseus for a few years.)

Camille • A dog owned by stage and screen actress Helen Hayes (*A Farewell to Arms*).
  • A Rhodesian ridgeback of television actor John James (Jeff Colby on *Dynasty* and *The Colbys*).

Camp • The favorite dog of author Sir Walter Scott. It was a black and tan, part English terrier, part English bulldog. Scott wrote that the dog was "extremely sagacious, faithful and affectionate."

Canache • In Greek mythology, one of the many hounds of Actaeon, the hunter whom the goddess Artemis turned into a stag. Canache was a "barker," according to *Room's Classical Dictionary*.

Candida • An English mastiff owned by British screen actor Dirk Bogarde (*The Servant*).

Candy • *Midnight Express* actor Bo Hopkins's golden retriever.

Canute • British author Vita Sackville-West's elkhound. It was named after the first Danish king of England.
   • U.S. vice president Thomas E. Dewey's dog.

Captain • One of U.S. president George Washington's dogs.
   • The cocker spaniel of film comedic pioneer Harold Lloyd.
   • The Old English sheepdog of actress Jeanette MacDonald (*Naughty Marietta*).
   • The Great Pyrenees dog owned by television comedic actress Betty White (*Golden Girls*). Its nickname was Cappy.

Captain Bobby • A mixed basset-schnauzer of film actress Cloris Leachman (*The Last Picture Show*). Its full name was Captain Bobby Snout.

Captain Doberman • A canine character in a Mickey Mouse short produced by the Disney studio.

Captain Pendragon • The name of silent-screen star Rudolph Valentino's pet Irish wolfhound.

Cardigan • One of General George Armstrong Custer's dogs, named after a British cavalryman in the Crimean War.

Carface • A cigar-chomping bulldog in the 1996 film *All Dogs Go to Heaven 2*. (The dog's voice was done by actor Ernest Borgnine.)

Carlo • Poet Emily Dickinson's dog, given to her by her father in 1850.

Carlos • A dog belonging to television game-show host Bob Barker.

Carlotta • A spaniel of editor and publisher John Lehmann.

Carlton • The white bulldog in the 1946 film *The Spiral Staircase*, which starred Dorothy McGuire and George Brent.

Carnoustie • Actress Joan Fontaine's West Highland white terrier. A golfer, Fontaine named the dog after a golf course in Scotland.

Carol • King George VI's Welsh corgi, born on Christmas Day, and named after the traditional Yuletide song.

Caroline • Producer-actor John Houseman's dachshund.

Caron • A water retriever owned by France's Charles IX. Also see **Comte**.

Casey • The name of dogs owned by the singing couple Steve Lawrence and Eydie Gormé, and by movie actor Tim Holt (*The Treasure of Sierra Madre*).

Casper • One of movie and television actor Robert Wagner's King Charles spaniels.

Cassie • A dog owned by actor Charles Bronson and his wife, Jill Ireland.

Cassy • Pop singer David Cassidy's dog.

Caswell Laddy Boy • The Airedale terrier of U.S. president Warren G. Harding.

Catcher • A Siberian husky owned by actress Kate Jackson (*Charlie's Angels*).

Catfish • The name of writer Lewis Grizzard's dog, famous for drinking out of the toilet bowl.

Cavall • In T.H. White's *The Sword in the Stone*, one of King Arthur's many dogs.

Centime • One of movie actress Natalie Wood's dogs. (A *centime* is the French equivalent of a penny.)

Cerberus • In Greek mythology, the three-headed dog that guards the gate to the underworld.

Cesare • The King Charles spaniel of fashion photographer Francesco Scavullo. See **Caesar**.

Chablis • A Bichon frisé of sports announcer Frank Gifford and his talk-show host–singer wife, Kathie Lee Gifford, named after a dry white wine.

Champ • The Doberman pinscher of actress Tanya Roberts (*Charlie's Angels*).
• The name of dogs owned by musician-record company executive Herb Alpert and by film actor Edward G. Robinson.

Champion • In Ellery Queen, Jr. mystery stories, the name of Djuna's black Scottie dog.

Champion Tinetern Tiptoe • An Airedale terrier of U.S. president Woodrow Wilson.

Chance • One of actress-singer Carol Lawrence's dogs.
• The pizza-loving bulldog (voice-over by Michael J. Fox) in the 1996 Disney movie *Homeward Bound 2: Lost in San Francisco*. His big line is "Dogs rule and cats drool."

Chang • A Pekingese of comedic actress Betty White (*Golden Girls*).

Charcoal • A Chow Chow owned by designer Bijan.

Chardonnay • A Bichon frisé of sports announcer Frank Gifford and his talk-show host wife, Kathie Lee Gifford, named after a dry white wine. See **Chablis**.

Charles • Actor Richard Thomas's King *Charles* spaniel.

Charley • The title character, a gray standard poodle, in writer John Steinbeck's best-selling book *Travels with Charley*. Charley was the name of his real-life dog.

Charlie • U.S. presidential daughter Caroline Kennedy's dog when she lived at the White House.
• *Golden Girls* actress Bea Arthur's German shepherd.
• One of actress Doris Day's poodles.
• The cockapoo of actress Sandy Duncan (*The Hogan Family*).
• The mixed-breed dog of television personality Leeza Gibbons.
• Actress-singer (Broadway's *West Side Story*) Carol Lawrence's dog.
• One of three King Charles spaniels owned by Katie Wagner, daughter of actor Robert Wagner. See **Casper** and **Chelsea**.

Charlie Brown • The poodle of comedic actor Red Buttons (*Sayonara*) and the name of dogs owned by actress Nanette Fabray and television actor Earl Holliman (*Police Woman*).

Charlie Potatoes • A dog of movie and television actor Robert Blake (*In Cold Blood*).

Charlotte • In the 1977 film *The Deep*, starring British actress Jacqueline Bisset and Nick Nolte, the dog owned by Robert Shaw (as Treece). The real name of the dog was **Saucey**.

Charo • A poodle owned by stage and screen actress Helen Hayes (*Airport*).

Chaucer • Chevy Chase's on-screen schnauzer in the 1978 movie *Foul Play*, costarring Goldie Hawn.

Checkers • The name of Richard M. Nixon's black-and-white-spotted cocker spaniel, made famous when the future U.S. president admitted in a speech on September 23, 1952, that the dog was a gift from a supporter in Texas and that he and his family liked the dog too much to give it up even though it was an illegal political gift.

Chelsea • A dog of British comedic actor Dudley Moore (*Arthur*).
•The third King Charles spaniel owned by Katie Wagner, daughter of actor Robert Wagner. See **Casper** and **Charlie**.

Cheo • A dog owned by British actor James Mason.

Chester • Television actress Fran "*The Nanny*" Drescher's Pomeranian.
• One of actress Sally Struthers's chow chows.

Chesty Pagett • The U.S. Marine Corps' mascot bulldog.

Cheyenne • An Australian cattle dog owned by actress Kelly McGillis (*Witness* and *Top Gun*).

Chico • A large white poodle owned by English writer John Lehmann. He inherited the dog from his mother.
• A dog owned by Lou Costello of the comedy team Abbott and Costello.

Chief • One of Lassie author Albert Payson Terhune's many collies.

Chili • Cabaret singer Bobby Short's Dalmatian.

China • A greyhound of actress Bo Derek.
• A dog owned by Joanne Carson, ex-wife of television talk-show host Johnny Carson.

Ching • Film actress Valerie Perrine's Great Dane.
• King George VI's Tibetan lion dog. See **Choo-Choo**.

Ching Ching • One of actress-turned-diplomat Shirley Temple's dogs.

Ching Ching II • Another dog of Shirley Temple.

Chinkapen • One of U.S. president Lyndon B. Johnson's dogs.

Chinook • The white German shepherd costar with actor Kirby Grant in a few feature movies about a Mountie and his dog, including *Trail of the Yukon* (1950), *Yukon Manhunt* (1950), *Snow Dog* (1951), and *Yukon Vengeance* (1955). See **White Shadow**.

Chipper • A dog featured on the science-fiction fantasy television show *Land of the Giants* from 1968 to 1970. Its owner was twelve-year-old Barry Lockridge, played by Stefan Arngrim.

• One of singer-actress Doris Day's dogs.

Chips • The first American sentry dog sent to Europe with the Third Infantry Division in World War II. The dog, which flushed out a machine-gun crew in Sicily, was awarded a Silver Star and a Purple Heart.

Chiquita • A poodle owned by stage and screen actress Helen Hayes. (*Chiquita* in Spanish usually refers to something small.)

Chong • A black Chow Chow owned by British prime minister David Lloyd George. Given to him by Sir Philip Sassoon, it regularly attended cabinet meetings.

Choo-Choo • A Tibetan lion dog, father of **Ching**, owned by King George VI. It was so named because "he made noises exactly like a train" as a puppy.

Chop Suey • The Lhasa apso owned by pop pianist and dog-lover Liberace. See **Chow Mein**.

Chopper • An English bulldog owned by rap singer Ice-T.

Chou Chou • The poodle in the 1945 movie *The Clock*, which starred Judy Garland.

Chow Mein • Entertainer Liberace's cocker spaniel. See **Chop Suey**.

Chris • The spaniel owned by Nobel Prize-winning author John Galsworthy (*The Forsyte Saga*). John, the canine hero of Galsworthy's *The Country House*, was based on Chris.

Chrissie • One of actress-singer Shirley Jones's dogs.

Christabel • One of the two Monroe family dogs on the television series *My World . . . and Welcome to It*. Also see **Irving**.

• A poodle owned by humorist James Thurber.

Christy • A Dalmatian that John Tesh and Connie Selleca gave their son, Gib on Christmas Day, hence the dog's name.

• A dog owned by model-actress Brooke Shields (whose real first name is Christa).

• One of corporate-buyout mogul Henry Kravis's dogs.

Christy Love • The dog of actress Holly Robinson (*21 Jump Street*).

Chuckie • A Chow Chow owned by *All in the Family* actress Sally Struthers.

Chuleh • A Pekingese owned by author Beatrix Potter, creator of Peter Rabbit.

Cif • A German shepherd owned by *10* actress Bo Derek.

Cigar • A dog that was owned by actor Edward G. Robinson, who was an avid cigar smoker.

Cinderella • One of film and stage actress-dancer Ann Miller's dogs.

Cinders • The Jones family dog in the television series *Casey Jones*.

Cindy • A dog given to director Garry Marshall by Cindy Williams whom he directed in the television series *Laverne and Shirley*.

• One of FBI director J. Edgar Hoover's cairn terriers.

• A boxer owned by naturalist and author Dian Fossey,

who was portrayed in the film *Gorillas in the Mist* by actress Sigourney Weaver.

• A mixed-breed dog owned by *Some Like It Hot* actress Marilyn Monroe.

• A family dog owned by television comedian Sid Caesar (*The Show of Shows*).

Cindy-Cleo • A female Labrador retriever that served as a guide dog for fourteen years and eight months, a record according to the *Guinness Book of World Records*.

Cinnamon • A dog owned by Joanne Carson, ex-wife of television talk-show host Johnny Carson.

• A dog owned by singer Della Reese, who has a preference for "spicy" names. See **Allspice** and **Cajun**.

Clancy Muldoon • Actress Shannen Doherty's golden retriever.

Clarissa • A dog mentioned in James Thurber's story "How to Name a Dog."

Clementine • Legendary stage and screen actor John Barrymore's dog.

Cleo • The name of the basset hound owned by Socrates Miller, played by actor Jackie Cooper, in the 1955–58 television series *The People's Choice*. Cleo made humorous observations throughout the show, although no one on camera could hear the comments.

• Owners of dogs named Cleo have included actor Charlton Heston, comedy duo George Burns and Gracie Allen, singer Carol Lawrence, Pulitzer Prize–winning drama critic Brooks Atkinson, and San Francisco 49ers football team owner Edward De Bartolo, Jr.

Clipper • A German shepherd owned by U.S. president John F. Kennedy while in the White House.

Cliquot • Movie actress Joan Crawford's white French poodle, which had its own coat monogrammed C.C. The name possibly comes from *Veuve Cliquot*, a French champagne.

Cloe • One of U.S. president George Washington's dogs. (The name may have been short for Clover or Chloe, a name from Greek mythology.)

Close Encounter • The winningest show dog of all time, according to the *Guinness Book of World Records*. The Scottish terrier won 203 Best-in-Breed awards.

Clovis Lee • A springer spaniel of artist David Bates. The dog lacked a tail but Bates always painted the tail on in his portraits.

Clown • A cocker spaniel of French actress Brigitte Bardot and movie director Roger Vadim.
• A poodle owned by put-down clown Don Rickles.

Clumsy • In T.H. White's *The Sword in the Stone*, one of King Arthur's many dogs.

Clyde • A dog once owned by actor Burt Reynolds and *Laugh-In* actress Judy Carne.
• A golden retriever owned by television actress Tiffani-Amber Thiessen (*Beverly Hills 90210*). See **Bonnie**.

Cobo • One of actor-producer Michael Landon's dogs.

Cocktail • A wirehaired terrier owned by 1920s comedic movie actor Edmund Lowe (*Flagg and Quirt*).

Coco • The tenth most popular name for a dog in the U.S.

• The name of a cocker spaniel owned by actor Fredric March (*The Best Years of Our Lives*).

• A Lhasa apso of comedian Bob Hope.

• A Rottweiler owned by Debbi Fields of Mrs. Fields's Cookies fame.

• A poodle of entertainer Liberace and a dog of media personality Sandra Bernhard.

Coconut • A poodle owned by television actress Joyce De Witt (*Three's Company*).

Cody • The golden retriever of television and movie actor Michael Paré (*The Greatest American Hero* and feature *Eddie and the Cruisers*).

Cole • The Labrador retriever of lyricist-composer Martin Charnin (*Annie*).

Colette • A dog owned by movie and television actor Brian Keith (*The Wind and the Lion*).

Colle • In T.H. White's *The Sword in the Stone*, one of King Arthur's many dogs.

• In Geoffrey Chaucer's *Canterbury Tales*, one of the dogs in the "Nun's Priest's Tale."

Colonel Blimp • A terrier of screen actress Elizabeth Taylor (*Butterfield 8*).

Columbus • A toy poodle of singer-dancer-actor Sammy "Candy Man" Davis, Jr.

Commission • A dog owned by screen legend Clark Gable.

Comte • A water retriever owned by Charles IX of France, from the French word for "count." See **Caron**.

Conan • The Labrador retriever of weight-lifter-turned-actor Arnold Schwarzenegger, who took the name from his starring role in the 1982 film *Conan the Barbarian*.

Conus • A Rottweiler owned by television comedian Sid Caesar in his drinking days. See **Sascha**.

Cookie • A Rottweiler owned and appropriately named by Debbi Fields, founder of Mrs. Fields's Cookies.

Cooper • An Australian cattle dog owned by movie and television actor Mark Harmon (*Moonlighting*). Also see **Frank**, **Paddy** and **Red**.
  • A dog owned by second-generation humorist Wil Shriner.

Cooter • One of musician-producer Herb Alpert's dogs.

Cora • A cairn terrier owned by Prince Edward, later known as the Duke of Windsor.

Corky • A Welsh corgi once owned by opera diva Beverly Sills. The opera singer had to part with the dog because of its tendency to be destructive.
  • A Yorkshire terrier owned by television evangelists Jim and Tammy Faye Bakker. Corky's girlfriend was a poodle named **Peaches**.
  • A dog that appeared in the 1950 movie *Behave Yourself*, starring Shelly Winters and Farley Granger.
  • A dog owned by *Our Gang* actor Carl "Alfalfa" Switzer.

Cormac • A dog owned by singer Robin Gibb of the Bee Gees.

Cornelius • Playwright Tennessee Williams's bulldog, named after Williams's intimidating father.

Coty • A dog owned by television actor Ian Ziering (*Beverly Hills 90210*).

Country • One of *Happy Days* actor Anson Williams's basset hounds.

Crab • The only canine character in William Shakespeare's plays—in *The Two Gentlemen of Verona*. About the dog, its owner in the play, Launce, says, "I think Crab my dog be the sourest natured dog that lives."

Crackers • One of King George VI's Welsh corgis, born on Christmas Day. (Crackers were traditional Christmas favors in England.) See **Carol**.

Cricket • Screen actress Natalie Wood's sheepdog and one of television actress Betty White's dogs.

Croissant • A dog owned by Loretta Swit of television's *M*A*S*H* series.

Cub • A border collie owned by television actor John James (Jeff Colby on *Dynasty* and *The Colbys*).

Cube • A Rottweiler owned by television actor Brian Austin Green (*Beverly Hills 90210*).

Cujo • The title character, a Saint Bernard, in Stephen King's novel *Cujo*.
 • A dog of actress Mariette Hartley, best remembered for her appearances with James Garner in the Polaroid commercials.

Curley • *Rocky* and *Rambo* star Sylvester Stallone's mutt.

Cyclone • A dog of Arizona conservative and former U.S. presidential candidate Barry Goldwater.

Cyrano • One of actress Shirley Jones and comedian-husband, Marty Ingels's dogs, which, like Edmund Rostand's character Cyrano de Bergerac and most canines, has a large nose.

D

Daffodil • One of many King Charles spaniels owned by the Gladys, Duchess of Marlborough.

Dai • A Pembrokeshire corgi owned by British prime minister David Lloyd George. (*Dai* is Welsh for the name David.)

Dainty • One of singer David Cassidy's dogs.

Daisey • A dog of actress Marcia Rodd (*Trapper John, M.D.*).

Daisy • A Scottish terrier owned by Katharine White, wife of writer E.B. White (*Charlotte's Web.*) The dog's mother was **Jeannie**, owned by writer James Thurber, who dedicated his book *Is Sex Necessary?* to both dogs. White wrote Daisy's obituary, which was published in *The New Yorker* magazine.

• Dagwood Bumstead's family dog in the Chic Young comic strip *Blondie*, which began in 1930 and in the *Blondie* feature movies, which began in 1938 and ran until 1950.

• The family dog of *Uncle Tom's Cabin* author Harriet Beecher Stowe.

• Writer Dorothy Parker's Scottish terrier.

• A Yorkshire terrier of movie actress Elizabeth Taylor and ex-husband Richard Burton.

• A golden retriever of actress Mariette Hartley.

• A French poodle of stage and screen actress Tallulah Bankhead (*Little Foxes*).

- A dog of *Mommie Dearest* author Christina Crawford.
- A collie of actress-singer Doris Day (*The Pajama Game*).
- A wirehaired fox terrier owned by Russian-born stage and screen actress Alla Nazimova (*The Bridge of San Luis Rey*).

Daisy-June • One of *Send Me No Flowers* actress Doris Day's dogs.

Dan • Veterinarian-turned-author James Herriot's black Labrador that always carried sticks in its mouth when it walked. Herriot's best-seller *All Things Bright and Beautiful* was dedicated to Dan (and Hector.) Also see **Hector** and "**Handsome Dan.**"

Dancer • A little gray poodle belonging to comedic television actress Betty White (*Golden Girls*), given to her by her parents.
- A dog of television actor Max Gail (Sergeant Stanley Wojohowicz on *Barney Miller*).

Dash • A mongrel, noted for its odd behavior, owned by poet Thomas Hood, and later by writer and essayist Charles Lamb.
- It was also the name of a dog that U.S. president Benjamin Harrison gave his grandchildren.
- A King Charles spaniel owned by Princess Victoria when she was coronated Queen of England. She made reference to Dash in her 1833 diary.
- A golden retriever of television comedic actress Mary Tyler Moore.

Dave • In novelist Jack London's *Call of the Wild*, the companion sled dog of **Buck**.

Davie • U.S. president Woodrow Wilson's Airedale.

Davy Crockett • One of two pugs owned by the Duke and Duchess of Windsor, named after the American frontiersman. See **Disraeli**.

Dawg • Hi and Lois Flagston's dog in the comic strip *Hi and Lois*.

Deacon • One of *Legends of the Fall* movie actor Brad Pitt's dogs.

Deckel • A dachshund owned by Queen Victoria. A gravestone on the grounds of Windsor Castle honors the dog.

Delilah • A dog owned by "coochie-coochie" singer Charo, widow of bandleader Xavier Cugat. The dog is named after Samson's mistress.
  • A streetwise stray dog (voice-over by Carla Gugino) in the 1996 Disney movie *Homeward Bound 2: Lost in San Francisco*.

Demi • A dog once owned by movie actor Rock Hudson (*Strange Bedfellows*), probably short for *demimonde*, a class of women who were sexually indiscreet.

Demon • Writer Ron Goulart's German shepherd in his "How Come My Dog Don't Bark?"

Deputy Dawg • A cartoon character hound dog which made its debut on television's *Terrytoons* in 1960.

Derek • A poodle owned by actor-dancer Patrick Swayze (*Dirty Dancin'*).

Detroit • The mangy family dog on the television series *The Fitzpatricks*, which ran in the 1977–78 season.

Diablo • A spaniel owned by the "It" girl actress Clara Bow (*Man Trap*). (*Diablo* means "devil" in Spanish.)

Diamond • The name of English mathematician and philosopher Sir Isaac Newton's spaniel.
• In T.H. White's *The Sword in the Stone*, one of King Arthur's many dogs.
• The Labrador retriever of gossip commentator Bill Harris (*Entertainment Tonight* and *At the Movies*).

Diana of Wildwood • The original name of U.S. president Calvin Coolidge's Shetland sheepdog. See **Calamity Jane**.

Dick • The spaniel mascot of the *U.S.S. Constitution* in 1840.
• The Great Dane of television actor Wallace Ford.

Didi • *Show Boat* actress Kathryn Grayson's dog.

Digby • The Wheaton cairn terrier of actress Shelley Duvall (*Popeye*).

Digger • In the television cartoon series *Valley of the Dinosaurs*, the name of the Butler family's pet dog.

Dillon • Actress Doris Day's dog, which lost a leg in an auto accident.

Dinah • A golden retriever and former guide dog owned by actress Betty White, one of television's *Golden Girls*. Dinah was the subject of the book *Dinah's Story*, co-authored by Ms. White and Tom Sullivan, the original owner of the guide dog and a *Good Morning America* special correspondent.

Dingo • A dog owned by actress Peggy McKay (Stacy on *The Lazarus Syndrome*). (A dingo is a wild dog found in Australia.)

Dinkey • A Pomeranian of silent-screen star Constance Talmadge (*Intolerance*).

Dino • One of several Siberian Huskies owned by actor Eddie Velez (*Extremities*).

Diogenes • In Charles Dickens's "Dombey and Son," Florence Dombey's brutish but loyal dog. (Diogenes was a Greek philosopher.)

Dippy Dawg • See **Goofy.**

Dirty Dawg • One of Hanna-Barbera's cartoon canines.

Disraeli • The name of the "bugged" bulldog in the spy spoof *The Spy with a Cold Nose* (1966).
• One of two pugs owned by the Duke and Duchess of Windsor, named after the nineteenth-century British statesman. See **Davy Crockett.**

Diswilliam • A poodle owned by television actress and producer Mary Tyler Moore.

Diveidi • A Chow Chow owned by British prime minister David Lloyd George. The name means "mischief" in Welsh.

Dixie • A dog owned by actress Mary Kate McGeehan (Linda Caproni on *Falcon Crest*).

Djedda • Opera singer Maria Callas's brown poodle, given to her by Greek shipping magnate Aristotle Onassis. (The name was reportedly inspired by a town in Saudi Arabia where Onassis negotiated shipping rights of oil and almost cornered the world oil market.)

Doctor Sam • One of entertainer Sammy Davis, Jr.'s toy poodles.

Dog Bright • A dog immortalized in the nursery rhyme:
Poor Dog Bright,
Ran off with all his might,
Because the cat was after him,
Poor Dog Bright.

Doggie Daddy • A dog in Hanna-Barbera cartoons.

Doll • See Dolly.

Doloras • One of actress Tallulah Bankhead's dogs.

Dolly • English author Nancy Mitford's French bulldog.

Domino • A dog of singer-actress Olivia Newton-John (*Grease*).

Don't Cry • A dog owned by *CHiPS* star Erik Estrada.

Don't Know • One of humorist Mark Twain's dogs. See **I Know** and **You Know**.

Donna • A dog of Olympic diver Greg Louganis.

Donnie • Ann Sothern's Scottie in her 1944 film *Maisie Goes to Reno*.

Dookie • A corgi given to Queen Elizabeth when she was seven years old. Its full name was Rozavel Golden Eagle. See **Tafferteffy**.

Dopey • One of singer-actor Bobby Sherman's dogs.

Dorarich Butch • A Sealyham terrier owned by legendary screen actor Humphrey Bogart (*Casablanca*).

Doris • The Lhasa apso of television actress Michael Learned (*The Waltons*).

Dos • The Australian cattle dog of cookie entrepreneur Debbi "Mrs." Fields.

Dotti • An Akita that won a 1994 Delta Society award for helping a blind cardiologist perform his medical duties.

Dottie • The dog of ex-adman and Nixon aide H.R. Haldeman.

Dragée • One of Gladys, Duchess of Marlborough's many King Charles spaniels.

Drago • See "**Arthur Pendragon**."

Drifter • The retriever of Joan Embery, "goodwill ambassador" of the San Diego Zoo.

Dromas • In Greek mythology, one of the many hounds of Actaeon, the hunter whom the goddess Artemis turned into a stag. Dromas was a "runner," according to *Room's Classical Dictionary*.

Droopy • A cocker spaniel owned by actress Lauren Bacall and Humphrey Bogart.

Drujok • One of two Samoyeds owned by Russian-born stage and screen actress Anna Sten (*The Brothers Karamazov*).

Duane • Bee Gees singer Barry Gibb's dog.

Dublin • *Starsky and Hutch* actor David Soul's golden retriever, named after some Irish real estate.

Duchess • A poodle owned by Hollywood cartoon feature producer and pioneer Walt Disney.

Duck • The Scottish deerhound of *Out of Africa* author Isak Dinesen.

Dudley • The sheep dog on the television show *The Rich Little Show*.
• A basset griffon vendeen owned by actress Mary Tyler Moore.

Duffer • The Wheaton terrier of television actor Eugene Roche (*Perfect Strangers* and *Julie*). (Duffer is a term for a clumsy person, especially a weekend golfer.)

Duffy • A Scottish terrier owned by Franklin and Eleanor Roosevelt early in their marriage.

Duke • The third most popular name for a dog in the U.S.
• In Booth Tarkington's novel *Penrod*, Penrod Schofield's dog was named Duke. The dog was "small and shaggy and looked like an old postman."
• Duke was also the name of the Jed Clampett's hound dog in the television series *The Beverly Hillbillies*.
• One of singer Mariah Carey's Doberman pinschers.
• A dog owned by comedic actor Robin Williams (*Good Morning Vietnam*).
• The name of actor John Wayne's childhood pet, an Airedale, after whom Wayne received the nickname Duke.
• A dog owned by film actress Joan Bennett (*The Woman of the Window*).
• Silent screen actress Clara Bow's Great Dane.
• The featured Great Dane in the 1965 movie *The Ugly Dachshund*, who thinks it is a dachshund.
• It was also the name of Kelly's dog in Jack Moore's comic strip *Kelly*.
• One of the dogs in the novel *Swiss Family Robinson*.

• An English mastiff owned by U.S. president Rutherford B. Hayes.

• A black Labrador owned by English romance novelist Barbara Cartland. It was a gift from the Earl of Mountbatten.

• Elly May Clampett's dog in the television series *The Beverly Hillbillies*.

• The Great Dane of former television talk-show host Mike Douglas.

Dum Dum • A dog in Hanna-Barbera cartoons.

Dumpling • One of U.S. president Lyndon B. Johnson's beagles.

Dushok • One of two Samoyeds owned by Russian-born stage and screen actress Anna Sten (*The Brothers Karamazov*).

Dusty • In Carl Anderson's *Henry* cartoon, Henry's white dog.

• The canine sidekick of Shield, "The Boy Detective," in the comic book series *The Shield*.

• The border collie of standup comedian-turned-actor Michael Keaton (*Batman*).

Dusk • *Out of Africa* author Isak Dinesen's Scotch deerhound, a wedding present. It was eventually killed by a zebra.

Dutchess • The nonhousebroken dog of U.S. president Franklin D. Roosevelt.

Dylan • The Llewellyn setter of movie actress Sally "Hot Lips" Kellerman (*M*A*S*H*).

Dynomutt • The Blue Falcon's "Dog Wonder" (a mechanical pet dog) in Hanna-Barbera's television cartoons.

E

Eaglehurst Gillette • A setter owned by U.S. president Herbert Hoover.

Easy • A dog of television actor Max Gail (Sergeant Stanley Wojohowicz on *Barney Miller*).

Eclair • A poodle of television actress Janine Turner (*Northern Exposure*).

Ed • The dog of P.A.W.S. activist Courtney Thorne-Smith. P.A.W.S. stands for Pets Are Wonderful Support, an organization that helps HIV/AIDS-infected people get along with pets.

Eddie • The name of the Jack Russell terrier on the television series *Frasier*. Its real name is Moose.
• Movie actress Judy Garland's collie.
• A chow chow of television's *All in the Family* actress Sally Struthers.

Edgar • One of U.S. president Lyndon Baines Johnson's beagles.

Edison • The shaggy dog of Caractacus Potts in the 1968 movie *Chitty Chitty Bang Bang*.

Edward • In Anne Tyler's novel *The Accidental Tourist*, on which the 1988 movie was based, the Welsh corgi that helps bring the couple together.
• A dog of actress-director Ida Lupino (*High Sierra*).

E'en So • A Pekingese owned by movie stars Elizabeth Taylor and Richard Burton. The dog understood commands in Welsh and was blind in one eye.

Eiko von Blutenberg • A dachshund bought by writer Dorothy Parker who later changed its name to Robinson.

Einstein • In the 1985 movie *Back to the Future*, starring Michael J. Fox, the mixed-breed dog owned by the mad scientist played by actor Christopher Lloyd, named after German physicist Albert Einstein.

Elfie • Television actress Shannen Doherty's German shepherd.

Elmer • One of **Daisy**'s five puppies in the *Blondie* cartoon strip.

Elmo • A dog featured in the television cartoon series *The Funky Phantom*.

Elsa • A Lhasa apso owned by actress Elizabeth Taylor.

El Tigre • One of singer-actress Doris Day's dogs. (*El tigre* means "the tiger" in Spanish.)

Elvis • The pet dog of the Elvis Hole-in-the-Wall gang in the television series *Butch Cassidy and the Sundance Kids*.
   • A golden retriever owned by *General Hospital* actor Jack Wagner.

Emily • A Lhasa apso owned by heiress and art patron Peggy Guggenheim.

Emma • A poodle owned by quiz-show host Allen Ludden who married actress Betty White of television's *Golden Girls*.

Engelbert • U.S. general George S. Patton's dog.

Erda • A German shepherd owned by author-artist Maurice Sendak (*Where the Wild Things Are*).

Ernest • The *female* dog on television's *Dave's World*.

Ernie • Writer George Plimpton's yellow Labrador retriever and an avid bird watcher!

Eros • A greyhound owned by Albert, husband of and Prince Consort to Queen Victoria. (Eros is the Greek god of love.)

E.T. • The German shepherd of producer Gene Roddenberry, who created *Star Trek*. (E.T., of course, is short for Extra Terrestrial.)

Ethel • An Airedale terrier of comedic actor Ronnie Schell (Private Duke Slater on *Gomer Pyle U.S.M.C.*).

Evalita • A dog owned by actress Beverly D'Angelo (*Coal Miner's Daughter*).

Eve • A dog owned by actor Anthony Edwards (*E.R.* and *Revenge of the Nerds*, Parts I and II).

Explorer • A collie owned by author Albert Payson Terhune (*Lad: A Dog*). See **Thane**.

Ezra Pound • A mutt owned by writer F. Scott Fitzgerald and his wife, Zelda, named after the writer-poet Ezra Pound.

F

Fair Ellen • One of author Albert Payson Terhune's dogs.

Faithful • The Newfoundland owned by Ulysses S. Grant's son Jesse.

Fala • U.S. president Franklin D. Roosevelt's Scottish

terrier, whose full name was Murray, the Outlaw of Fala Hill. Originally named Big Boy, it was given to him by his cousin Margaret Stuckley. The Roosevelts reportedly renamed the dog after an ancestor. Fala (or Fal) was privy to a lot of high-level international meetings, including the one in 1941 with Winston Churchill when Roosevelt and Churchill signed the Atlantic Charter aboard the *U.S.S. Augusta*.

Fallon • One of actor John Forsythe's toy poodles, named after his daughter Fallon Carrington on television's *Dynasty* series.

Famous • Audrey Hepburn's high-strung Yorkshire terrier, which required tranquilizer pills to calm down, the price of fame.

Fang • A German shepherd owned by actress Joan Fontaine (*Rebecca*).
• A canine secret agent on the television series *Get Smart*, starring Don Adams. The dog was also known as Agent K-13.

Fannie • One of television actor (*Police Woman*) Earl Holliman's many dogs.

Fanny • A Rhodesian ridgeback of Princess Grace Kelly and Prince Rainier.

Farfel • The dog dummy that sang in an old Nestle's commercial (". . . Nestle's makes the very best c-ch-hooc-co-ol-laat-te."). The dog's ventriloquist was named Danny O'Day.

Farley • A dog of television actor Earl Holliman (*Police Woman*).

Farkas • The wolf in the 1977 movie *Lucan*.

Faro • Actor Burt Lancaster's dog in the 1955 movie *The Kentuckian*, the only movie that he directed.

Farouk • The dog in the *Ironsides* television series, named after the Egyptian king.

Fatty • One of several golden retrievers owned by television actress Staci Keanan (*Going Places* and *My Two Dads*).

Faunus • A dog of poet Elizabeth Barrett Browning (*Sonnets from the Portuguese*).

Fawn Hall • Actor Dennis Quaid's golden retriever, so called because it shredded everything, as the real Fawn Hall, a government administrative assistant, did with government documents during the Iran-Contra scandal.

Feather • A Yorkshire terrier of actress Marcia Rodd (*Trapper John, M.D.*).

Feathers • Writer Carl van Vechten's cat, mentioned in his book *The Tiger in the House*, published in 1920.

Feets • A cocker spaniel (with large paws!) owned by writer Lawrence Sanders, author of mystery thrillers such as *The First Deadly Sin*.

Feller • A cocker spaniel puppy given to U.S. president Harry Truman by a woman from Missouri, his home state. He gave the dog to the White House physician, Brigadier General Wallace Graham.

Ferdinand • A dog owned by actress Peggy McKay (Stacy on *The Lazarus Syndrome*).

Ferdinando • A dog given to Isabella Rossellini by her actress-mother Ingrid Bergman when Isabella was in a body cast for two years.

Fern • A mixed-breed dog owned by comedic actress Carol Burnett.

Fido • A stereotypical name for a loyal dog, from the Latin word for "faithful." U.S. president Abraham Lincoln owned a yellow mixed-breed dog named Fido. Coincidentally, the dog was "assassinated"—stabbed to death by a drunk.

Fifi • One of actor Robert Wagner and actress Jill St. John's dogs.

Fiona • An Airedale terrier owned by writer Richard Condon, author of *Prizzi's Honor*, *Arigato*, and *The Manchurian Candidate*.

Flame • The dog in the *My Pal* movie series in the early 1950s.

Flannel • A dog owned by author Stephen Crane (*The Red Badge of Courage*).

Flapjack • The name of the dog in the toy line based on Pillsbury's little "Dough Boy."

Flash • The featured dog in the television cartoon series *Emergency Plus Four*.

Flashy Sir • A champion greyhound honored in the Greyhound Hall of Fame in Abilene, Texas. Each year the organization gives out the Flashy Sir award to the greyhound with the best distance record.

Flea Bailey • A Tibetan terrier owned by Lia Belli, the fifth wife of famed lawyer Melvin Belli. (Note the similarity of the dog's name and the name of another lawyer—F. Lee Bailey!).

Flic • A boxer owned by Algonquin "Round Table" writer Dorothy Parker. (*Flic* is French slang for policeman.)

Flip • In the *Happy Hooligan* comic strip, Happy Hooligan's pet dog.
• One of actor Gregory Peck's dogs.

Flipper • Movie star Sylvester Stallone's Labrador, which actually drowned in Biscayne Bay behind Stallone's Miami mansion in 1996.

Flora • The "best of dogs," according to writer and cat-lover Edward Lear (*A Book of Nonsense*). He encountered the dog while vacationing on the island of Corsica. He noted that it was a "spotty little beast of excellent qualities."

Florence • A Labrador retriever owned by television personalities Gary Collins and Mary Ann Mobley.

Flossy • The black and white spaniel owned by British author Anne Brontë.

Flotsam • The canine featured in the television series *On Our Own*. (Flotsam is a term for wreckage of a ship found floating on water.)

Floyd • A basset hound owned by comedic actor Harry Anderson (*Night Court*).

Fluff • A dog of actress of Berlin-born American actress Katherine Cornell (*The Barretts of Wimpole Street*).

Fluffy • One of Queen Victoria's six Pomeranians. See **Beppo, Gilda, Lulu, Mino**, and **Nino**.

Fluffy Ruffles • A Pomeranian that failed the screen test to star with Charlie Chaplin for his classic 1918 movie *A Dog's Life*. See **Scraps**.

Flush • The red cocker spaniel owned by Elizabeth Barrett Browning, mentioned in Rudolph Besier's book *The Barretts of Wimpole Street*. The dog accompanied Browning and her husband, Robert, on their honeymoon. Virginia Woolf wrote about the dog in her piece "Flush."

Fly • A sheepdog that Peter Rabbit author Beatrix Potter kept on her sheep farm.
• One of stage actress Sarah Bernhardt's dogs.

Foodini • The dog puppet on television's *Lucky Pup* show, which ran from 1948 to 1951.

Forester • One of George Washington's many dogs.

Foxhugh • A Maltese of rock 'n' roll legend Elvis Presley.

Foxy • A collie of U.S. president Calvin Coolidge.

Frank • An Australian cattle dog owned by movie and television actor Mark Harmon (*Flamingo Road*). Also see **Cooper**, **Paddy**, and **Red**.

Frankie • A Labrador retriever owned by comedic television star Paul Reiser (*Mad about You*).

Freckles • A dog owned by Robert F. Kennedy, the brother of U.S. president John F. Kennedy.
• One of U.S. president Lyndon B. Johnson's beagles.
• A dog owned by "God Bless America" singer Kate Smith.

Fred • The name of Little Ricky's puppy in the *I Love Lucy* television series.

• A King Charles spaniel of publisher-author William F. Buckley, Jr.

• A reddish dachshund owned by writer E.B. White (*Charlotte's Web*). It lived to the ripe age of fourteen and was often mentioned in White's writings, e.g., "Death of a Pig" and various *New Yorker* columns.

Fred Bassett • The British equivalent of Snoopy, Fred Bassett is a comic strip hound that was created in 1963 by Alex Graham.

Freddie • In the comic strip *Hubert*, the sheepdog belonging to Hubert.

Freebo • One of U.S. president Ronald W. Reagan's dogs.

Freeway • The dog owned by Robert Wagner and Stefanie Powers in their television series *Hart to Hart*, so named because it was found on a freeway. The dog's real name was Charlie and he was not discovered at Schwab's drugstore—he was found in a dog pound!

• A mixed-breed dog owned by television actress Ming-Na Wen of *The Single Guy*.

• A cocker spaniel owned by actress Leslie Charleson (*General Hospital*). She chose the name because of the time spent on freeways going to and from the studio.

• A Great Dane owned by Olympic diver Greg Louganis.

Fremont • In the television series *Dennis the Menace*, Mr. Wilson's dog.

Freya • An elkhound owned by writer Vita Sackville-West.

Friskey • Former U.S. vice president Spiro T. Agnew's dog.

Frisky • A dog owned by television personalities Gary Collins and Mary Ann Mobley.

Fritzie • Screen actor (*The Thin Man*) William Powell's dog.

Frosty • A poodle owned by singer Pat Boone (*Love Letters in the Sand*).

Fuji • The dog of the Osmond Brothers on their Saturday morning television cartoon show. (The Osmonds were given an Akita named Fuji, which turned out to be very antisocial! The name is from an extinct volcano that is the highest mountain in Japan.)
   • An Akita owned by pro basketball player Byron Scott.

Fula • A female Besenji, one of the earlier members of the breed also known as Congo terrier.

Fumbles • The dog of the Huddles family in the Hanna-Barbera television cartoon series *Where's Huddles?*

Fussy • The dog of British stage and screen actress Ellen Terry.

Fuzz • The German shepherd police dog that appeared in the 1973–74 television police drama series *Chase*.

Fuzzy • A Belgian sheepdog of U.S. president Ronald W. Reagan.

G

G. Boy • Short for Government Boy, a cairn terrier owned by FBI chief J. Edgar Hoover.

Gaby • Actress Glenn Close's Coton de Tulear dog.
  • A dog belonging to actress Louise Sorel (Don Rickles's wife on *The Don Rickles Show*).

Gala • One of the first two dogs trained as Seeing Eye dogs. See **Buddy**.

Gandalf • One of two English setters that won a 1995 Delta Society award for making hospital visits to AIDS and cancer patients at the National Cancer Institute in Bethesda, Maryland. See **Hambleton**.

Gandhi • A dachshund owned by actress Marion Davies, girlfriend of publisher William Randolph Hearst. (Mahatma Gandhi was a Hindu leader in India for many years.)

Gangster • A boxer owned by the creator and portrayer of movie hero Rocky Balboa—Sylvester Stallone.

Garm • In Norse mythology, the menacing dog who guarded the entrance to the underworld.

Garryowen • The red Irish wolfhound, owned by Giltrap, in James Joyce's *Ulysses*.

Gatchina • A borzoi or Russian wolfhound given to Princess Alexandra of England by her brother-in-law Alexander III, the Czar of Russia.

Gatsby • A dog of *Pretty Woman* movie actress Julia Roberts, a reference to Jay Gatsby, the F. Scott Fitzgerald character.

Gee Gee • A poodle owned by actress Elizabeth Taylor when she was married to actor Michael Wilding (*In Which We Serve*).

Geist • The dachshund of nineteenth-century British Victorian poet Matthew Arnold, who wrote the elegy "At Geist's Grave" when the dog died.

Gelert • A legendary wolfhound that belonged to the Welsh prince Llewellyn in the thirteenth century. The prince killed the dog when he thought it killed his infant son, only to find out that the hound had killed a wolf that was trying to attack the child.

Gem • The name of U.S. president Theodore Roosevelt's wife's dog—a rat terrier.

Gemmy • A Bichon frisé of novelist Barbara Taylor Bradford (*Angel*).

General Pompey • One of screen actor Charlton Heston's canines, named after the Roman general who became one of the first members of the first triumvirate in the first century B.C.

Genghis Khan • A Shih Tzu of actress Zsa Zsa Gabor.

Genya • The champagne-colored French poodle of New York deejay Alison Steele.

Geoffrey • One of movie director Alfred Hitchcock's Sealyham terriers. Geoffrey and another Sealyham named Stanley appeared with the director in his cameo appearance in his 1963 movie *The Birds*. See **Stanley**. (Hitchcock's production company, Shamley, was a partial anagram of Sealyham.)

George • Actress Mary Robson's Airedale in the 1938

Howard Hawks's comedy movie *Bringing Up Baby*, starring Katherine Hepburn and Cary Grant. The real name of the dog was **Skippy**.

• Another dog of P.A.W.S. activist Courtney Thorne-Smith. P.A.W.S. stands for Pets Are Wonderful Support, an organization that helps HIV/AIDS-infected people get along with pets.

• A Yorkshire terrier owned by British novelist John Gardner who believed that George was "the *only* name for a dog."

• A terrier of British actor Ronald Colman (*A Tale of Two Cities*).

• One of television actor Michael Gray's poodles.

• Other canine George owners include actress Melissa Gilbert (*Little House on the Prairie*) and actor Earl Holliman (*Police Woman*).

George Brandt • A dog of movie actress Janet Leigh (*Psycho*).

George Tirebiter • In the 1940s, the canine mascot of the University of Southern California Trojans football team, so named because it loved to chase cars and bite the tires.

Georgia • A Lhasa apso of Welsh-born stage and screen star Richard Burton.

Gerland • In T.H. White's *The Sword in the Stone*, one of King Arthur's many dogs.

• One of the dogs in the "Nun's Priest's Tale" of Geoffrey Chaucer's *Canterbury Tales*. See **Colle** and **Talbot**.

Gerlert • In T.H. White's *The Sword in the Stone*, one of King Arthur's many dogs.

Giallo • A Pomeranian written about and owned by Romantic poet Walter Savage Landor.

Gigi • Playwright Tennessee Williams's Boston bulldog (not a poodle!), which often flew first class with him—named after the character created by French writer Colette and popularized by Lerner and Loewe.

• Opera singer Beverly Sills's poodle, which was fond of diving into the toilet bowl!

• A dog owned by cosmetic mogul Mary Kay Ash.

• Anthropologist and *In the Shadow of Man* author Dr. Jane Goodall's French poodle.

Gilbert • In Disney cartoons, **Goofy**'s nephew—the one wearing a mortarboard.

Gilby • A Maltese of comedic actor and comedian Bob Hope.

Gilda • A Pomeranian owned by Queen Victoria of England.

Gillie • A fox terrier owned by British writer Saki (real name H. H. Munro) as a youth.

Gin • One of French actress Brigitte Bardot's dogs.

Ginger • The dog owned by Ralph Kramden's mother-in-law, Mrs. Gibson, in the television series *The Honeymooners*.

• A Belgian Schippenke owned by comedic actress-producer Lucille Ball.

• A cockapoo of dancer-actor-choreographer Gene Kelly (*Singin' in the Rain*) and a dog of actor Lorne Greene (*Bonanza*).

Ginger Boy • U.S. General Omar Bradley's dog.

Ginnie • A pointer owned by the ill-fated General George Armstrong Custer.

Giorgio • A German shepherd of television actress Linda Gray (*Dallas*).

Gismo • One of *Goonies* actor Corey Feldman's dogs.

Glen • A Scottish collie owned by U.S. president Herbert Hoover.

Gnasher • One of Heathcliff's dogs in Emily Brontë's novel *Wuthering Heights*.

Goalie • The dog of New York mayor Rudolph Giuliani (he is, of course, a New York Rangers fan!).

Gogo • Actress Greer Garson's dog in her 1945 movie *Valley of Decision*.

Golden Blackie • One of screen actor Vincent Price's many dogs.

Goldie • One of actor Vincent Price's dogs.

Goofy • The name of Mickey Mouse's silly canine friend in Disney cartoons. Originally named **Dippy Dawg**, the black hound made his movie debut in *Mickey's Review* in 1932.
• Singer-actor Bobby Sherman's bloodhound.

Googy • A dog of television actress Eva Gabor (*Green Acres*).

Gorby • Actress Victoria Principal's dog, named after Soviet leader Mikhail Gorbachov.

Gorgon • The talking dog owned by Barnaby Baxter in the comic strip *Barnaby*.

Gracie • *Little House on the Prairie* actress Melissa Gilbert's dog.

Granite • A champion Alaskan sled dog that helped win the 1,158-mile dog sled race in Alaska in 1988.

Gray Dawn • One of writer Albert Payson Terhune's collies and subject of his book *The Way of a Dog*.

Grendel • The puppy featured on the television situation comedy *Thirtysomething*. (Grendel is the name of the monster in *Beowolf.)*

Gretel • A Keeshond owned by pianist-entertainer Liberace.

Greyfriar's Bobby • The eponymous Sky terrier in author Eleanor Atkinson's novel. There is a statue in the dog's honor in Edinburgh, Scotland.

Griggs • A Louisiana Catahoulas dog of Paul Newman and Joanne Woodward.

Grim • A mouse-colored greyhound given to Rutherford B. Hayes. Despite his name, he was "good-natured and neat in his habits" and had "social qualities and talents." Grim, unfortunately, met his Reaper when he remained steadfast on the tracks of an oncoming train as it severed his otherwise healthy body.

Grip • A dog of movie director Wes Craven (*Nightmare on Elm Street*).

Grits • A puppy given to Amy Carter, daughter of U.S. president Jimmy Carter. It was given to her by one of her teachers. Grits and the White House didn't get along so it was returned to the teacher. Grits and Amy's Siamese cat, Misty Malarkey Ying Yang, didn't see "eye to eye." See **Misty Malarkey.**

Grock • A wirehaired terrier owned by British prime minister (1916–22) David Lloyd George.

Grunk • Singer Dinah Shore's favorite dog; its name has graced the license plates of her car.

Guapa • A Pyrrenean mountain dog of actress Deborah Kerr (*The King and I*) and a dog owned by French actress Brigitte Bardot. (*Guapa* means "pretty" in Spanish.)

Gucci • A Chow Chow of actor James Hampton (*China Syndrome*), named after the fashionable brand of Italian leather goods.

Gulliver • Diana Rigg's Great Dane in her television series *Diana*. The dog, in fact, was owned by her brother Roger.

Gunn • Actress Bo Derek's West Highland white terrier.

Gus • Robert Vaughan's dog in the television series *The Protectors*.
 • The featured dog in the mid–1970s movie *Won Ton Ton*.
 • A dog owned by Robert Duvall, who played the role of Gus McCrae in the popular television mini-series *Lonesome Dove*.
 • A Labrador belonging to U.S. senator Phil Gramm of Texas.

Gwen • A Welsh terrier owned by Prince Edward of England, who later became Duke of Windsor and King Edward VIII. ("Gwen" is Welsh for white.)

Gwyllgi • The "dog of darkness" in Welsh folklore, a ghostlike figure usually visible by horses.

Gypsy • Actress Suzanne Pleshette's Tibetan terrier.

H

Hachiko • A loyal Akita whose statue stands at a Tokyo train station. Hachiko went to meet his owner every day at the train station in Tokyo, even nine years after his master's death in 1925.

Hailey • A Newfoundland dog of television actress Sally Struthers (*All in the Family*).

Hambleton • "Hambone" is one of two English setters that won a 1995 Delta Society award for making hospital visits to AIDS and cancer patients at the National Cancer Institute in Bethesda, Maryland. See **Gandalf**.

Hamish • A cairn terrier owned by Edward, Prince of Wales (who later became Edward VII of England).
• A dog of U.S. president Woodrow Wilson.

Hamlet • *Ivanhoe* author Sir Walter Scott's greyhound.
• The name of stage actress Sarah Bernhardt's dog.

Hamlet II • A dog owned by British actress Hayley Mills (*Pollyanna*).

Handsome • One of television actress-movie director Penny Marshall's dogs.

Handsome Dan • The name of the Yale football team's original mascot bulldog since 1892. There have been at least thirteen Handsome Dans since then.

Hannah Morgan • A dog owned by actress-singer Edie Adams, wife of the late Ernie Kovacs.

Hans • The German shepherd that inspired Seeing Eye dogs. It was owned by Dorothy Eustis, the pioneer of Seeing Eye dogs.

Hansie • A dachshund owned by movie actor Vincent Price.

Hap • A Labrador retriever that survived a 1976 boating accident, thanks to its master, Captain Cyril Lebrecque. Two crew members drowned while Lebrecque saved the dog, prompting legal action by the families of the deceased. The captain was found innocent.

Happy • A fox terrier owned by George, Duke of York (later King George V of England).
  • A Boston Bull terrier given to movie actor Vincent Price by his sister when he was a teenager.
  • One of singer David Cassidy's dogs.

Haroun • An Irish wolfhound owned by Rudolph Valentino, and named after one of the heroes of *The Arabian Nights*.

Harry • The name of actor Paul Newman and wife Joanne Woodward's wire fox terrier.
  • A mixed black Labrador/Great Dane in the Patsy Award Hall of Fame. It was owned and trained by Karl Lewis Miller, a noted trainer.
  • A black Scottish cockapoo that won a 1995 Delta Society award for helping a deaf woman function on a daily basis.
  • The name of one of actress Bo Derek's canines.

Harum Scarum • An Airedale owned by movie actress Bo Derek.

Harvey • A boxer given to actor Humphrey Bogart and Lauren Bacall as a wedding present by writers Louis Bromfield and George Hawkins. During their dating period, Bogie called Bacall Harvey, after the invisible rabbit in the Mary Chase play *Harvey*. Bacall had to be "invisible" during her early relationship with Bogie because he was still married to another woman!

• A yellow Labrador retriever owned by Charles, the Prince of Wales.

Hasi • Swedish-born actress Elke Sommer's poodle.

Hazber • A poodle owned by Oscar-winning actress Joan Fontaine (*Rebecca*).

Heathcliff • Actress June Allyson's cocker spaniel, named after the hero of the Emily Brontë novel *Wuthering Heights*, on which her favorite movie was based.

Heather • A collie owned by George, Duke of York (later King George V of England).

Hector • One of two German shepherds owned by U.S. president Rutherford B. Hayes, named after the great Trojan hero.

• Veterinarian-turned-author James Herriot's Jack Russell terrier. Herriot's best-seller *All Things Bright and Beautiful* was dedicated to Hector (and Dan, the other shepherd).

• A Doberman pinscher owned by Hungarian-born horror film star Bela Lugosi.

• The dumb, brown dog that starred in the 1965 animated television show *Hector's House*.

• The dog who sailed from Vancouver to Japan in search of its master, and the subject of Kenneth Dodson's 1958 book *Hector the Stowaway Dog*.

Heidi • The ninth most popular name for a dog in the U.S. It was also the name of President Dwight D. Eisenhower's Weimaraner dog. Heidi stained one rug too many and was exiled to the family farm in Gettysburg, Pennsylvania.

• The name of one of the dachshunds in the 1966 Disney movie *The Ugly Dachshund*.

• Movie actor Charlton Heston also named one of his dogs Heidi, as did television actors William Shatner (*Star Trek*) and Emma Samms (*Dynasty*).

• The Samoyed of television actor Jimmy McNichol (*The Fitzpatricks* and *California Fever*).

Heineken • One of singer-actress Doris Day's dogs, named after a popular brand of Dutch beer.

Helda • An Alsatian sheepdog that served the French in World War I as an artillery spotter.

Helen • A dachshund owned by newspaper publisher William Randolph Hearst for fifteen years. Its epitaph at San Simeon reads, "Here lies dearest Helen, my devoted friend. W.R.H."

Help and Hand • A Scottish deerhound owned by King Robert the Bruce.

Henrietta • A King Charles spaniel owned by actor-poet Richard Thomas (John Boy in *The Waltons*).

Henry • A Yorkshire terrier owned by actress Demi Moore and actor Bruce Willis.

• A dog owned by British diplomat Harold Nicolson.

Her • One of U.S. president Lyndon B. Johnson's beagles, immortalized on the cover of *Life* magazine. LBJ made dog lovers cringe when he was photographed holding up one of the beagles by its ears. See **Him**.

Hero • One of actress Bo Derek's German shepherds.

Hey Dog • In the Steve McQueen television series *Wanted: Dead or Alive*, the name of Jason Nichols's mutt.

Higgins • The featured dog in the 1963–70 television series *Petticoat Junction*. The dog also played the leading role in the 1974 movie *Benji*. Animal trainer Frank Inn found Higgins in an animal shelter.

Him • One of U.S. president Lyndon B. Johnson's beagles, immortalized on the cover of *Life* magazine. LBJ made dog lovers cringe when he was photographed holding up one of the beagles by its ears. See **Her**.
• A Sealyham terrier that movie director Alfred Hitchcock gave to actress Tallulah Bankhead whom he directed in the 1944 movie *Lifeboat*.

Hobo • The name of the Nash family dog in the 1960 movie *Please Don't Eat the Daisies*, which starred Doris Day and David Niven.

Hogan • A dog owned by screenwriter David Kelley (*L.A. Law*).

Hokey Wolf • A wolf featured in Hanna-Barbera cartoons.

Holly • Admiral Byrd's lead sled dog on his first Antarctic expedition.

Homer • One of British actor Rex Harrison's basset hounds, named after the Greek epic poet.

Hondo • A golden retriever of football coach Dan Reeves, named after author Louis D'Amour's western hero (played by John Wayne in the movies).

Honey • A corgi given to Prince Charles by his mother Queen Elizabeth II.
• Dogs named Honey have been owned by actress-singer Doris Day and actress-Elvis-ex-wife Priscilla Presley.

Honey Bear • One of *McMillan and Wife* costar Susan Saint James's dogs.

Honey Pie • A dog of actress Susan Richardson (*Eight Is Enough*).

Hong Kong Phooey • The "Mutt of Steel" and the secret identity of Henry Pooch, the police station janitor, in Hanna-Barbera cartoons.

Hoopla • One of actress Helen Hayes's dogs.

Hoover • Composer-pianist Burt Bacharach's Lhasa apso. See **Noover**.

Horrible • A mutt taken in by the Petrie family in an episode of the television comedy series *The Dick Van Dyke Show*.

Horme • Greek historian Xenophon's dog, which was of "the greatest intelligence and fidelity."

Hotfoot • The lead dog of the sled team that won the first 1,158 mile Alaskan race known as the Iditarod.

Hub • U.S. president Warren G. Harding's Boston terrier.

Huckleberry Hound • The blue-haired star of the Hanna-Barbera *Huckleberry Hound* television series launched in 1958.

Huey • A dog owned by retired television personality Phil Donahue.

Hughie • The Sheltie of *L.A. Law* executive producer Rick Wallace.

Hugo • Actress Marilyn Monroe's basset hound. When

her marriage to playwright Arthur Miller broke up, Miller maintained custody of the dog.

Humphrey • The canine sidekick of the *Superkatt* comic book hero back in the 1940s.

Hylactor • In Greek mythology, one of the many hounds of Actaeon, the hunter whom the goddess Artemis turned into a stag. Hylactor was a "barker," according to *Room's Classical Dictionary*.

I

Iggy • The cross-eyed dog in the comic strip *Count Screwloose of Tooloose*. It wears a hat reminiscent of the one worn by Napoleon's.

Igloo • The name of Admiral Byrd's fox terrier, which accompanied Byrd to his explorations in both the Arctic and Antarctic.

I Know • One of author Mark Twain's dogs. See **Don't Know** and **You Know**.

Igor • The bullmastiff of actress Laraine Day (*Dr. Kildare*).

Iman • Russian Czar Nicholas II's favorite collie.

Inga • A dog of Austrian-born movie director-writer Billy Wilder (*The Lost Weekend*).

Ingo • The German shepherd owned by actress and World Wildlife Fund activist, Catherine Bach (*The Dukes of Hazzard*). (Coincidence: Ingo rhymes with Ringo and actress Barbara Bach, not related, is Ringo Starr's wife.)

Inni • A mixed-breed dog of French actress Brigitte Bardot.

Io • Author Maurice Sendak's golden retriever. (Io was the woman changed into a white heifer by Hera, the wife of Zeus, after Zeus fell in love with her.)

Irish • The Irish setter in the comic strip *Radio Patrol*.

Irish Terrier • The aptly but uncreatively named Irish terrier of Irish-American playwright Eugene O'Neill.

Irving • One of the two Monroe family dogs on the television series *My World . . . and Welcome to It*. Also see **Christabel**.

Islay • One of Queen Victoria's dogs.

Issa • A dog owned by Roman epigrammatist Martial (Marcus Valerius Martialis).

Ivan • The German shepherd on the television series *The Inspector*.

Ivory • A greyhound owned by actress Bo Derek.

J

J. Edgar • A beagle given to U.S. president Lyndon B. Johnson by J. Edgar Hoover, longtime director of the FBI. It won an American Kennel Club award, the only presidential dog to win the honor.

Jack • The name of the Ingall's family collie dog in the television series *Little House on the Prairie*. The dog's real name was **Bandit**.
• A Jack Russell terrier owned by singer Mariah Carey.

• The golden retriever of television actor Joey Lawrence (*Gimme a Break* and *Blossom*).

• A spaniel owned by movie and television actor Fred MacMurray (*My Three Sons*).

• Jack was also the name of U.S. president Theodore Roosevelt's terrier.

• An Irish terrier (and terror!) owned by England's King Edward VII. (It once chewed up the coat of a foreign ambassador!)

• A Sealyham terrier owned by King George V of England.

Jackie • One of U.S. president Gerald R. Ford's golden retrievers.

Jacko • One of Paul Bunyan's three dogs—the reversible one.

Jackson • An Irish setter owned by British singer Olivia Newton-John.

Jacques • One of pianist-entertainer Liberace's canines.

Jaggers • A cairn terrier owned by Edward, Duke of Windsor.

Jagss • A Labrador retriever of actor Stephen Macht (*Cagney and Lacey*) based on the first letters of the first names of his immediate family, including himself: Jessie and Julie (J), Ari (A), Gabriel (G), Suzanne (S), and Stephen (S).

Jaguar • A Labrador retriever of chef-restaurateur Wolfgang Puck.

Jake • One of football coach Dan Reeves's golden retrievers. See **Hondo**.

James • One of British mystery writer Dame Agatha Christie's dogs.

Jan • A boxer owned by Spanish artist Pablo Picasso.

Jane • A Welsh corgi owned by Princess Elizabeth (later Queen Elizabeth II) of England and her sister, Princess Margaret. The dog was run over and killed by one of the workers at Windsor Park.

Jasmine • One of *Sugar Babies* actress-dancer Ann Miller's dogs.

Jason • A Labrador retriever owned by Indian-born British actress Vivien Leigh (*Gone with the Wind*).

Jasper • The Gregg family's dog in the television series *Bachelor Father*.
  • A dachshund owned by producer-actor John Houseman (*Paper Chase*).

Jeannie • A Scottish terrier owned by humorist James Thurber and, in fact, mentioned in his *Thurber's Dogs*. See **Daisy**.

Jennie • Author Maurice Sendak's Sealyham terrier, to which his book *Higglety Pigglety Pop! or, There Must Be More to Life* is dedicated. The dog appears in other Sendak books such as *Mrs. Piggle-Wiggle's Farm* and *Where the Wild Things Are*.
  • The name of dogs owned by actor Earl Holliman (*Police Woman*) and by writer James Thurber.

Jennifer • Television actress Bea Arthur's Doberman pinscher.
  • A Kerry blue terrier owned by movie director John Huston and his actress wife Evelyn Keyes (*Gone with the Wind*).

• One of writer Sidney Sheldon's German shepherds.

Jenny • A Pomeranian owned by David Hasselhoff (*Baywatch*).

Jerry • One of fictional detective Bulldog Drummond's three dogs, the only bulldog. Also see **Bess** and **Jock**.
• A dog owned by actress Evelyn Keyes and movie director John Huston (The Maltese Falcon).
• Writer F. Scott Fitzgerald and wife, Zelda, owned a mixed-breed dog named Jerry.

Jessamyn • A poodle owned by humorist Erma Bombeck.

Jessie • A golden retriever owned by actor Dennis Quaid (*The Right Stuff*). He nicknamed the dog **Fawn Hall** because "she shreds everything."
• One of actress Valerie Harper's dogs.
• A Scottish terrier owned by U.S. president Theodore Roosevelt, often used to herd the Roosevelt children home.

Jet • A black Labrador retriever featured in crime detective writer Rex Stout's short story "A Dog in the Daytime, a.k.a. Die like a Dog." The dog's original name was Bootsy.
• A Labrador retriever of pro football player Jack Youngblood.

Jezebell • A boxer owned by screen actor Alan Ladd (*The Great Gatsby*).

Jiggs • The mascot, a white bulldog, of the U.S. Marine Corps. The dog died in 1927 and was replaced by Jiggs II.
• A Wheaton terrier owned by actress Louise Sorel, who played Don Rickles's wife on *The Don Rickles Show*.

Jigs • A Great Dane owned by actress Mary Astor's character in the 1936 movie *Dodsworth*.

Jip • In Charles Dickens' novel *David Copperfield*, Dora Spenlow's black spaniel, which was fond of prancing on the dinner table.
• The name of Dr. Doolittle's dog in Hugh Lofting's *The Story of Doctor Dolittle*, published in 1920 and made into a movie in 1967. The dog had an especially strong sense of smell and helped save a man stranded on an island.
• A dog owned by U.S. president Abraham Lincoln.

Jock • The Scottish terrier in the 1955 Disney feature cartoon *Lady and the Tramp*.
• A terrier owned by author Nancy Mitford (*The Sun King*) in her youth.
• A terrier owned by fictional detective Bulldog Drummond. Also see **Bess** and **Jerry**.
• Also see **Auld Jock**.

Jocko • A Sealyham terrier owned by humorist Will Rogers.

Joe • The German shepherd that starred in the Saturday morning television series *Run, Joe, Run*.
• The dachshund of World War II U.S. Air Force General Claire Chennault.
• A dog owned by actress Cloris Leachman (*Last Picture Show*).
• Horror film actor Vincent Price's favorite dog, about whom he wrote the book *The Book of Joe*.
• A wirehaired terrier owned by 1920s comedic movie actor Edmund Lowe (*Dinner at Eight*).

Joey • A Shih Tzu owned by actress Susan Clark and her husband, pro-football-player-turned-actor Alex Karras.
• Another wirehaired fox terrier of movie actor Edmund Lowe (*What Price Glory?*).

Jo-Fi • A chow owned by Austrian psychoanalyst Sigmund Freud.

Johnny • A Scottish terrier owned by actor Lionel Barrymore (*Grand Hotel*).
   • A Sealyham terrier (full name Ilmer Johnny Boy) owned by England's Princess Margaret.
   • An English bulldog owned by film actor Vincent Price (*The Tower of London*).

Johnson • The golden retriever of *Entertainment Tonight* cohost Bob Goen.

Joker • A poodle owned by comedian-actor and "joker" Don Rickles.

Jo-Jo • A black poodle given to flamboyant entertainer Liberace after he mentioned on national television that he loved poodles.

Jolly-Jane • A Shetland sheepdog owned by U.S. president Calvin Coolidge.

Jonathan Rebel • The name of the puppet dog on the Bobby Goldsboro television show.

Jones • A Norwich terrier owned by writer E. B. White (*Charlotte's Web*).

Jonesey • A dog owned by singer Jack Jones, son of actor-singer Allan Jones (*A Night at the Opera*).

Joseph • A Labrador retriever owned by *Top Gun* actor Tom Cruise.
   • A poodle owned by *Valley of the Dolls* author Jacqueline Susann.

Josephine • The black poodle owned by author

Jacqueline Susann and immortalized in her book *Every Night, Josephine!*

• A bull terrier featured in writer James Thurber's story "Josephine Has Her Day," and in the book *Thurber's Dogs*.

Joy • A spaniel owned by Alexis, the son of Czar Nicholas and his wife, Alexandra.

Juan • A dog owned by television game-show host Bob Barker, who gives his dogs Spanish names.

Jubilee Morn • A Pekingese owned by the Duke and Duchess of Marlborough.

Juda • One of *Cagney and Lacy* actor Stephen Macht's Labrador retrievers.

Judge • A pug owned by humorist James Thurber.

• One of the earliest Boston terriers on record—owned by Robert C. Hooper, a dog breeder, in the 1870s.

Julie • A hunting dog owned by *Day of the Locust* author Nathanael West. When West and his wife were killed in an auto accident in 1940, the dog was the sole survivor and was adopted by West's brother-in-law S.J. Perelman, the humorist.

• A Bichon frisé owned by movie actor-turned-diplomat John Gavin (*Psycho*).

• One of humorist James Thurber's dogs.

Julius • The Boyle family's dog in the television cartoon series *Wait till Your Father Gets Home*.

• A Great Dane owned by television comedian Sid Caesar of the great program *Your Show of Shows*.

Jumbo • The small black and white dog owned by Freckles in Merrill Blosser's strip *Freckles and His Friends*.

Junior • An Australian shepherd owned by Demi Moore and Bruce Willis.

• Actress Maureen O'Sullivan's toy fox terrier.

• A featured dog, the leader of a pack of wild dogs, in the 1964 movie *Island of the Blue Dolphins*.

• A German shepherd owned by actress-producer Lucille Ball (*I Love Lucy*).

Juno • In Emily Brontë's *Wuthering Heights*, Heathcliff's aggressive pointer, named after the Roman queen of heaven and wife of Jupiter.

Jupiter • A sheepdog owned by journalist Jimmy Cannon, named after the Roman supreme deity.

K

Kabar • Silent-screen actor Rudolph Valentino's Doberman pinscher, which had the distinction of being the first dog to be buried at the Pet Park in Los Angeles, California.

Kabul • An Afghan hound that appears in several of artist Pablo Picasso's paintings of his wife, Jacqueline. (Kabul is the capital of Afghanistan.)

Kachina • A Tibetan Lhasa terrier owned by Peggy Guggenheim during her marriage to surrealist painter Max Ernst. When they divorced, Ernst won custody of the dog.

Kaiser • A mixed-breed dog owned by nineteenth-century British Victorian poet Matthew Arnold, whose last poem was the elegy "Kaiser Dead."

Kamikaze • The name of the first Akita brought to the United States—in 1939 by Helen Keller who had just toured Japan. The word *Kamikaze* is Japanese for "divine wind" or "golden wind," and took on a new meaning after the bombing of Pearl Harbor. See **Kenzan Go**.

Karl • A black German shepherd owned by writer Norman Mailer (*The Naked and the Dead*).

Karty • One of television actor Lorenzo Lamas's dogs.

Kasmir • A dog that Mohammed permitted to enter paradise, according to Muslim literature.

Kate • A golden retriever owned by clothing designer Bill Blass.
• A Sealyham terrier owned by the Duke of Windsor (later King Edward VIII) as a child.

Katie • A Brittany spaniel of actress Susan Dey (*The Partridge Family* and *Love and War*).
• A Yorkshire terrier of movie and television actor Richard Basehart (*Being There*).
• One of *Police Woman* actor Earl Holliman's many dogs.

Kato • The Akita owned by the late Nicole Brown Simpson. It wailed around the time it was estimated that Simpson and Ronald Goldman were slashed to death. The dog was named after Kato Kaelin, O.J. Simpson's houseboy and witness at Simpson's trial.

Kayo • Harpo Marx's black-spotted, white dog in the 1932 movie *Horse Feathers*.

Kazak • The "hound of space" mastiff in author Kurt Vonnegut's novel *The Sirens of Titans*.

Keeper • Novelist Emily Brontë's devoted bull mastiff, it followed her coffin during her funeral procession.

• An Irish wolfhound owned by Swedish actress Mai Zetterling (*Only Two Can Play*).

Kelly • The dog in the 1958 movie *Kelly and Me*.
• A fox terrier of author-playwright Jean Kerr.

Kep • A collie owned by author Beatrix Potter and is featured in her "The Tale of Jemima Puddle-Duck.

Kendall • One of the two dogs owned by film actress Margot Kidder (*Superman*).

Keno • The Russian wolfhound of author Jane Ardmore (*The Self-Enchanted*).

Kenzan Go • Another Akita that Helen Keller brought back from Japan in 1939. See **Kamikaze**.

Kewpie • In the comic strip *The Born Loser*, Brutus Thornapple's dog.

Kiche • A she-wolf featured in Jack London's novel *White Fang*.

Kiddo • One of TV's *MacMillan and Wife* costar Susan Saint James's dogs.

Kiki • World-champion boxer Sugar Ray Leonard's schnauzer.
• The name of dogs owned by actor-director-writer Orson Welles and actress Kathryn Grayson.

Killer • In the 1975–76 television series *The Cop and the Kid*, the dog of Lucas Adams, played by actor Tierre Turner.
• A German shepherd of film actress Bo Derek.
• A Pomeranian of *Baywatch* television star David Hasselhoff.

• A poodle of *The Unsinkable Molly Brown* actress-singer Debbie Reynolds.

• A Pomeranian of singer Tammy Wynette ("Stand by Your Man").

Killie • An Irish setter owned by writer T.H. White (*The Once and Future King*). See **Brownie**.

Kiltie • A collie owned by U.S. government official Caspar Weinberger, the secretary of defense during the Ronald Reagan administration.

Kim • One of U.S. president Lyndon B. Johnson's many beagles.

Kimberly • A black Labrador owned by England's Earl of Mountbatten.

King • The second most popular dog name in the U.S. It was also the name of the Alaskan husky that was the leader of the dog-sled team of Sergeant Preston of the Yukon of cinema and television.

• The name of the dog in the 1958 movie *The Proud Rebel*, starring Alan Ladd and Olivia de Havilland.

• Entertainer Jimmy ("the Schnozzola") Durante's Irish setter.

• One of Canadian-born *Bonanza* television actor Lorne Greene's dogs.

King Arthur • A Dalmatian named after the medieval king and owned by Adlai Stevenson, a governor of Illinois who ran for the U.S. presidency in 1952 and 1956.

King Cole • A bulldog and "merry old soul" owned by U.S. president Calvin Coolidge.

King Kong • A Shih Tzu named after the silver screen's

legendary giant gorilla and owned by actress Marisa Berenson (*Barry Lyndon*).

King Timahoe • An Irish setter given to U.S. president Richard M. Nixon by his staff. He named the dog after the village in Ireland where his "mother's Quaker ancestors came from."

King Tut • U.S. president Herbert Hoover's German shepherd, named after Tutankhamen, the king of Egypt in the eighteenth dynasty. The dog was featured prominently in Hoover's campaign photos. He was also famous for patrolling the White House grounds and for biting visitors to the White House.

Kinga • A German shepherd of actor Blair Underwood (Jonathan Rollins on *L.A. Law*).

Kirk • A Doberman pinscher of William Shatner who named his Doberman pinscher after his Captain Kirk character in *Star Trek*.

Kis Lany • A German shepherd owned by actresses Eva Gabor and Zsa Zsa Gabor in their early days.

Kiss • See **Buddy**.

Kitty • A dog owned by Debbi Fields, the cookie entrepreneur ("Mrs. Fields")—a most unusual name for a dog.

Kleine • A cocker spaniel of Arte Johnson, who imitated a German on television's *Laugh-In*. *Kleine* is German for "small."

Knave • In Albert Payson Terhune's class novel *Lad: A Dog*, the "showy, magnificent" collie whose behavior was not always good.

Knockwurst • A dachshund of film actress Rita Hayworth (*The Lady from Shanghai*), a good name for a "wiener" dog.

Knudle • Another one of comedic actor (*Laugh-In*) Arte Johnson's cocker spaniels. (*Knödel* means "dumpling" in German.)

Kris • A Saint Bernard owned by Hollywood dog trainer Karl Lewis Miller.

Kronen • A Great Dane of television actress Ruta Lee (*Coming of Age*).

Krypto • Superboy's yellow-collared superdog ("Dog of Steel") in comic books. He had X-ray vision, incredible strength, could fly, and, of course, had a great sense of smell.

Krystle • One of actor John Forsythe's toy poodles, named after his television wife, Krystle Jennings Carrington, on television's *Dynasty* series.

L

Labes • A canine character in Aristophanes's play *The Wasps*, one of the earliest literary references to a dog.

Labros • In Greek mythology, one of the many hounds of Actaeon, the hunter whom the goddess Artemis turned into a stag. Labros was "boisterous," according to *Room's Classical Dictionary*.

Lachne • In Greek mythology, one of the many hounds of Actaeon, the hunter whom the goddess Artemis turned into a stag. Lachne was "shaggy," according to *Room's Classical Dictionary*.

Lacy • A terrier owned by *Ace Ventura Pet Detective* actress Sean Young.

Lad • The collie immortalized in Albert Payson Terhune's novel *Lad: A Dog*, based on the character of his own collie, Sunnybank Lad. Lad had "benign dignity that was a heritage from endless generations of high-strain ancestors . . . He had uncanny wisdom . . . he had a soul."

Ladadog • The name of the Nash family sheepdog in the 1965–67 television series *Please Don't Eat the Daisies*.

Laddie • A classic name for a male collie or Scottish terrier, it was the name of a Scottish terrier owned by Queen Victoria of England. Laddie is Scottish for "boy" or "young man."
• The name of the Williams family dog, a terrier, on the television situation comedy series *Make Room for Daddy*, starring Danny Thomas.

Laddie Boy • The name of U.S. president Warren G. Harding's Airedale. Its full name was Caswell Laddie Boy. The dog attended cabinet meetings and had its own chair. A statue of the dog, paid for by the pennies contributed by newspaper delivery boys (Harding was a newsman earlier in his career), was sculpted by Bashka Paeff and it can be seen at the Smithsonian Institution. Also see **Laddie Buck**.

Laddie Buck • The name of U.S. president Calvin Coolidge's Airedale. Grace Coolidge later changed the dog's name to **Paul Pry** because he pried into everyone's business. Laddie Buck was the half-brother of Warren Harding's Airedale **Laddie Boy**.

Lady • The *most* popular name for a dog, *usually* a female one, in the U.S. It was the name of the female cocker spaniel and love interest in the 1956 Walt Disney animated feature film *Lady and the Tramp*.

• One of U.S. president George Washington's hounds.

• A German shepherd owned by U.S. president Ronald W. Reagan.

• The collie "wife" of author Alfred Payson Terhune's **Lad**.

• Movie actor Tyrone Power's German shepherd.

• The dog in the 1956 movie *Goodbye, My Lady*, starring Brandon de Wilde who loves the dog but eventually has to give it up.

• One of comic actor-director Jerry Lewis's two Shih Tzus. See **Angel**.

• Scottish-born singer Sheena Easton's dog.

• Other owners of dogs named Lady include actor Earl Holliman (*Police Woman*) and singer Donny Osmond (the Osmond Brothers).

Lady II • Singer Donny Osmond's German shepherd.

Lady III • Singer Donny Osmond's Belgian police dog.

Lady Ashley • A beagle owned by television actress Eva Gabor (*Green Acres*).

Lady Bug • One of actress Sylvia Sidney's pugs.

Lady Di • One of Liberace's many dogs, a West Highland white terrier.

Lafayette • The friend of the country cat Napoleon in the 1970 Disney movie *The Aristocats*.

Laika • The first dog to orbit Earth—in Russia's Sputnik II in November 1957. The dog died in space because the satellite was not equipped to return to land.

Lambchop • A Great Dane owned by Olympic swimmer Greg Louganis.

Lambchops • The name of ventriloquist Shari Lewis's hand-puppet poodle.

Lampon • In Greek mythology, King Midas's hunting dog, which died of thirst trying to access an underground spring. The name means "flash" in Greek.

Lance • The German shepherd of singer Robert Goulet and actress Carol Lawrence.

Lara • The male Newfoundland owned by U.S. president James Buchanan. Lara had the ability to sleep with one eye open.

Lassie • The collie in Eric Knight's 1938 story "Lassie Come‑Home" and star of the 1942 movie and many subsequent features and TV series. In 1969 Lassie became the first animal elected to the Animal Hall of Fame. It is #81 on the list of popular dog names in the U.S. Lassie, of course, is Scottish for "girl" or "young woman."
    • Comedic actor Lou Costello (Abbott and Costello) owned a dog named Lassie.

Laughing Gravy • The mongrel star in the 1931 Laurel and Hardy comedy *Laughing Gravy*.

Laura • The Labrador retriever of Princess Anne.

Laverne • The name of a dog owned by actor-producer Michael Landon.

Layla • A predominantly black Newfoundland that won a 1994 Delta Society award for being a "therapy dog" at a Syracuse, New York, daycare center.

Lazlo • A dog of actress Susan Clark (*Babe*) and pro-football-player-actor Alex Karras (*Babe*).

Leader • U.S. senator Robert Dole's miniature schnauzer. The name was inspired by Dole's being the Senate majority *leader*.

Leasel • One of singer Rick Springfield's dogs.

Lebbo • Ballerina Anna Pavlova's bulldog.

Lebros • In Greek mythology, one of the many hounds of Actaeon, the hunter whom the goddess Artemis turned into a stag. Lebros was "mangy," according to *Room's Classical Dictionary*.

Leica • Television talk-show pioneer Jack Paar's photogenic German shepherd, which made occasional appearances on *The Tonight Show*.

Lelaps • In Greek mythology, one of the many hounds of Actaeon, the hunter whom the goddess Artemis turned into a stag. Lelaps was a "tempest," according to *Room's Classical Dictionary*.

Leo • The canine actor who played Buck in the 1972 film version of Jack London's *Call of the Wild*, starring Charlton Heston.

Leroy Brown • The Labrador retriever of singer Frank Sinatra, named after the bad guy in the song "Bad, Bad Leroy Brown."

Lethal Ron • One of singer Rick Springfield's dogs.

Leucite • In Greek mythology, one of the many hounds of Actaeon, the hunter whom the goddess Artemis turned into a stag. Leucite was "white," according to *Room's Classical Dictionary*.

Liberty • A golden retriever given to U.S. president

Gerald R. Ford by White House photographer David Kennerly.

Lickety Spitz • A Finnish spitz owned by singer Dolly Parton. See **Mark Spitz.**

Lilac • One of movie actress (*Gilda*) Rita Hayworth's dachshunds.

Liline • The English toy spaniel of King Charles IX.

Lillie • Comedic actor Cheech (of Cheech & Chong) Marin's dog.

Lilly • Singer-actress Liza Minnelli's cairn terrier which made newspaper columns when Sweden would not let the dog enter the country because of quarantine laws.

Lily Langtry • A white poodle owned by Eleanor "Cissy" Patterson, newspaper publisher and socialite. It was named after the British actress who had a love affair with King Edward VII of England.

Lincoln • The Airedale terrier owned by actor Stephen Dorff (*What a Dummy*).

Linus • A cocker spaniel owned by film and television director Garry Marshall (*Pretty Woman*), named after the character in the *Peanuts* comic strip.

Lion • In writer William Faulkner's novel *Go Down, Moses*, a "great blue dog" named for its leonine prowess and strength.
  • One of King Arthur's dogs, according to English writer T.H. White.

Lisa • A black poodle in writer Patricia Highsmith's *A Dog's Ransom*.

• A dachshund owned by movie actor Vincent Price (*Tower of London*).

• One of two Yorkshire terriers owned by Hollywood producer Darryl F. Zanuck. See **Tina**.

Little Beagle • A beagle owned by U.S. president Lyndon B. Johnson.

Little Chap • Guess what?! Another beagle owned by large-eared U.S. president Lyndon B. Johnson.

Little Tyke • The son of bulldog Big Spike in comic books.

Lizzie • The dog of Kitty Brown who hosts the "Kitty Chat" segment of Fox/FX's *The Pet Department Show*.

Lobo • The dog that accompanied the Horace Heidt band. (*Lobo*, by the way, means "wolf" in Spanish.)

• A guard dog bought by singer Michael Jackson's father after the Sharon Tate murder.

• A German shepherd owned by Charlton Heston's family in his youth. When Heston was nine years old, the dog was shot by "an angry neighbor" whose dog Lobo "mauled in a fight."

Lochinvar Bobby • One of singer-actor Bobby Sherman's dogs, partially named after a hero mentioned in Sir Walter Scott's narrative poem "Marmion."

Loch Lomond • A bearded collie, owned by film actress Bo Derek, named after the lake in western Scotland.

Loki • A dog of actor Gary Collins and Mary Ann Mobley.

• The dog of actor Jared Martin (Dusty Farlow on *Dallas*).

Lola • A white greyhound owned by French writer Colette. She bought it from the manager of a circus.

Looty • One of the first Pekingese brought to England—in 1860 when Britain was at war with China. The fawn and white dog was a gift to Queen Victoria.

Lord Nelson • The dog featured in the mid-1960s television series *Please Don't Eat the Daisies*, named after the British admiral.

Lottie • A French bulldog owned by English writer Nancy Mitford.

Love • A German shepherd of former television talk-show host Mike Douglas.

Lowey • King Charles spaniel of writer-political commentator William F. Buckley, Jr.

Low Pressure • The most prolific dog on record—a champion male greyhound that sired over three thousand puppies, according to the *Guinness Book of World Records*. The dog was nicknamed Timmy.

Luath • The yellow Labrador retriever in writer Sheila Burnford's *The Incredible Journey*.
• In T.H. White's *The Sword in the Stone*, one of King Arthur's many dogs.

Lucan • One of the Doberman pinschers in the 1985 movie *Remo Williams: The Adventure Begins*.

Lucille • A Dalmatian owned by television personality and producer Dick Clark.

Lucky • A sheepdog puppy given to U.S. president Ronald W. Reagan while in office. The dog didn't pass "Obedience Training 101" and was soon dispatched to the Reagan's ranch in Santa Barbara, California.

• Movie actor Paul Newman's golden retriever.

• The names of dogs owned by actor Al Pacino and actress Ava Gardner.

• The black and white mascot of the *National Enquirer*. It was found in a dog pound in 1972 and received its name in a contest for which the publication received 20,000 letters.

• A dog owned by wild-animal trainer Clyde Beatty.

Lucky Pup • The star canine puppet on television's *Lucky Pup* show, which aired from 1948 to 1951 on CBS. (The pup was lucky because it inherited $5 million from a recently deceased circus queen.)

Lucy • A Bichon frisé owned by singer Tanya Tucker.

• A dog owned by television actor-producer Michael Landon (*Bonanza*).

• One of several cocker spaniels owned by television and movie director Garry Marshall.

• An Airedale terrier owned by television actor and *I Love Lucy* fan Ronnie Schell (Private Duke Slater on *Gomer Pyle, U.S.M.C.*). See **Ethel**.

• Former television talk-show host Mike Douglas's silky terrier.

• A dog owned by television actor Thom Bray (*Breaking Away* and *Riptide*).

Lucy Brown • A poodle owned by comedic actor Red Buttons. The name is mentioned in the song "Mack the Knife," popularized by singer Bobby Darin.

Luffra • In T.H. White's *The Sword in the Stone*, one of King Arthur's many dogs.

Luigi Deflorio • Actress Sandra Bullock's Jack Russell

terrier, so named, according to Bullock, "because he's like a sweet old Italian man."

Luke • The name of comedic actor Roscoe "Fatty" Arbuckle's dog. The dog appeared with Arbuckle in some of his comedies produced by Mack Sennett.
   • The Chow Chow of film actress Merle Oberon (*The Scarlet Pimpernel*).

Lulu • On *The Honeymooners* television series, Ed Norton's pet dog, which got lost at Coney Island.
   • A fox terrier owned by French novelist Françoise Sagan (*Bonjour tristesse*).
   • One of Queen Victoria's six Pomeranians. See **Beppo, Fluffy, Gilda, Mino,** and **Nino.**
   • Champion welterweight boxer Sugar Ray Leonard's little Chihuahua.
   • The name of a dog owned by actress Kristy McNichol (*Empty Nest*).

Lu-Lu • The Shih Tzu of actress Shirley Jones and her husband, comedian Marty Ingels.

Lump • A dachshund owned by Spanish painter Pablo Picasso. The dog appears in the artist's interpretations of Velasquez's famous painting *Las Meninas*. (A story goes that Picasso painted a rabbit to see how his city dog would react. The dog attacked the canvas!).

Luna • An Australian shepherd that won a 1995 Delta Society award for providing comfort and therapy to its owner after a paralyzing spinal injury.

Luncheon Tom • A terrier mix owned by British writer Nancy Mitford and her family.

Lunyu • Psychoanalyst Sigmund Freud's Chow Chow.

Lupe • One of television game-show host Bob Barker's dogs.

Luska • A black and white Siberian husky owned by King Edward VII of England.

Lycisa • In Greek mythology, one of the many hounds of Actaeon, the hunter whom the goddess Artemis turned into a stag. Lycisa was "wolf-like," according to *Room's Classical Dictionary*.

Lyle • A West Highland white terrier owned by socialite and ex-debutante Cornelia Guest.

M

Mac • *Charlotte's Web* author E.B. White's first dog in his childhood.

MacBarker • The dog of cartoon character Mr. Magoo.
• The Dalmatian of actress Gina Gallego (Alicia Sanchez on *Flamingo Road*).

Machito • An Alsatian owned by actress Evelyn Keyes during her marriage to bandleader Artie Shaw, her fourth husband. The name is Spanish for "little he-man."

Macho • The name of dogs owned by French actress Brigitte Bardot and Hungarian-born actress Zsa Zsa Gabor. *Macho* means "manly" in Spanish.

Mackie • A dog of English actress Gertrude Lawrence (Broadway's *The King and I*).

Madame Moose • One of U.S. president George Washington's many dogs.

Madame Sophia • A bulldog owned by playwright Tennessee Williams (*The Night of the Iguana*).

Madeleine • A pug owned by television talk-show host Sally Jessy Raphael.

Madison • A Welsh terrier owned by author-illustrator Tomie de Paola.
   • An Australian shepherd of acting couple Demi Moore and Bruce Willis.

Maf • A white poodle given to actress Marilyn Monroe by singer Frank Sinatra. The name is short for Mafia, the organized crime syndicate with which Mr. Sinatra has *no* affiliation.

Maggie • A pet dog of Eleanor Roosevelt, the wife of U.S. president Franklin D. Roosevelt.
   • The name of dogs owned by actors Dustin Hoffman (*The Graduate*), Melissa Sue Anderson (*Little House on the Prairie*), and Earl Holliman (*Police Woman*).
   • The schnauzer of former football pro Bob Waterfield.
   • One of television actor Michael Gray's poodles.

Magillacuddy • The dog of singer Maureen McGovern ("There's Got to Be a Morning After" from *The Poseidon Adventure*).

Magnolia • The English sheepdog of actress Tallulah Bankhead (*Lifeboat*).
   • The bearded collie of Tony Dow, Wally Cleaver on television's *Leave It to Beaver*.

Magnum • One of the Doberman pinschers in the 1985 movie *Remo Williams: The Adventure Begins*.

Maida • A dog owned by General George Armstrong Custer and killed in battle.

• A bloodhound owned by author Sir Walter Scott. It was, as Scott described, "the finest dog of the kind in Scotland; perfectly gentle, affectionate and good-natured."

Major • U.S. president Franklin D. Roosevelt's police dog. An aggressive dog, it bit a U.S. senator (Hattie Caraway) on the leg and tore the pants off a British prime minister (Ramsay MacDonald) and was banished from the White House, to retire at the Roosevelt home in Hyde Park, New York.

• The German shepherd owned by actress Irene Dunne (*I Remember Mama*).

• The German shepherd of author Patricia Ellis (*Keeping Up with the Joneses*).

Major Homer Q. Putnam • The childhood dog of film pioneer Cecil B. DeMille and his brother William. The name came from a character in one of their father's plays.

Makeba • A pit bull of actor Malcolm-Jamal Warner, from a name popularized by South African black singer Miriam Makeba.

Manchu • A black Pekingese owned by Alice Roosevelt, daughter of U.S. president Theodore Roosevelt. It was given to her by the last empress of China.

Man Friday • A dog owned by movie actor Errol Flynn (*Captain Blood*).

Mannie • A dog owned by television actor Earl Holliman (*Police Woman*).

Marco • One of Queen Victoria's Pomeranians.

Marco Polo • Silent-screen actor Douglas Fairbank's large mastiff, named after the Venetian explorer.

Mariko • A dog owned by television actress Kate Vernon (*Falcon Crest* and *Who's the Boss?*).

Mariposa • A Shih Tzu of actress Elizabeth Taylor. (*Mariposa* means "butterfly" in Spanish.)

Mark Spitz • A Finnish spitz, named after the Olympic swimmer, owned by singer Dolly Parton. See **Lickety Spitz**.

Marksman • A red setter owned by Franklin D. Roosevelt in his youth.

Marmaduke • The Great Dane in the Brad Anderson comic strip for over forty years.

Martha • An English sheepdog that inspired Paul McCartney's song "Martha."

Martika • One of *Star Trek* actor William Shatner's Doberman pinschers.

Martini • Model Cheryl Tiegs's wirehaired fox terrier.

Marty Wiener • One of fitness guru Richard Simmons's many Dalmatians.

Mary • A dog owned by actor-producer Michael Landon.

Mary Elizabeth • A Scottish terrier of television actress Elinor Donahue (*Father Knows Best*).

Mas • One of television actor Lorenzo Lamas's dogs.

Mat Burke • Playwright Eugene O'Neill's Irish terrier, named after a character in his play *Anna Christie*.

Matej • A dog of *One Flew over the Cuckoo's Next* movie director Milos Forman.

Mathe • A greyhound of King Richard II.

Matilda • The bulldog mascot of the British Bulldogs, a professional wrestling team.

Matt • A Bichon frisé owned by James Arness who named the dog after his character Marshall Matt Dillon in the television series *Gunsmoke*. See **Miss Kitty**.

Maude • A poodle owned by actress-producer Mary Tyler Moore.

Maui • See **Murray**.

Max • A popular name for a dog, it is the second most popular name for a male dog in England.
   • A dachshund owned by nineteenth-century British Victorian poet Matthew Arnold and mentioned in his elegy "Poor Matthias," published in 1882.
   • A black Labrador owned by actress Deirdre Hall.
   • The "Bionic Dog," the German shepherd owned by television's *The Bionic Woman*. It is short for Maximillion because the dog cost one million dollars to build.
   • One of boxer Sugar Ray Leonard's cocker spaniels.
   • *Patton* star George C. Scott's mastiff.
   • A miniature poodle owned by comedic actor Don Adams, who played Maxwell Smart on the television series *Get Smart*.
   • The German shepherd of screenwriter and author Sidney Sheldon (*The Other Side of Midnight*).
   • A Chow Chow of author-trendsetter Martha Stewart.
   • The German shepherd of German tennis pro Steffi Graf.

• The Rottweiler of actor John Larroquette (*Night Court*).

• A dog of actor Brian Mitchell ("Jackpot" on *Trapper John, M.D.*).

Maybelline • A dog owned by *American Bandstand* host and television producer Dick Clark, who named the dog after Chuck Berry's song and not after the cosmetic company.

McCormick • A Lhasa apso of television actor Jonathan Taylor Thomas (*Home Improvement*).

Meatball • On the television series *Baa Baa Black Sheep*, the name of "Pappy" Boyington's (Robert Conrad) dog.

Mecca • A Rottweiler of actor Malcolm-Jamal Warner (*The Cosby Show*), named after the birthplace of Mohammed.

Medve • A black poodle owned by humorist James Thurber that was "a rich source of literary material ("And So to Medve"). She won best of breed for standard poodles at the 1929 Westminster Dog Show. The name is Hungarian for "bear."

Meeny • One of actress Kathryn Grayson's dogs.

Meg • A frisky Scottish terrier, also called Meggie, owned by Franklin and Eleanor Roosevelt—famous for biting newspaper reporter Bess Furman on the nose.

• A Scottish terrier owned by film actress Bette Davis (*Whatever Happened to Baby Jane?*).

Megan • A dog owned by television actor Jonathan Brandis (Lucas Wolenczak on *Seaquest DSV*).

Meggie • See Meg.

Meko • A mutt that won a 1994 Delta Society award for helping a hearing-impaired woman function on a daily basis.

Melampus • In Greek mythology, one of the many hounds of Actaeon, the hunter whom the goddess Artemis turned into a stag. Melampus was the "black-foot," according to *Room's Classical Dictionary*.

Melaneus • One of the many hounds of Actaeon, the hunter whom the goddess Artemis turned into a stag. Melaneus was "inky," according to *Room's Classical Dictionary*.

Melanie • The name of one of fitness guru Richard Simmons's Dalmatians, named after the character Melanie Hamilton in the novel *Gone with the Wind*. (Actress Olivia de Havilland played Melanie in the movie version.)

Melisande • A Prussian sheepdog in author Albert Payson Terhune's *Lad: A Dog*.

Melon • An Irish setter owned by chef-restaurateur Wolfgang Puck.

Merle • A dog owned by actress Emma Samms (*Dynasty* and *Models, Inc.*).

Merlin • A cairn terrier named after the Arthurian seer Merlin the Magician and owned by actor Bert Lahr, who played opposite Toto (another cairn terrier) in the 1939 movie *The Wizard of Oz*.
   • A dachshund owned by Adlai E. Stevenson, governor of Illinois and U.S. presidential candidate in 1952 and 1956.

Merry • An Akita given to Sean Lennon by Beatle John Lennon and wife, Yoko Ono, as a Christmas gift.

Merrylegs • In English novelist Charles Dickens's *Hard Times*, the performing circus dog that disappears with its owner, Jupe. It later returns alone, haggard, and near blind.

Me-Too • A Tibetan spaniel owned by actor Stewart Granger (*King Solomon's Mines*) and actress Jean Simmons (*Great Expectations*).

Mica • A cocker spaniel owned by actress Katharine Hepburn (*Guess Who's Coming to Dinner*).

Mick the Miller • A stuffed racing greyhound on display in London's Natural History Museum.

Michael Moo • A sheepdog owned by television actress Linda Gray (*Dallas*).

Midnight • A cockapoo owned by comedic actor Dom DeLuise (*Blazing Saddles*).
• A dog owned by African-American model and actress Tyra Banks (*Higher Learning*).

Mighty Manfred • The name of Tom Terrific's dog in cartoons.

Miiko • An Akita owned by actor Hal Williams (Smitty in *Sanford and Son* and Sgt. Major Ted Ross in *Private Benjamin*).

Mika • A dog owned by singer Pia Zadora.

Mike • The name of Theodore Roosevelt's daughter's bull terrier. It was also the name of an Irish setter given to Bess Truman, Harry Truman's daughter, by Postmaster General Bob Hannigan.

• A poodle owned by comedian and comedic actor Bob Hope (*The Paleface*).

• A wirehaired fox terrier of Russian-born actress Alla Nazimova (*The Bridge at San Luis Rey*).

• A dog owned by silent-screen actress Miriam Cooper, wife of director Raoul Walsh.

Mikie • One of actor-producer Michael Landon's many dogs.

Mildew Wolf • A cartoon canine in Hanna-Barbera cartoons whose voice is that of comedic actor Paul Lynde.

Miles • A dog owned by comedian-turned-promoter Marty Ingels.

Millie • U.S. President and Mrs. George Bush's English springer spaniel. Her full name was Mildred Kerr. She became a best-selling "author" (*Millie's Book*) in 1990 and appeared on the cover of *Life* magazine when she gave birth to puppies. See **Ranger**. Also see **C. Fred Bush**.

• A French bulldog owned by writer Nancy Mitford (*The Sun King*).

• A Labrador retriever of U.S. president Ronald W. Reagan.

Mimsy • A yellow Labrador owned by King George VI when he was still the Duke of York. (He subsequently owned other yellow Labs.)

Min • Writer Henry David Thoreau's Maltese.

Ming • A Shih Tzu of British actor Michael York (*Cabaret*).

Mink • One of movie actress Rita Hayworth's dachshunds.

Minka • A dog owned by comedic actor Dudley Moore (*Arthur*).

Miniccio • A dog owned by stage actress Sarah Bernhardt.

Minnie • A black Labrador retriever owned by actress Karen Black (*Five Easy Pieces*).
• A Chihuahua owned by Sylvia Fairbanks who had the distinction of being married to two movie screen stars—Douglas Fairbanks and Clark Gable.
• A dog owned by movie actress Anjelica Huston (*Prizzi's Honor*).

Mino • One of Queen Victoria's six Pomeranians. See **Beppo**, **Fluffy**, **Gilda**, **Lulu**, and **Nino**.

Minuet • A French poodle named after the triple-meter dance rhythm occasionally played by its owner pianist-entertainer Liberace.

Mischi • Another dog owned by pianist-entertainer Liberace.

Mishka • A Scottish terrier owned by actress Zsa Zsa Gabor.

Miss Brinda • A defect-plagued dog owned and loved by playwright Tennessee Williams.

Miss Kitty • One of television actor James Arness's Bichon frisés, named after his female lead in the long-running television series *Gunsmoke*. See **Matt**.

Miss MacTavish • The Scottish terrier of detective Philo Vance in the detective novels of writer S.S. Van Dine (real name: Willard Huntingdon Wright).

Miss Magoo • The name of Lhasa apsos owned by actress Eva Gabor and by actress-singer Carol Lawrence.

Miss Mouse • A Yorkshire terrier owned by actress-singer Carol Lawrence.

Miss Wiggles • A spaniel of singer Frank Sinatra.

Mrs. Bouncer • A "preposterously small" Pomeranian owned by author Charles Dickens's daughter Mary.

Mrs. Peel • A dog owned by actor Jamie Farr (*M*A*S*H*).

Missy • A miniature poodle of actress Claudette Colbert (*It Happened One Night*).
• A dog owned by actress Janet Gaynor (*Seventh Heaven*).

Mr. Binkie • The name of the Scottie in the 1939 movie *The Light That Failed*, based on the Rudyard Kipling story.

Mr. Chairman • The family dog of the Gilbreth family in the 1950 movie *Cheaper by the Dozen*. They purchased the dog for $5.

Mr. Deeds • A dachshund owned by film actress Fay Wray (*King Kong*).

Mr. Kelly • A sheepdog of singer-poet Rod McKuen.

Mr. Mack • The chromium bulldog corporate logo of the Mack Truck Corporation.

Mr. Moon • One of *Streetcar Named Desire* playwright Tennessee Williams's bulldogs.

Mr. Peabody • In cartoons a genius dog that wears a

red bow tie and glasses and is the master of a boy named Sherman.

Mr. Pet • A boxer owned by singer Natalie Cole and her father, Nat King Cole.

Mr. Punch • A pug owned by British prime minister Winston Churchill.

Mr. Stubbs • A dog of Mike Brady, actor Robert Reed of television's *The Brady Bunch*.

Mr. T. • The springer spaniel of Steve Allen and Jayne Meadows. The dog's bark was often heard on Allen's mischievous recorded telephone messages.

Misty • A gray poodle owned by writer and Algonquin "Round Table" member Dorothy Parker.
  • A golden retriever of U.S. president Gerald R. Ford.

Mitou • A male Pekingese owned by *Ethan Frome* author Edith Wharton. See **Miza**.

Mitzi • Actor George Hamilton's Yorkshire terrier. It appeared with Hamilton on Cybill Shepherd's television show *Cybill* and had to move its bowels in its key scene.
  • A dog owned by public television kiddie-show host Mr. Rogers.

Miza • A female Pekingese owned by *Ethan Frome* author Edith Wharton. See **Mitou**.

Mocha • A Weimaraner of "Superman" actor Dean Cain (*Lois and Clark*).

Moe • A Doberman pinscher of U.S. president John F. Kennedy.

Moka • A dog of actress Diana Barrymore (*Between Us Girls*).

Molly • A golden retriever owned by soap-opera (*Days of Our Lives*) actress Deirdre Hall.
• A Weimaraner of television personality and producer Dick Clark (*American Bandstand*).
• A bearded collie of actress Bo Derek.

Mona • An Airedale terrier owned by novelist Richard Condon, author of *Prizzi's Honor* and *The Manchurian Candidate*.

Monche • One of French actress Brigitte Bardot's many dogs.

Mony • A dog owned by singer-actor Rudy Vallee (*The Vagabond Lover*).

Moogie • A terrier owned by movie actress Linda Blair (*The Exorcist*).

Moonbeam • A dog of film producer David Wolper (*If It's Tuesday, It Must Be Belgium*).

Moose • The real name of the Jack Russell terrier on the television situation comedy *Frasier*. See **Eddie**.
• A dog of movie actress-singer Kathryn Grayson (*Show Boat*).

Mooter, The • A dog owned by actor Jackie Joseph (the original *Bob Newhart Show*).

Mop • One of Queen Victoria's Pomeranians.

Mopsy • One of U.S. president George Washington's hounds, sometimes spelled Mopsey.

Morgan • A dog of film actress Ava Gardner (*The Sun Also Rises*).

Moritza • A black Belgian shepherd owned by British actor Basil Rathbone while living in the U.S. The actor and dog were featured in a Calvert Reserve Whiskey ad.

Moss • One of two dogs owned by writer Thomas Hardy. It was beaten to death by a homeless man. See **Wessex**.

Mosstrooper • The first Border terrier registered by the British Kennel Club in 1913. Its owner was listed as Mary Rew.

Moujik • A Boston terrier owned by French clothing designer Yves St. Laurent. The dog was featured in a painting by Andy Warhol.

Moya • A yellow Labrador that won a 1995 Delta Society award for being a guide dog to a blind woman.

Muddy Water • A mixed-breed dog of writer F. Scott Fitzgerald and his wife, Zelda.

Muff • A dog owned by the Duke of Kent. Its full name was Choonam Li Wu T'song but the Duke's daughter Alexandra preferred to call the dog Muff.

Muffin • A dog given to actress Tori Spelling by her father, producer Aaron Spelling. A product of Beverly Hills, it is rumored that the dog has a "cap job" on its teeth and gets its claws manicured once a week!
  • A Yorkshire owned by Johnny Carson during his marriage to wife Joanne.
  • A cockapoo owned by U.S. president Ronald W. Reagan.
  • One of the Apple family dogs in the television series *Apple's Way*.

• A cocker spaniel featured in two of author Peter Israel's mystery novels.

Muffy • Actress Lee Remick's dog in the 1959 movie *Anatomy of a Murder*. The dog was taught to wear a flashlight.
• One of actress Doris Day's poodles.
• A Chow Chow owned by actress Uma Thurman (*Pulp Fiction*).

Muggs • James Thurber's feisty Airedale in *The Dog That Bit People* from *My Life and Hard Times*, published in 1933. He also mentioned the dog in his book *Thurber's Dogs*. He was also known as Muffin Muggs.

Muggsie • A collie owned by actress Marilyn Monroe during her first marriage to Jim Dougherty.

Mugsy • A dog of singer Jay Osmond of The Osmond Brothers.

Mule Ears • A collie of U.S. president Calvin Coolidge.

Mumshay • A spaniel owned by sisters actress June Havoc and ecdysiast Gypsy Rose Lee.

Murphy • The dog on the cover of John Denver's Greatest Hits album—it was Denver's own pet.

Murray • The mixed-breed collie on the television situation comedy *Mad about You*. Its real name is **Maui**.
• The full name of U.S. president Franklin D. Roosevelt's dog **Fala** was Murray, the Outlaw of Fala Hill.

Music • A female greyhound in William Wordsworth's poems "Incident Characteristic of a Favorite Dog" and "Tribute to the Memory of the Same Dog." The dog, owned by Wordsworth's sister Dorothy, tried to save a friend named Dart, which had fallen through the ice on a pond.

Mustard • The name of three terriers in Sir Walter Scott's *Guy Mannering* (1815), a common name for Dandie Dinmonts.

Musty • The name of the mastiff in the movie *Dangerous Days*.

Mutt • A perfect name for some dogs. It is the name of a black and white mongrel in Farley Mowat's *The Dog Who Wouldn't Be*, published in 1957.

• It was also a mongrel dog owned by writer E.B. White during his college days at Cornell University.

• A mongrel, sometimes known as Mut (one *t*), that appeared with comedic actor Charlie Chaplin in *A Dog's Life*.

Muttly • The canine accomplice of Dick Dastardly in Hanna-Barbera cartoons.

Myron • The white dog owned by Dick and Dora Charleston (played by actors David Niven and Maggie Smith) in the 1976 movie *Murder by Death*.

N

Nabisco • A dog owned by financier Henry Kravis whose firm helped finance the R.J. Reynolds-Nabisco merger.

Nadia • A dog of television actor Leif Garrett (*Three for the Road*).

Nana • In J.M. Barrie's *Peter Pan*, the Newfoundland

dog that takes care of the Darling children Wendy, John, and Michael.

• A bull terrier of French singer Serge Gainsbourg, known for singing a duet with actress Brigitte Bardot and a song about Bonnie and Clyde.

Nancy • A cockapoo of comedic actor Dom DeLuise (*Fatso*).

Napoleon • The huge Irish wolfhound dog in Clifford McBride's comic strip *Napoleon*.

Nastasha • A Samoyed owned by actress Julie Parrish (*Good Morning World*).

Natasha • An Australian shepherd of television comedian Flip Wilson.

Nato • A dog of U.S. General George C. Marshall, a major commander in World War II, and architect of postwar recovery plans, including the North Atlantic Treaty Organization (NATO).

Negus • One of two black Scottish terriers owned by Eva Braun, the mistress of German tyrant Adolf Hitler. (Negus was the term for the emperor of Ethiopia, from an Amharic word for "king.") See **Stasi**.

Neil • The ghostly and occasionally "tipsy" Saint Bernard owned by George and Marian Kirby on the *Topper* television series (1953–56). Neil's favorite drink was a martini, although brandy snifters were evident. The dog's real name was Buck and it was the "grandson" of the dog that appeared in the 1935 movie *Call of the Wild* starring Clark Gable.

Nell • One of two German shepherds owned by Rutherford B. Hayes.

• A Yorkshire terrier owned by actor Richard Basehart (*Moby Dick*).

Nero • The name of a Roman emperor and one of legendary Paul Bunyan's three hounds.

• A part Maltese, part mongrel white terrier owned by Jane Welsh Carlyle and cited by Virginia Woolf in *Flush* (1933).

Nick • A mixed-breed dog given to choreographer Jerome Robbins (*West Side Story*) by friends.

• A German shepherd of television actor Devon Gummersall (*My So-Called Life*).

Nicky • A poodle of game-show host Allen Ludden (*Password*).

• A Yorkshire terrier of singer Maureen McGovern.

Nielsen • Actor Bill Kirchenbauer (*Just the Ten of Us*) gave his dog this name hoping that his show's ratings (as in A.C. Nielsen) would be good.

Nikki • A mixed-breed dog of actor James Garner (*Maverick*).

Nimrod • A large hound owned by British author Sir Walter Scott (*Ivanhoe*). The dog killed Scott's cat, Hinse of Hinsefield. (In the Bible, Nimrod was the great-grandson of Noah and a great hunter.)

Nini • One of French actress Brigitte Bardot's dogs.

Nino • One of Queen Victoria's six Pomeranians. See **Beppo, Fluffy, Gilda, Lulu,** and **Mino.**

Nip • A black and white sheepdog owned by author Beatrix Potter, creator of Peter Rabbit.

Nipper • The RCA Victor dog on the "His Master's Voice" logo of RCA. The logo was inspired by the nineteenth-century painting *His Master's Voice* by Francis Barraud who used his mixed-breed terrier as the model.

Nipper Dog • A dog of actress Mary McDonough (Erin on *The Waltons*).

Nitro • One of *Dallas* actor Jack Scalia's Rottweilers. See **Tara**.

Noel • One of Liberace's French poodles.

Nogi • A combination Boston terrier and French bull-dog owned by writer Dorothy Parker.

Nonne • A hunting dog owned by French king Louis XIV. The name comes from the French word for "nun."

Noofy • A Newfoundland dog owned by composer-pianist Burt Bacharach.

Noover • A Lhasa apso of songwriter Carole Bayer Sager. See **Hoover**.

Norma • One of the dachshunds in the 1966 Disney movie *The Ugly Dachshund*.

Nox • A black retriever in G.K. Chesterton's "The Oracle of the Dog" from *The Incredulity of Father Brown* (1926). The dog helped Father Brown solve the murder of Colonel Druce.

Nugget • A dog of singing duo Steve Lawrence and Eydie Gormé.

Nuisance • A dog of Hungarian-born movie producer Alexander Korda (*The Private Life of Henry VIII*).

Nutmeg • A dog owned by singer Della Reese, who has a preference for "spicy" names.

O

O'Casey • The pet dog of Lucas Tanner (played by actor-turned-talk-show-host David Hartman) in the television series *Lucas Tanner*. Tanner's dog was also known as Bridget in some of the segments.

Odie • The dog in the *Garfield* comic strip drawn by Jim Davis.

Odin • A German shepherd of actress-singer Carol Lawrence. (Odin is the chief deity of Scandinavian culture and is the god of wisdom, culture, war, and the dead.)

Odysseus • A dog that wandered in and out of gossip-columnist Liz Smith's life, named after the Greek epic hero.

Ofer • The mascot of the Los Angeles Rams football team.

Offisa Bull Pupp • In George Herriman's *Krazy Kat* comic strip, an English bulldog police officer.

Oh Boy • A white English bulldog owned by U.S. president Warren G. Harding.

Okra • A black dog featured in the Pat Conroy novel *The Great Santini*, named after the chief ingredient of gumbo soups and stews. (The word "gumbo" is from a Bantu word *kingumbo*, meaning "okra.")

Old Bill • The fox terrier mascot of the British Navy during World War I. Originally named Fritz, he was found alive on a wrecked German ship.

Old Bob • The gray sheepherding collie in Alfred Ollivant's *Bob, Son of Battle* (1898).

Ol' Bullet • The dog in the *Barney Google and Snuffy Smith* comic strip.

Old Flint • The first official Bedlington terrier owned in England—by a man named Squire Trevelyan in the 1780s.

Old Yeller • The name of the yellowish-colored hunting dog fond of yelling in Fred Gipson's novel *Old Yeller*, on which the 1957 Walt Disney movie *Old Yeller* was based.

Oliver • A poodle owned by actress-turned-princess Grace Kelly (*Rear Window*).
• One of Los Angeles Lakers' announcer Chick Hearn's Bichon frisés.

Olivia • A Shih Tzu of heiress Wallis Annenberg, daughter of publisher Walter Annenberg.

Orbit • The robot dog of the Partridge family on the television cartoon series *Partridge Family: 2200 A.D.*

Oreo • A canine "cookie" of a dog owned by actor Jonathan Prince (*Alice* and *Throb*).

Orthrose • In T.H. White's *The Sword in the Stone*, one of King Arthur's many dogs.

Oscar • The name of the St. Bernard in Thorne Smith's novel *Topper*.
• A West Highland white terrier given to Katie Wagner by her mother, actress Natalie Wood
• A dog owned by actress Jean Harlow (who never won an Oscar).

Osceola • A German shepherd owned by author Isak Dinesen (*Out of Africa*) in her youth. It was named by her father after the leader of the American Seminole Indian tribe.

Oshkosh • See **Rob Roy**.

Ossie • A dog of singer Donny Osmond of the Osmond Brothers.

Othello • A spaniel owned by writer Virginia Woolf, named after the Moor in the Shakespearean tragedy.

Otto • Sergeant Snorkel's pet bulldog in the *Beetle Bailey* comic strip.
 • A German shepherd found dead in Ross MacDonald's detective novel *The Sleeping Dog*.

P

Pablo • A poodle of actor and art buff (Pablo as in Picasso?) Vincent Price.

Pachytus • In Greek mythology, one of the many hounds of Actaeon, the hunter whom the goddess Artemis turned into a stag. Pachytus was described as "thick-skinned," according to *Room's Classical Dictionary*.

Paderewski • A poodle of actor and music buff Vincent Price, who named the dog after the famous Polish pianist Ignace Paderewski.

Paddy • An Australian cattle dog owned by movie and television actor Mark Harmon (*Beyond the Poseidon Adventure*) Also see **Cooper, Frank,** and **Red**.

Paisley • The cocker spaniel featured on the early 1950s television series *Marge and Jeff*.

Pal • The real name of the original movie star Lassie.

Palo Alto • A bird dog owned by U.S. president Calvin Coolidge.

Pamper • A toy poodle owned by actress Bo Derek.

Panache • A Bichon frisé of *Newhart* actress Mary Frann who staged a naming contest with cast and crew of *Newhart*—the name Panache was best. (*Panache* is French for an ornamental plume or tuft of feathers.)

Panda • The name of dogs owned by actors Hugh O'Brian, Vincent Price, and Kathryn Grayson.

Pandy • A poodle owned by horror film actor Vincent Price (*The House of Wax*).

Pansy • A Lhasa apso of Hollywood dress designer Bob Mackie.
   • One of actor Vincent Price's many poodles.

Papillon • A dog of Debbi Fields of Mrs. Fields Cookies fame. (*Papillon* is French for "butterfly.").

Pard • In the 1941 movie *High Sierra*, a dog befriended by the character Roy Earle (played by Humphrey Bogart).

Paris • A Doberman pinscher of actor William Shatner, and a dog owned by actor Brian Keith.

Park Barbarian • A terrier of actor Ronald Colman (*A Tale of Two Cities*).

Partner • A dog that won a 1995 Delta Society award for helping Oklahoma City bomb blast victims recover from their injuries.

Pasha • A Yorkshire terrier owned by Tricia Nixon, daughter of U.S. president Richard M. Nixon. (*Pasha* is a Turkish title that notes high rank.)

Pasop • An Alsatian owned by writer Isak Dinesen (*Out of Africa*). The dog was named after the dog in her story "The Deluge at Norderney" and was also known as Rommy.

Pasquate • A poodle of movie actor Vincent Price.

Pat • A German shepherd owned by U.S. president Herbert Hoover.
 • A dog owned by silent-screen actress Miriam Cooper, wife of director Raoul Walsh.

Patapon • A red setter of French actress Brigitte Bardot.

Patches • The dog of actress Nichelle Nichols (Uhura on television's *Star Trek*).

Pati • A toy terrier owned by French writer Colette.

Patience • A poodle of film actor Vincent Price.

Patrick • An *Irish* wolfhound owned by U.S. president Herbert Hoover.
 • An *Irish* wolfhound given to Princess Mary by the Irish Wolfhound Breeding Association.
 • An *Irish* setter of entertainer-entrepreneur Merv Griffin.

Patty • A dog of comedian Dick Martin (Rowan and Martin).

Paul • The French toy bulldog sired by Peter and owned by Edward VII of England. See **Peter**.

Paul Pry • An Airedale terrier of U.S. president Calvin Coolidge. See **Laddie Boy**.

Pax • In the television series *Longstreet* starring James Franciscus, the name of blind insurance investigator Mike Longstreet's Seeing Eye dog.

Peaches • The poodle girlfriend of television evangelists Jim and Tammy Faye Bakker's Yorkshire Terrier named **Corky**.

Peanut • A mutt owned by actress Bo Derek.

Pechicho • A dog of English naturalist and author W.H. Hudson (*Green Mansions*).

Pecosa • A beagle of Luci Baines Johnson, daughter of U.S. president Lyndon B. Johnson. (*Pecosa* means "freckled" in Spanish.)

Pedro • Detective Sexton Blake's pet dog.

Pee-Wee • The white dog, owned by a young baseball fan, that was accidentally struck by a ball hit by William Bendix, as Babe Ruth, in the 1948 movie *The Babe Ruth Story*.
   • A terrier of movie actress Elizabeth Taylor (*Who's Afraid of Virginia Woolf?*).

Pee Dee • A dog of pop crooner Jack Jones (*The Impossible Dream*).

Peggy • U.S. president Ronald W. Reagan's Irish setter, which he owned when he was a radio announcer in Des Moines, Iowa. (It was reportedly named after a woman named Margaret Cleaver, a former girl-friend.)

• A Scottish terrier of U.S. president Franklin D. Roosevelt.

• A cocker spaniel owned by King Edward VII of England.

Pegleg Pete • The evil, peg-legged bulldog in the Walt Disney animated films *Steamboat Willie* (1928) and *Gallopin' Gaucho* (1929).

Penelope • One of actor Vincent Price's many poodles.

Penny • A Jack Russell terrier owned by actress Audrey Hepburn.

• A sheepdog of actress Natalie Wood (*Marjorie Morningstar*).

Penrod Pooch • The dog, also known as Penry, in Hanna-Barbera cartoons. Its voice is that of actor Scatman Crothers.

Pepe • A dog owned by composer Cole Porter.

• A Mexican Chihuahua owned by writer Gertrude Stein.

• One of television game-show host Bob Barker's dogs.

• A German shepherd owned by actress Yvonne De Carlo (*Criss Cross*).

Pepper • The sixth most popular name for a dog in the U.S., it is also the name of the Dandie Dinmont terriers in Sir Walter Scott's novel *Guy Mannering* (1815).

• The Dandie Dinmont of author Isak Dinesen, named after the Peppers of Sir Walter Scott.

• A New Zealand terrier given to Hollywood producer Aaron Spelling by actor Ricardo Montalban, a star of Spelling's successful *Fantasy Island* television series.

- Singer Merle Haggard's toy terrier.
- The name of dogs owned by author Christina Crawford and by singer David Cassidy.

Peppy • A variation of Pepper, but clearly a spunkier canine, it is the fourth most popular name for a dog in the U.S.
- A wirehaired fox terrier of television actor Michael Gray.

Percival • One of movie actor Vincent Price's poodles, named after one of King Arthur's knights who sought the Holy Grail.

Perites • One of Alexander the Great's dogs, named after a city that the statesman founded.

Perry • One of film actor Gregory Peck's dogs.

Pesky • One of the dachshunds in the 1966 Disney movie *The Ugly Dachshund*.

Pet • A dachshund of Norwegian actress Liv Ullmann.

Pete • "Pete the Pup" in the Hal Roach *Our Gang* comedies popular in the 1930s. The dog had a black ring around one eye.
- The dog featured in the movie *The Silent Call*.
- A bull terrier owned by U.S. president Theodore Roosevelt, who occasionally champed at trousers of a French ambassador and other dignitaries.
- A German shepherd of actress Debra Winger (*Officer and a Gentleman* and *Legal Eagles*).

Peter • A wirehaired terrier owned by mystery writer Agatha Christie and a member of her O.F.D.—Order of Faithful Dogs.
- A French toy bulldog owned by England's King

Edward VII. It was hurt in an accident and had to be put to sleep; it was survived by a son named Paul.

• A cocker spaniel of film star Katharine Hepburn (*The Lion in Winter*).

Peter Pan • A wirehaired fox terrier, named after the J.M. Barrie character, and owned by U.S. president Calvin Coolidge.

Petey • One of actress Sylvia Sidney's pugs.

• The name of dogs owned by humorist Wil Shriner and by actress Halle Berry (*Boomerang*).

Phantom • A boxer puppy that actor Rex Harrison and his wife, Lilli Palmer, gave to actor and *bon vivant* David Niven. It was named after Niven's military unit when he was in the Normandy invasion in World War II.

Phearless • A Lhasa apso of comedienne Phyllis Diller.

Phoebe • In T.H. White's *The Sword in the Stone*, one of King Arthur's many dogs.

• A mixed-breed dog of television comedienne Carol Burnett.

Phylax • The childhood dog of Nobel Peace Prize–winning missionary and musician Albert Schweitzer.

Picayune • A poodle of film actor Vincent Price.

Piccolo • A poodle owned by writer and diarist Anaïs Nin. (*Piccolo* means "small" in Italian.)

Pidge • In the 1955 movie *The Lady and the Tramp*, Tramp's "pet" name for Lady, the love of his life.

Pierre • Gospel singer Albertina Walker considers her

poodle "a big part of my life and . . . a member of the family."

• A poodle owned by silent-screen actress Miriam Cooper, wife of director Raoul Walsh.

Pilsner • A terrier named after a pale, light lager beer by its owner—former child movie actress Linda Blair (*The Exorcist*).

Pinker • A cocker spaniel given to writer Virginia Woolf by Vita Sackville-West.

Pinkie • A dog of cowboy movie actor Tom Mix.

Pinto • The name of dogs owned by actors Earl Holliman (*Police Woman*) and Vincent Price (*House of Wax*). (Pinto is a term for a spotted or mottled horse.)

Pip • A perennially popular name for a dog. Actor Robert Vaughn and singer Donny Osmond are among those luminaries who own canines named Pip.

Pippin • A cairn terrier owned by *Born Free* author Joy Adamson.

Pitty Pat • The name of one of fitness guru Richard Simmons's Dalmatians, named after the nickname of Aunt Hamilton in Margaret Mitchell's *Gone with the Wind*. (She was played by actress Laura Hope Crews in the movie version.)

Pixie • A white poodle that Greek shipbuilder Aristotle Onassis gave to opera diva Maria Callas.

Pluto • Mickey Mouse's world famous canine friend, who made his movie debut in the Walt Disney 1930 cartoon *The Chain Gang*. (He was named Rover in his first two movie appearances.) Pluto, by the way, never

spoke. (In mythology, Pluto was the Roman god of the underworld.)
- *Night Court* actor John Larroquette's golden retriever.
- A Rottweiler of actor Craig T. Nelson (*Coach*).

Poacher • One of *Police Woman* actor Earl Holliman's dogs.

Pockets • A poodle owned by comedic actress Kaye Ballard (*The Mothers-in-Law*).

Poemenis • In Greek mythology, one of the many hounds of Actaeon, the hunter whom the goddess Artemis turned into a stag. Peomenis was a "shepherd," according to *Room's Classical Dictionary*. Sometimes listed as Pomenis ("leader").

Poker • A dog owned by Scottish-born singer Sheena Easton.

Polly Purebred • The girlfriend of cartoon's Underdog.

Pomero • A white Pomeranian owned by English author and poet Walter Savage Landor (*Imaginary Conversations*).

Poncho • A dog owned by child-actress-turned-diplomat Shirley Temple (*Stand Up and Cheer*).

Pongo • A Staffordshire bull terrier of actress Anne Bancroft and movie director-writer Mel Brooks.

Ponne • One of French King Louis XIV's dogs. See **Bonne** and **Nonne**.

Poochie • One of television personality-entrepreneur Merv Griffin's Irish setters.

Pooh Bear • A dog owned by Joanne Carson, former wife of late-night television host Johnny Carson.

Pookie • A cairn terrier owned by Prince Edward during his courtship with Wallis Simpson.
    • A West Highland white terrier of merger mogul Henry Kravis.
    • A pug of cartoonist and comic book publisher Stan Lee.
    • A mastiff owned by *Dynasty* and *Equal Justice* actor George Di Cenzo.

Pookles • One of actress Rita Hayworth's dogs.

Poor Pooh • A Jack Russell terrier owned by Prince Charles. The dog made news when it disappeared, prompting one newspaper to write, "At Least He's Still Got His Mistress."

Pops • 1930s and 1940s bandleader Glenn Miller's dog.

Portia • A Saint Bernard owned by actor Charlton Heston (*The Ten Commandments*), named after the heroine of Shakespeare's *The Merchant of Venice*.

Possum • A mongrel owned by author Jack London (*The Call of the Wild*). (Shortly after London died in 1916, Possum was found drowned in a pool.)

Potatoes • One of film actress Natalie Wood's dogs.

Poucette • A French bulldog owned by writer Colette. The name means "little thumb" in French.

Powder Puff • A dog owned by sexy actress Jayne Mansfield (*Will Success Spoil Rock Hunter?*). The dog was killed in the same auto accident that decapitated Mansfield.

• A dog owned by author Stephen Crane (*Red Badge of Courage*).

• Entertainer-pianist Liberace's schnauzer.

Prairie • One of rock singer Axl Rose's dogs.

Precious • A schnauzer owned by pianist-entertainer Liberace.

Precious Penelope • Television actress Shannen Doherty's Labrador retriever.

Precious Pupp • The Hanna-Barbera cartoon dog living at 711 Pismo Place with its owner Granny Sweet.

Preppy • One of *Dynasty* and *Equal Justice* actor George DiCenzo's mastiffs.

President • The Great Dane owned by U.S. president Franklin D. Roosevelt.

Pretzel • Singer Ruth Etting's dog.

Prince • The fifth most popular name for a dog in the U.S., and the name of silent-screen actor Rudolph Valentino's German shepherd.

• The Great Dane in the 1939 movie classic *Wuthering Heights*. In the movie version of Jack London's *Call of the Wild*, it was the name of Buck's rival dog.

• The German shepherd living on the Wameru game reserve on the television series *Daktari*.

• The Doberman pinscher in writer Paul Fairman's *The Dark Road Home*.

• The collie of Canadian-born actor Jack Pickford (*Brown of Harvard*).

• One of English poet William Wordsworth's dogs.

Princess • A royal and popular name for a female dog, and the eighth most popular one in the U.S.

• A stray dog found by Harlan Day (played by actor Derek Scott) in the 1947 movie *Life with Father*.

• One of singer Mariah Carey's Doberman pinschers.

• A dog owned by movie star Tyrone Power (*The Eddie Duchin Story*).

Prissy • One of fitness guru Richard Simmons's many Dalmatians, named after the servant in Margaret Mitchell's *Gone with the Wind*. (Prissy was played by actress Butterfly McQueen in the movie version.)

Professor Peabody • The dog in television's *Rocky and Bullwinkle*.

Promise • The name of the pointer in the 1940 movie *The Biscuit Eater*, which was remade in 1972.

Prudence • A dog of movie actor Vincent Price.

Prudence Prim • The favorite dog, a white female collie, of Grace Coolidge, the wife of U.S. president Calvin Coolidge.

Prunella • A Shar-pei of pianist-entertainer Liberace, probably because the breed of dog looks shriveled up—like a prune!

Psean • One of screen actor Vincent Price's poodles.

Pterelas • A hound of Actaeon. The name means "winged" in Greek.

Puddle • A golden cocker spaniel owned by actress Lauren Bacall (*To Have and Have Not*).

Puffy • One of singer Janet Jackson's dogs.

Pumpkin • The King Charles spaniel of television's Mary Hart (*Entertainment Tonight*).

• The King Charles spaniel of Ethel Kennedy, wife of Robert F. Kennedy.

Punch Burger • A part German shepherd, part Keeshond that its owner, Laura van Sant, entered in the U.S. presidential race in 1988 to protest the quality of the other candidates.

Punky • Actress Betty Grable's dog, said to have been responsible for her losing the part of Adelaide in the film *Guys and Dolls*. Grable was supposed to meet with producer Sam Goldwyn but instead took ailing Punky to a veterinarian. She missed the meeting, thereby irritating the legendary producer. (Vivian Blaine got the part.)

• One of comedic actress Kaye Ballard's poodles.

Pupi • The toy poodle of salon entrepreneur Georgette Klinger.

Puppy • A dog owned by television actor Earl Holliman (*Police Woman*).

Purty • One of several dogs owned by movie actor Brad Pitt (*A River Runs through It*).

Pushface • Actress Carole Lombard's Pekingese in the 1936 film *My Man Godfrey*.

Pushinka • A dog that was given to Caroline Kennedy, daughter of U.S. president John F. Kennedy, by Soviet premier Nikita Khrushchev. It was a puppy of **Strelka**, one of the first dogs to go on a space flight. The name means "fluffy" in Russian.

Pushka • The pampered poodle of salon entrepreneur Georgette Klinger.

Pussycat • The sheepdog of television actor Gardner McKay (*Adventures in Paradise*).

Q

Queenie • In the comic strip *Dondi*, Dondi's dog.
• A dog in writer William Bankier's story "The Dog Who Hated Jazz."

Quick Draw McGraw • A dog in the Hanna-Barbera cartoons.

Quince • A pointer owned by English writer T.H. White.

Quizzical • A King Charles spaniel of writer Armand Deutsch (*Me and Bogie*).

R

Rab • The vigilant dog in Dr. John Brown's *Rab and His Friends*. He stayed at the bedside of his dying owner Ailie.

Rascal • The dog of Brian Foster in the Hanna-Barbera cartoon feature *C.H.O.M.P.S.*, on whom the electronic watchdog CHOMPS was based. CHOMPS was an acronym for Canine Home Protection System.

Rags • Bobbie Lee Hartley's dog in the movie *Ode to Billy Joe*.
• The name of actress June Havoc's dog in the television series *Willy*.
• A combination French bulldog and Boston terrier owned by writer Dorothy Parker in her youth.
• The mechanical dog ("I'm Rags, your dog. Woof, woof!") in Woody Allen's movie *Sleeper*.

• A dog of television actor Tim Reid (Gordon "Venus Flytrap" Sims on *WKRP in Cincinnati*).

Rajah • The pet collie of Tarzan author Edgar Rice Burroughs, named after the word for a Hindu prince or ruler .

Ralph • The invisible dog on television's *Flip Wilson Show*.
• The beagle of television actress Sara Gilbert (*Roseanne*).

Rama • The German shepherd of heavyweight boxer Ken Norton.

Rambler • In the 1977–78 television series *The Life and Times of Grizzly Adams*, Grizzly's hound dog.

Ramullah • The dog of international playboy Ali Khan.

Randy • One of many dogs owned by television actor Earl Holliman (*Police Woman*).

Ranger • One of Millie's puppies—Millie being the famous dog owned by U.S. president George Bush.

Raoulle • The barking dog featured in the 1978 film *The Buddy Holly Story*, starring Gary Busey.

Rasputin • In the television series *Ivan the Terrible*, the dog owned by Ivan Petrovsky, played by actor Lou Jacobi. (Rasputin was the "mad monk" who strongly influenced Czar Nicholas II.)

Rat • An Australian terrier of novelist, essayist, and social critic Gore Vidal (*Burr*), given to him by acting couple Paul Newman and Joanne Newman. Actress Greta Garbo called the dog "Ratzski" because "Rat is so brutal a name."

Ready • The bulldog in the comic strip and television series *Ruff and Ready*.

Rebel • The German shepherd and friend of Champion in the television series *The Adventures of Champion*.

Rebell • A Great Dane owned by Nazi-sympathizer Unity Mitford, of the English literary Mitford family.

Recession • A basset hound of comedian Bob Hope, named after one of the multimillionaire's biggest fears.

Red • The canine protagonist in writer Jim Kjelgaard's story "Big Red."
  • An Australian cattle dog owned by movie and television actor Mark Harmon (*St. Elsewhere*). Also see **Cooper**, **Frank**, and **Paddy**.

Red Bandit • One of several Siberian huskies owned by actor Eddie Velez (*Extremities*).

Red Dog • An Australian cattle dog of actor Mark Harmon (*Flamingo Road*) and actress Pam Dawber (*Mork and Mindy*).

Reggie • A Lhasa apso of film star Elizabeth Taylor.
  • A dog of television actor Abe Vigoda (*Barney Miller* and *Fish*).
  • A golden retriever owned by actress Robin Riker (Bobbi Turner on *Thunder Alley*).

Rek • A dog of Czech film director Milos Forman (*One Flew over the Cuckoo's Nest*).

Ramses • One of movie actor Charlton Heston's many dogs.

Ren • A dog owned by Bee Gees singer Barry Gibb.

Renaldo • The name of Cisco Kid's white dog in the television series *The Cisco Kid* (which starred actor Duncan *Renaldo*, whose original name was Renaldo Duncan!).

Rescue • Actress Arlene Dahl's Great Dane in the 1953 film *Here Come the Girls*.

Rex • Latin for King, it is the twenty-first most popular name for a dog in the U.S. It was the name of First Lady Nancy Reagan's King Charles spaniel.
  • A King Charles spaniel owned by actor Michael J. Fox.
  • Writer James Thurber's bull terrier in his youth and later mentioned in his *My Life and Hard Times* and *Thurber's Dogs*.

Rhett Butler • One of fitness guru Richard Simmons's Dalmatians, named after the main character of Margaret Mitchell's novel *Gone with the Wind*. (Butler, of course, was played by Clark Gable in the movie version.)

Rhubarb • The Alsatian dog that starred in *You Can Never Tell*.

Rieley • The golden retriever of golf legend Arnold Palmer.

Riff • The late actor's Bruce Lee's schnauzer, which was a brother of actor Steve McQueen's dog.

Rikki Tikki Tavi • Spy novelist Robert Ludlum's German shepherd, from the name of the mongoose in Rudyard Kipling's *Jungle Book*.

Rin Tin Tin • A German shepherd found by American soldiers in France during World War II. It began starring in American silent movies in 1923 (*Where the North Begins*) and appeared regularly for many years, as did the dog's son Rin Tin Tin, Jr. A television series, *The Adventures of Rin Tin Tin*, premiered in 1955. The fourth "Rinty" won the TV Patsy Award in 1958 and 1959. The original Rin Tin Tin bit Warner Brothers studio head Jack Warner. Its footprints were imprinted at Grauman's Chinese Theater in Hollywood.

Rip • A comic-strip police dog created by Perry Mason author Erle Stanley Gardner.

Rita • One of many King Charles spaniels owned by Gladys, Duchess of Marlborough.

Rivets • The dog mascot of the Society for Prevention of Cruelty to Animals.

Rob • The bearded collie of actress Bo Derek.

Rob Roy • The name of Calvin Coolidge's favorite dog, a white collie originally named Oshkosh, after where it was born. It was named after Sir Walter Scott's outlaw character Rob Roy.

Robin • A Sealyham terrier owned by heiress Peggy Guggenheim.

Robinson • A dachshund of writer and wit Dorothy Parker.

Rocco • A dog of actress-singer Bernadette Peters (*Dames at Sea*).

Rocco van Hammerich • An Alsatian tracking dog and former body guard of former German chancellor Helmut Schmidt.

Rocket • A Siberian husky of actress Kate Jackson (*Charlie's Angels*).

Rocky • A Belgian Malinois dog famous for its drug enforcement work on the Texas-Mexico border.

• A Rottweiler of actor Leonardo Di Caprio (*What's Eating Gilbert Grape?*).

• A dog owned by television actor Richard Paul (Mayor Sam Booth on *Murder, She Wrote*).

Rogan • A dog of British screen actor Dirk Bogarde (*Death in Venice*).

Rollo • *Call of the Wild* author Jack London's dog in his early days.

Roosevelt • A mixed-breed dog of film actress Sally Kellerman (*M*A*S*H*).

Rosalita • Actor Kevin Costner's Labrador retriever. The dog's mother was "actress" who played Kevin's dog in the movie *Revenge*.

Rosie • A cocker spaniel of actress Brenda Vaccaro (*Once Is Not Enough*).

Rover • A common name for a dog in days of old, ever since U.S. president George Washington gave the name to one of his hounds. (Rover was an obsolete old English word for "pirate" or "robber," in addition to its extant meaning "wanderer.")

• The original name of Walt Disney's Pluto.

• The name of U.S. president Lyndon B. Johnson's first dog, a collie.

• A Pekingese of screen actress Dorothy Gish (*Orphans of the Storm*).

Rowf • A black dog that is a main character in Richard Adams's novel *The Plague Dogs*. See **Snitter**.

Rowlf • One of Muppet creator Jim Henson's early

puppets, a hound, which was featured on the television musical variety program *The Jimmy Dean Show*.

Roxie • A dog of television actress Morgan Brittany (*Dallas*).

Roxy • One of singing duo Steve Lawrence and Eydie Gormé's dogs.

Royal • A collie owned by author Sir Walter Scott (*Ivanhoe*).

Ruby • One of Czech-born tennis great Martina Navratilova's dogs.
• A Belgian sheepdog of television actress Bea Arthur (*Maude*).
• A dog owned by French-born diarist Anaïs Nin (*Delta of Venus*).
• A dog owned by *Red Badge of Courage* author Stephen Crane.

Ruby Rough • One of two Chow Chows owned by Calvin Coolidge.

Rudy • One of film actress-singer Doris Day's dachshunds.

Ruff • Dennis the Menace's dog in the Hank Ketcham comic strip—he's dreadfully afraid of cats.

Ruffy • A terrier of actress Irene Dunne (*Cimarron*).

Rufus • One of Jim Henson's Muppets.
• A Golden retriever of actor Marc Singer (*Beastmaster*).

Rufus I and Rufus II • Childhood chocolate-brown poodles of British prime minister Winston Churchill.

When a servant let Rufus I off its leash, it was run over and killed. When Churchill screened the movie *David Copperfield*, he covered the eyes of Rufus II, sitting on his lap, when Bill Sikes tried to drown his dog.

Rump Roast • A dog owned by lawyer Melvin Belli.

Rumples • A dog of actress Kathyn Grayson (*Kiss Me, Kate*).

Runge • A German shepherd owned by author and illustrator Maurice Sendak (*Where the Wild Things Are*). The dog was named after Philipp Otto Runge, an eighteenth-century German artist.

Russia • A borzoi (a *Russian* wolfhound) of actress Bo Derek (*10*).

Rusty or Rusti • A good name for an Irish setter or similarly colored dog.
   • A Shih Tzu of *Baywatch* star David Hasselhoff.
   • A dog of rock singer Mark Lindsay of Paul Revere and the Raiders.

Ryan • A collie of actor Mark Harmon (*Beyond the Poseidon Adventure*).
   • One of Olympic diver Greg Louganis's Great Danes.

S

Sacha • A poodle of actress (*Rosemary's Baby*) and writer (*Adam's Rib*) Ruth Gordon.

Sadie • A toy poodle that was given to singer-actress Barbara Streisand by the crew of *Funny Girl*. The name is from her song "Sadie, Sadie, Married Lady" in the movie.

Sailor Boy • A Chesapeake retriever owned by U.S. president Theodore Roosevelt.

Sakki • The Akita of television actress Amanda Bearse (*Married . . . with Children*).

Sale Gosse • A poodle of television interviewer Barbara Walters.

Sally • A Yorkshire terrier owned by actress Elizabeth Taylor and hubby, Richard Burton.
• A red cocker spaniel owned by author A.J. Cronin (*The Citadel*). Also see **Silly Sally**.

Sam • The tenth most popular name for a dog in the U.S., and the name of one of the Apple family dogs in the television series *Apple's Way*.
• The German shepherd of John F. Kennedy, Jr., occasionally seen in New York's Central Park chasing Frisbees.
• A golden Labrador in the *Sam* series in 1977–78.
• A poodle of straw-hatted southern comedienne Minnie Pearl.
• A dog owned by television actor Earl Holliman (*Police Woman*).
• A Springer spaniel owned by *Knight Rider* actress Patricia McPherson.
• It was one of two family dogs in Bill Keane's comic strip *The Family Circus*.
• The name of John Wayne's dog in the 1954 western *Hondo*.
• The dog that costarred with Mel Gibson in the 1987 movie *Lethal Weapon*. See **Smilin' Sam**.

Samantha • One of talk-show host Johnny Carson's Yorkshire terriers when he was married to Joanne.
• An Old English sheepdog of actress Katherine Ross (*Butch Cassidy and the Sundance Kid*).

• A dog of actress Mary McDonough (Erin on *The Waltons*).

Sammy • A Wheaton terrier of *Beverly Hills 90210* actress Tori Spelling.

• The dog of film cowboy Ken Maynard (*In Old Santa Fe*).

Samson • A good name for a strong dog, based on the Biblical figure (Judges 13–16) noted for his great strength.

• A Burmese mountain dog of actor William Devane (*Family Plot*).

• A German shepherd of television actor Laurie Burton (*Rituals*).

• A water spaniel of humorist James Thurber (*The Secret Life of Walter Mitty*).

• U–2 spy pilot Francis Gary Powers's childhood dog. (The name was significant during the exchange with Colonel Rudolf Abel on February 10,1962. American officials asked Powers the name of his high school football coach to help prove that he was the real Powers. He was unable to remember the coach's name but he did mention the name of his dog, which convinced officials that he was the real person and not a planted spy.)

• One of the Doberman pinschers in the 1985 movie *Remo Williams: The Adventure Begins*.

Sancho • The wolf in the 1971 movie *The Wild Country*, which also featured a very young actor Ron Howard.

Sandringham • King George VI had several dogs named with the Sandringham prefix: Sandringham Glen; Sandringham Scion; Sandringham Spark, a clumber spaniel; Sandringham, a Labrador retriever; and Sandringham Stream.

Sandy • A popular name for a dog and the eighth most popular name for a female dog in England. It is most famous for being the name of Little Orphan Annie's dog in Harold Grey's comic strip and subsequent radio shows, plays and movies. (In the original Broadway musical the dog playing Sandy was actually named Sandy and its understudy was named **Arf**.)

• Also, it was the name of one of the bloodhounds that tracked down James Earl Ray after he escaped from prison on June 10, 1977.

• A cairn terrier owned by author A.J. Cronin (*The Citadel*).

• A Scottish terrier owned by Alice Roosevelt Longworth, the daughter of U.S. president Theodore Roosevelt.

• An Airedale terrier of U.S. president Woodrow Wilson.

• A Scottish terrier owned by author Beatrix Potter as a child.

• A dog of British comedienne Gracie Fields (*Sing as We Go*).

• A Samoyed of movie actor Patrick Wayne, son of screen legend John Wayne.

Sanford III • A dog of comedienne-actress Edie Adams (*The Apartment*).

Sarah • A West Highland white terrier owned by film director Alfred Hitchcock.

• A cocker spaniel owned by British novelist and poet Vita Sackville-West.

Sargeant • A dog owned by actor Earl Holliman, who played Lieutenant Bill Crowley to Angie Dickinson's Sgt. Pepper Anderson on television's *Police Woman*.

Sascha • A Siberian husky owned by television comedic actor Sid Caesar (*Your Show of Shows*).

Sasha • One of actress Valerie Perrine's Great Danes.
• Movie director George Cukor's standard poodle.
• A toy poodle of television actress Jennie Garth (Kelly Taylor on *Beverly Hills 90210*).
• The borzoi or Russian wolfhound of television actress Ruta Lee (*Coming of Age*).

Satan • A Belgian sheepdog owned by devilish playwright Tennessee Williams.

Satellite • The dog of French novelist Jules Verne (*Around the World in Eighty Days*).

Saucey • See **Charlotte**.

Saudi • One of movie actor Brad Pitt's dogs.

Sauer • A Doberman pinscher that tracked a thief in South Africa one hundred miles, the longest tracking incident by a dog according to the *Guinness Book of World Records*.

Sauki • A Shih Tzu of *Home Improvement* actor Zachary Ty Bryan.

Sausages • A dachshund that auditioned with comedic actor and director Charlie Chaplin for the canine lead in the film *A Dog's Life*.

Sauvignon • A schnauzer owned by Heloise, the "helpful hint" advice columnist and author. The name comes from the grape that is used to make a *cabernet sauvignon* wine or Bordeaux.

Savage Sam • Old Yeller's son featured in Fred Gipson's novel *Savage Sam* (1962).

Scamp • The name of one of U.S. president Theodore

Roosevelt's dogs, a terrier, while he was in office. It was also the name of the puppy in the Disney feature movie *The Lady and the Tramp*.

Scarlet • One of several golden retrievers owned by television actress Staci Keanan (*Going Places* and *My Two Dads*).

Scarlett • Another one of fitness maven Richard Simmons's Dalmatians, named after Scarlett O'Hara in Margaret Mitchell's novel *Gone with the Wind*. (Actress Vivien Leigh played Scarlett in the movie version.)

Schatzie • A dog owned by actress Bette Davis and her daughter B.D. The name means "little darling" in German.
• One of actress Doris Day's dachshunds.
• A miniature schnauzer owned by this author's family in the late 1950s. Also see **Schottzie**.

Schelsca • One of comedic actor Dudley Moore's dogs.

Schlubber • A mastiff of "Godfather" actor Marlon Brando.

Schnappsy • In Harold Knerr's comic strip *Dinglehoofer and His Dog*, Dinglehoofer's basset hound. Prior to World War II, the dog's name was Adolph but it was changed to avoid association with Hitler.

Schnick • A dachshund of movie actor Vincent Price.

Schnoodle • The nasty dog of Fräulein Rottenmeier in the 1982 Hanna-Barbera feature cartoon *Heidi's Song*.

Schottzie • Saint Bernard of Marge Schott, owner of the Cincinnati Reds baseball club.

Schunya • A German shepherd of film actor Bela Lugosi (*Dracula*).

Scipio • One of two talking dogs in Spanish writer Miguel de Cervantes's satirical *The Dogs' Colloquy*. The other dog was named **Berganza**.

Scooby-Doo • The goofy Great Dane in the Hanna-Barbera cartoon television series which debuted in the early 1970s.

Scooby-Dum • The dumb canine cousin of Scooby-Doo.

Scooby-Dear • A flirty female dog in the Scooby-Doo cartoons of Hanna-Barbera.

Scooter • A cairn terrier owned by actress Mary Kate McGeehan (Linda Caproni on *Falcon Crest*).

Scotch • A Scottish terrier owned by then-actor Ronald Reagan and his actress wife Jane Wyman. See **Soda**.

Scott • A Doberman pinscher of rock singer Mark Lindsay of Paul Revere and the Raiders.
• A border collie of Tom Hayden, political activist and former husband of Jane Fonda.

Scottie • The nickname for a Scottish terrier and a common name given to Scottish terriers by their owners. The eighty-first most popular dog name in the U.S. Also, the name of a collie owned by writer James Thurber's maternal grandfather.

Scrappy-Doo • The nephew of Scooby-Doo featured in Hanna-Barbera cartoons. (Scrappy-Doo's voice is that of deejay Casey Kasem, who began doing cartoon voice-overs before he became nationally famous as a deejay.)

Scraps • Charlie Chaplin's costar in the 1918 movie *A Dog's Life*. He was a white mongrel with a brown spot over one eye. Scraps appeared in dozens of movies.

Scruffy • On the television series *The Ghost and Mrs. Muir*, the name of the family dog.
• A mixed-breed dog of movie critic Leonard Maltin.
• The name of dogs owned by actress-singer Kathryn Grayson and by *Dynasty* actor George DiCenzo.

Scrummy • A yellow Labrador owned by the Duke of York, who later became King George VI of England. See **Stiffy**.

Seadog • The sailor dog on the original Cap'n Crunch breakfast cereal box.

Searcher • One of George Washington's many dogs.

Sebastian • A miniature poodle owned by actress Vivien Leigh (*Streetcar Named Desire*).

Sergeant Murphy • The motorcycle-riding canine police officer in Richard Scarry's picture books for young children.

Shadrack • An Airedale that movie director John Huston gave to actress Olivia De Havilland. (In the Bible, Shadrach or Shadrak was one of three men thrown in the furnace of Nebuchadnezzar.)

Shadow • The name of dogs owned by actors Corey Feldman (*Goonies*) and Earl Holliman (*Police Woman*).
• The taciturn golden retriever (voice-over by Ralph Waite) in the 1996 Disney movie *Homeward Bound 2: Lost in San Francisco*.

Shaggy • The 1960 Patsy winner that starred in the Disney movie *The Shaggy Dog*.

• One of television comedic actor Harvey Korman's dogs.

Shaka • A German shepherd of actor Blair Underwood (Jonathan Rollins on *L.A. Law*).

Shamgret Danzas • The tallest dog ever recorded, according to the *Guinness Book of World Records*. He stood "41$\frac{1}{2}$ or 42 inches when his hackles were raised" and weighed up to 238 pounds.

Shandygaff • Scottish terrier of 1930s movie actress Jean Muir (*A Midsummer Night's Dream*). The dog was not averse to licking a bit of ginger ale spiked with regular ale.

Shane • The golden retriever of television talk-show host Oprah Winfrey.

Shannon • President John F. Kennedy's Irish cocker spaniel, which was given to him by Eamon de Valera, the Prime Minister of Ireland. (Shannon is the name of the main river in Ireland.)

• A dog owned by singer Pia Zadora.

Sharkey • The boxer of television actor Shane Conrad (Cody Hawkes on *Jesse Hawkes*, which starred his father, Robert Conrad).

Sharp • A black Labrador owned by Queen Victoria.

Sheba • The most popular name for a female dog in the United Kingdom. (Curiously, it is also the name for a cat food manufactured by Mars, originally marketed only in Europe but now sold in the U.S.) Sheba is the biblical name for an ancient area of Arabia.

Sheeba • A Keeshond owned by Heloise of "Helpful Hint" fame.

Shelby • A golden retriever of clothing designer Bill Blass.

Shelley • A Bichon frisé of television producer Aaron Spelling.

Shep • A legendary collie that herded sheep in New York's Central Park before the muggers chased out the sheep.
• A dog in the 1954 movie *A Bullet Is Waiting*, starring Jean Simmons and Rory Calhoun.

Sherlock • The real name of the basset hound that Elvis "the Pelvis" Presley sang "Hound Dog" to on the July 1, 1956, broadcast of television's *The Steve Allen Show*.

Shinka • The Great Dane of actress Meredith MacRae and husband, Greg Mullavey (*Mary Hartman, Mary Hartman*).

Shira • An Akita of pro basketball player Byron Scott.

Shirley • One of actor-producer Michael Landon's dogs.
• One of comedic actress Kaye Ballard's poodles.

Sh*thead • Comedic actor Steve Martin's dog in the 1979 film *The Jerk*. (The dog was supposed to be named Lifesaver.)

Shock • A lapdog eulogized by poet and playwright John Gay, who wrote *The Beggar's Opera*.

Shuttz • A Doberman pinscher owned by television actor Willie Aames (*Eight Is Enough*).

Sid • A dog of television actor Max Gail (Sergeant Stanley Wojohowicz on *Barney Miller*).

Sidney • *Dirty Harry* screen actor Clint Eastwood's basset hound.

Silky • A terrier owned by *Baywatch* star David Hasselhoff.

Silly • One of singer-actor Bobby Sherman's dogs.

Silly Sally • A golden retriever of actress Shannen Doherty (*Beverly Hills 90210*).

Simba • A Pekingese owned by comedic actress Betty White.
 • A dog owned by movie actor James Stewart (*Rear Window*).

Simon • The Partridge family's mixed-breed shaggy dog.
 • Actor Paul Muni's (*The Life of Emile Zola*) Airedale, which understood commands in Yiddish.

Sinhue • A Welsh corgi owned by British actor Dirk Bogarde (*Death in Venice*).

Sirius • In mythology, the hunter Orion's dog. In astronomy, the "Dog Star" in the constellation Canis Major, the origin of the phrase "dog days of summer" (from Sirius's heliacal rising being in summer).
 • A dog owned by author Isak Dinesen's boyfriend Denys Finch Hatton, a big-game hunter.

Sir-Love-a-Lot • William Holden's dog in the 1973 Clint Eastwood–directed movie *Breezy*.

Sir Winston • A Papillon owned by Texas millionaire

T. Boone Pickens, named after British prime minister Sir Winston Churchill.

Sissy • A toy dachshund owned by *Baywatch* actor David Hasselhoff.

Skeeper • A dog owned by David Holt, host of television's *The American Music Shop* country-music program.

Skeets • A cocker spaniel of actress Brenda Vaccaro (*Once Is Not Enough*).

Skeezer • The therapeutic mutt featured in the 1982 feature movie *Skeezer*.

Skilaki • The miniature Yorkshire terrier of actress Marina Sirtis of *Star Trek: The Next Generation*. *Skilaki* is the Greek word for "little dog."

Skip • A mongrel owned by U.S. president Theodore Roosevelt. He found it while on a bear hunt.
• The dog featured in the Jerry Lewis movie *Visit to a Small Planet*.
• A loyal and loving dog owned by author and editor Willie Morris in his youth, written about in the posthumously published *My Dog Skip* in 1995.

Skipper • A dog owned by British actor James Mason.

Skippy • Once a very popular name for a dog, it is now #42 on the popularity list in the U.S. It was the real name of actress Mary Robson's dog **George** in the 1938 movie *Bringing Up Baby*, starring Katherine Hepburn and Cary Grant.
• In the 1934 movie *The Thin Man*, the real name of the wirehaired terrier that played **Asta**.
• A dog of *Beverly Hillbillies* Elly May Clampett.

Skookun • A cross between a dachshund and a wolfhound owned by Paul Bunyan of American folklore and bred with short front legs and long hind legs so it could run downhill with ease.

Skoshie • A poodle of actress Shirley Jones and Marty Ingels. The name is an Americanization of the Japanese word *sukoshi*, which means "little."

Skulker • The bulldog in Emily Brontë's novel *Wuthering Heights* that injures Catherine Earnshaw. See **Throttler**.

Sky • The beagle of pro football quarterback Roger Staubach, named after the Sky Ranch, where his team, the Dallas Cowboys, had its headquarters.

Slipper • A cairn terrier that Prince Edward gave to Wallis Simpson before their marriage.

Slivers • Little Nemo's dog in the comic strip *Little Nemo*.

Sluggy • A Scottish terrier of Humphrey Bogart.

Smiley • The shaggy dog of the Baxter family in the television series *Hazel*.

Smilin' Sam • One of singer David Cassidy's dogs.

Smoke • A German shepherd of actress Bo Derek.
  • A dog owned by television actor Earl Holliman (*Police Woman*).

Smokey • A good name for gray dogs:
  • A collie of film actor Paul Newman.
  • A family dog of this author—a gray schnauzer.

Snarf • The mischievous-looking bull terrier that appears in George Booth's *New Yorker* cartoons. It was named after a real-life dog named Snarfie Sue.

Sneakers • The dog in the 1984–89 television series *Highway to Heaven*, starring Michael Landon, who also produced the series.

Snert • Hagar the Terrible's dog in the comic strip *Hagar the Terrible*.

Snip • A cairn terrier owned by King George V of England.

Snitter • A black and white fox terrier and a main character in novelist Richard Adams's *The Plague Dogs*.

Snittle Timbery • See **Timber Doodle.**

Snoopy • Perhaps the most famous and beloved dog name in the world, it is the name of Charlie Brown's beloved beagle of Charles Schulz's *Peanuts* comic strip and subsequent TV specials. It is the seventh most popular name for a dog in the U.S.
  • A dog of rock legend Elvis Presley and daughter, Lisa Marie Presley.
  • A dog of actress Mary McDonough (*The Waltons*).

Snow • The Monroe family dog in the television series *The Monroes*.
  • A dog owned by actress Susan Strasberg, daughter of acting coach Lee Strasberg.

Snowflake • One of many King Charles spaniels owned by Gladys, Duchess of Marlborough.

Snowjob • An Alsatian owned by film and television comedian Bob Hope.

Snow White • One of singer Janet Jackson's dogs.

Snowy • A dog owned by singer-actress Doris Day.

Snuffles • Quick Draw McGraw's canine friend in television cartoons. He loved dog biscuits!

Snuffy • A cairn terrier that appeared in the 1958 film *Pal Joey*, starring Frank Sinatra and Kim Novak.
• One of the many dogs owned by pianist-entertainer Liberace.

Snugger • A mutt owned by movie actress Bo Derek.

Socrates • A dog of Lady Ottoline Morrell, a friend of writer Virginia Woolf and her Bloomsbury circle, named after the Greek philosopher.

Soda • Actor Monty Woolley's dog in the 1944 wartime movie *Since You Went Away*.
• A Scottish terrier owned by actor and future U.S. president Ronald Reagan and his actress wife, Jane Wyman. See **Scotch**.

Sojah • A Chow Chow of actress Tisha Campbell (*Martin*).

Sol-Leks • In Jack London's novel *Call of the Wild*, a sled dog that was blind in one eye.

Solo • In Hugo van Lawick's television film *The Wild Dogs of Africa*, a malnourished female puppy in a wild dog pack.
• A dachshund of movie director George Cukor who went "solo"—he was a lifelong bachelor.

Solomon • The brownish-black spaniel of television talk-show host Oprah Winfrey. (Solomon was a king of Israel, famous for his wisdom.)

Sonnie • A fox terrier owned by U.S. president Herbert Hoover.

Sophie • One of writer-humorist James Thurber's dogs.

Sooner • A mixed Labrador and golden retriever owned by actress Betty White.

Souci • A brindle bulldog owned by French writer Colette. The name is French for "worry."

Soufflé • A King Charles spaniel of Ethel Kennedy, wife of Robert F. Kennedy, a U.S. senator and U.S. attorney general.

Sounder • The family dog of the Calloways in the 1965 Disney feature movie *Those Calloways*.
  • The name of the sharecropper's dog in William H. Armstrong's book *Sounder* (1969), on which the 1972 movie, starring Cicely Tyson and Paul Winfield, was based.

Spanky • A dog owned by actor Bruce Penhall (Cadet Bruce Nelson on *CHiPS*).

Spannel • One of the two dogs that sailed to the United States on the Mayflower.

Spare-Ribs • The dog of Toots and Casper in the comic strip.

Sparkey • Film actress Rhonda Fleming's dog.

Sparkle • A dog of actor Gene Wilder and comedic actress Gilda Radner.
  • A King Charles spaniel of movie actor Kirk Douglas.

Sparky • A dog owned by singer Sheena Easton.

Sparko • The electric dog that was exhibited with Elektro, a seven-foot-tall Westinghouse robot exhibited at the New York World's Fair in 1939.

Spencer • Basketball star Kareem Abdul-Jabbar's Rottweiler.

Spice • A dog owned by singer Della Reese, who has a preference for "spicy" names. See **Allspice**, **Cajun**, **Cinnamon**, **Nutmeg**, and **Sugar**.

Spike • The name of cartoonist Charles Schulz's dog. Its claim to fame was that it made a Ripley's *Believe It or Not!* column for having an unusual diet. Not so coincidentally, Spike is the name of Snoopy's brother in Schulz's *Peanuts* comic strip.

• "The world's laziest dog"—comedienne Joan Rivers's Yorkshire terrier. The much-spoiled dog lives in a New York Eastside townhouse, has a man who carries it and takes it for walks, and travels in a Louis Vuitton cat carrier.

• The dog that is beaten badly and restored to health in the 1959 movie *A Dog of Flanders*, starring David Ladd, the son of film actor Alan Ladd.

• In Jack London's novel *The Call of the Wild*, the name of Buck's rival.

• The name of the Patsy-winning dog who played Yeller in the 1957 movie *Old Yeller*. The dog was also featured in the 1960 movie *A Dog of Flanders*.

Spitz • See **Lickety Spitz** and **Mark Spitz**.

Spooky • The Springer spaniel of singer-songwriter Mel Tormé.

Sport • The dog owned by Fred MacMurray and Claudette Colbert in the 1947 movie *The Egg and I*.

• A brown cocker spaniel owned by singer Kate "God Bless America" Smith.

• A stray dog that writer and diarist Anaïs Nin took in as a child.

Spot • Once a very popular name for a dog, Spot is now #56 on the list of most popular dog names in the U.S.

• The name of Dick and Jane's black and white dog in primer reading books used by most grammar schools in the 1930s, 1940s, and early 1950s.

• The name of the black and white dog owned by Dick and Jane (George Segal and Jane Fonda) Harper in the 1976 movie *Fun with Dick and Jane*. It was Henry's cat in the television cartoon series *Hong Kong Phooey*.

• The soldier's dog in the 1950 film *Rocky Mountain*.

• A cocker spaniel that actress Elizabeth Taylor owned as a child.

• A brown and white spaniel owned by author Beatrix Potter.

• The dog in Mert Walker's comic strip *Boner's Ark*.

• The German shepherd of Broadway actress-singer Carol Lawrence (*West Side Story*).

• The name of dogs owned by actor Rob Lowe, by actress Linda Darnell, and by Queen Victoria.

• See **Stricte**.

Spotty • A variation of **Spot**.

Spuds MacKenzie • The bull terrier ("Party Animal") in the Budweiser beer television commercials popular in the 1980s.

Spunky • A Scottie owned by U.S. president Dwight D. Eisenhower. Also the white cocker spaniel owned by the Fonz (played by Henry Winkler) in the television series *Happy Days*.

Sputnik • The beagle named after the Russian satellite by its owner Charles James, a designer who was considered "the couturier's couturier" in his day.

Stan • The dog owned by late-night television talk-show host David Letterman.
  • The dog in actor Robert De Niro's 1996 movie *The Fan*.

Stanley • One of movie director Alfred Hitchcock's Sealyham terriers. Stanley and another Sealyham named **Geoffrey** appeared with the director in his cameo appearance in his 1963 movie *The Birds*.

Star • *Baywatch* beauty Pamela Anderson's golden retriever.
  • *M*A*S*H* actor Wayne Rogers's dog.
  • One of actress Sylvia Sidney's pugs.

Stasi • One of two black Scottish terriers owned by Eva Braun, the mistress of Adolf Hitler. See **Negus**.

Sterling • One of *Star Trek* actor William Shatner's Doberman pinschers.

Stickeen • A mixed-breed dog of Scottish-born naturalist and conservationist John Muir, who helped found Yosemite National Park. Muir named the dog after the Stickeen Indian tribe, which raised the dog, and immortalized it in his 1909 novel *Stickeen*.

Stiffy • A yellow Labrador owned by Duke of York, who later became King George VI of England. See **Scrummy**.

Storm • The dog in the mid-1960s movie *Goodbye Charlie*.

Stormy • A Saint Bernard owned by *Golden Girls* actress Betty White.

Strange • A mutt owned by humorist Patrick McManus, who wrote about the "skunk dog" in *They Shoot Canoes, Don't They?*

Streaker • A dog owned by U.S. president John F. Kennedy.

Strelka • Russian for "Little Arrow," one of two Russian dogs put in orbit in 1960. The other dog was named **Belka** ("Squirrel"). Also see **Pushinka**.

Stricte • In Greek mythology, one of the many hounds of Actaeon, the hunter whom the goddess Artemis turned into a stag. Stricte meant "Spot," according to *Room's Classical Dictionary*. Also listed as Stricta in some sources.

Strip • In the Bud Blake comic strip *Tiger*, Tiger's black and white dog.

Strongheart • A German shepherd that was one of the first canine stars on the silver screen.

Strudel • A dachshund named after the German pastry by its owner, movie actor James Dean (*Rebel Without a Cause*).

Stumpy • A big brown dog in Beatrix Potter's *The Tale of Little Pig Robinson* (1930).

Sue • A female Welsh corgi owned by Queen Elizabeth II when she was a youngster. See **Sugar**.

Sugar • A female Welsh corgi and daughter of **Sue**, owned by Queen Elizabeth II.
  • A Maltese owned by actress Elizabeth Taylor.
  • A Maltese owned by singer-actress-dancer Ann-Margret (*Bye Bye Birdie*).

• A dog owned by singer Della Reese, who normally has a preference for "spicy" names. See **Allspice, Cajun, Cinnamon, Nutmeg,** and **Spice.**

Sultan • An Irish bloodhound owned by English novelist Charles Dickens. An undisciplined dog, it eventually had to be shot.

• A Persian deerhound in writer Michael Gilbert's story "The Emergency Exit Affair."

Summa • A collie of popular singer Pat Boone ("Love Letters in the Sand").

Summerann Thumberlina • The smallest living dog, as of 1995, according to the *Guinness Book of World Records.* The Yorkshire terrier weighs only twenty ounces and is eight inches long.

Sumner • One of rock singer Axl Rose's dogs.

Sunnee • A Chow Chow of Hollywood cartoon feature producer Walt Disney.

Sunnybank • Writer Albert Payson Terhune had several collies with the Sunnybank prefix: Sunnybank Jean, Sunnybank Lad, and Sunnybank Sigurd.

Sunshine • A collie of actress Susan Strasberg (*Picnic*).

• A golden retriever of movie and television producer David Wolper (*Roots*).

Suzette • A toy poodle owned by pianist-entertainer Liberace.

Suzie • A dog of comedy duo George Burns and Gracie Allen.

• The white poodle that actor Cary Grant gave to his bride, Betsy Drake, as a wedding present.

• One of stage and screen actor Al Pacino's dogs.

Suzie Wong • A Chow Chow named after the lead character in Paul Osborn's play *The World of Suzie Wong* by its owner, Liberace, the flamboyant entertainer.

Swallow • A dog owned by poet William Wordsworth.

Sweetheart • One of three dogs mentioned in Shakespeare's play *King Lear* (Act III, Scene 6). Lear thinks that his dogs, as well as his daughters, are turning against him ("The little dogs, and all . . . see, they bark at me.") See **Blanche** and **Tray**.

Sweden • A mutt owned by television actress K Callan (Martha on *Lois and Clark*).

Sweetie • A Rottweiler owned by actress-writer Carrie Fisher (*Postcards from the Edge*).

Sweetlips • An unusual name of one of U.S. president George Washington's many dogs.

Swizzle • In Hugh Lofting's *Doctor Doolittle's Circus*, a dog that belonged to a clown.

T

Tabby • An unusual name for a *dog* but it was the name of Abraham Lincoln's son Tad Lincoln's dog.

Taca • A Siberian husky owned by U.S. president Ronald W. Reagan.

Tackhammer • The name of Woody Woodpecker's canine foe.

Tafferteffy • A Pembrokeshire corgi that King George VI had mated with his pet dog Jane when the previous candidate, Dookie, did not rise to the occasion. Two puppies were the result of the merger and were born on Christmas Day.

Talbot • In T.H. White's *The Sword in the Stone*, one of King Arthur's many dogs.
• One of the dogs in the "Nun's Priest's Tale" of Geoffrey Chaucer's *Canterbury Tales*. See **Colle** and **Gerland**.

Tandy • A dog owned by U.S. president Harry S Truman.

Tara • One of film star Charlton Heston's dogs.
• The basset hound of stage and screen actor Rex Harrison.
• One of *Dallas* actor Jack Scalia's Rottweilers. See **Nitro**.

Taro • An Akita given the death sentence after viciously attacking a ten-year-old girl in 1991. Governor Christine Todd Whitman spared the dog's life in 1994 by granting clemency.

Tarzan • The Airedale terrier of writer Edgar Rice Burroughs, obviously named after his literary creation.

Tasha • Singer Barbara Mandrell's Yorkshire terrier.

Taster • One of U.S. president George Washington's many dogs.

T-Bone • The Saint Bernard named after a steak by its owner, Lucius Beebe, rich eccentric and author (*The Trains We Rode*), who loved the good life.

Tatters • One of many dogs owned by television actor Earl Holliman (*Police Woman*).

Taxi • The Labrador retriever of political activist Tom Hayden, former husband of actress Jane Fonda.

Tchu-Tchu • A dog owned by German-born missionary physician Albert Schweitzer. See **Phylax**.

Teddy • Screen actor and writer Kirk Douglas's poodle.
 • A poodle owned by Swedish movie director Ingmar Bergman (*Through a Glass Darkly*).
 • One of movie great Charlie Chaplin's dogs.
 • The Great Dane featured in many of Mack Sennett's movie comedies.

Telek • A Scotty given to then General Dwight D. Eisenhower by his close friend Kay Summersby during World War II.

Teresa • A Yorkshire terrier of actress Julie Harris (*The Member of the Wedding*)

Terrible Tim
 • See **Tiny Tim**.

Terry • The real name of the cairn terrier who played Toto in the movie classic *The Wizard of Oz* (1939).

Tess • Comedienne Lily Tomlin's Norwich terrier.

Tessa • One of humorist James Thurber's dogs.

Thane • Another collie, son of **Explorer**, owned by writer Albert Payson Terhune.

Thenne • One of French actress Brigitte Bardot's dogs.

Theron • In Greek mythology, one of the many hounds of Actaeon, the hunter whom the goddess Artemis turned into a stag. Theron was the "beast" or "beast slayer," according to *Room's Classical Dictionary*.

Thomas à Becket • A Yorkshire terrier owned by actress Elizabeth Taylor and named after the sainted Archbishop of Canterbury, one of two-time husband Richard Burton's favorite roles.

Thor • Manhunter's dog in comic books. (Thor was the Scandinavian god of thunder.)

Throttler • A bulldog in Emily Brontë's novel *Wuthering Heights*, and son of **Skulker**.

Thunder • One of boxer Sugar Ray Leonard's black cocker spaniels.

Thunderbolt • The dog star of the 1961 cartoon feature movie *101 Dalmatians*.

Tida • Television talk-show host Phil Donahue's Maltese.

Tiffany • A dog owned by Motown singer Diana Ross.
 • A Bichon frisé of television producer Aaron Spelling
 • In the movie *Benji*, the poodle girlfriend of Benji.

Tige • The pet bulldog of Buster Brown in the R.F. Outcault's comic strip originally published in 1902. A shoe manufacturer later adopted the Buster Brown and Tige names to market, quite successfully, shoes for many years.

Tiger • Usually a name for a cat, it was the Lane family's dog in the television series *The Patty Duke Show*.
 • The shaggy dog owned by the Brady family in *The Brady Bunch*. See **Blood**.

• The name of Judith Campbell Exner's dog. Exner was rumored to be a mistress of U.S. president John F. Kennedy.

• The name of one of movie actress Doris Day's poodles, and one of David Cassidy's dogs.

• The telepathic dog in the 1975 movie *The Boy and His Dog*. The dog was a regular on television's *The Brady Bunch*.

Tigger • A Jack Russell terrier of England's Prince Charles.

Tillie • One of National Institute of Dog Training founder Matthew Margolis's German shepherds. The dog was named after his wife's Aunt Tillie.

Tim • An orphaned dog given to ballet dancer Mikhail Baryshnikov by a staff member of the American Ballet Theatre.

Timber Doodle • The name of a dog owned by novelist Charles Dickens. Some sources indicate that the dog was also called **Snittle Timbery** and **Tumber**.

Timmy • A poodle owned by Princess Grace (Kelly) of Monaco. Also see **Low Pressure**.

Timothy • A Dandie Dinmont terrier owned by writer Dorothy Parker.

Tina • One of two Yorkshire terriers owned by Hollywood producer Darryl F. Zanuck. See **Lisa**.

Tinkerbell • A poodle named after Peter Pan's companion by its owner, actress-producer Lucille Ball.

Tinker Toy • One of actress-producer Lucille Ball's fox terriers, named after the brand of children's construction toy.

Tiny • One of actress-singer Doris Day's many dogs.

• An Old English sheepdog of U.S. president Franklin D. Roosevelt.

Tiny Tim • One of Calvin Coolidge's many dogs, its name was later changed to **Terrible Tim** for obvious reasons.

Tip • Movie actress (*Rosemary's Baby*) Mia Farrow's dog.

Tipler • One of U.S. president George Washington's many hounds.

Tippy • A black and white dog owned by movie actress Marilyn Monroe. It was shot by a neighbor who did not like the dog's barking.

Tito • One of film horror star Bela Lugosi's German shepherds.

Tlapka • The toy poodle of Ivana Trump, ex-wife of real-estate man Donald Trump. Tlapka means "paw" in Czech, Ivana's native tongue. She named another poodle Tlapka II.

Toby • A puppet dog character in the Punch and Judy shows.

• A part spaniel in Arthur Conan Doyle's *The Sign of Four* (1890). It helped Sherlock Holmes solve some crimes.

• An English setter owned by *Of Mice and Men* author John Steinbeck.

• In T.H. White's *The Sword in the Stone*, one of King Arthur's many dogs.

• A dog owned by stage and screen actor Burgess Meredith (*Of Mice and Men*).

• A poodle owned by *Golden Girls* comedic actress Betty White.

Toby-Chien • A bulldog owned by French writer Colette. It was often mentioned in her writings and had a prominent role in *Dialogue of the Beasts* (*Dialogue des bêtes*).

Todd Potter • One of film actor Brad Pitt's dogs.

Tokey • One of the dachshunds in the 1966 Disney movie *The Ugly Dachshund*.

Toky • One of singer Pia Zadora's Akitas.

Tolstoy • A lead sled dog, along with **Granite**, that helped win the 1,158-mile dog sled race in Alaska in 1988. The team was led by Susan Butcher.

Tom Anderson • Russian Empress Catherine the Great's English whippet, also known as Sir Tom.

Tom Dooley • The dog featured in the Disney feature movie *Savage Sam*, a sequel to *Old Yeller*.

Tonka • A Great Dane owned by actress Meredith MacRae and husband, Greg Mullavey.

Tony • Composer George Gershwin's wirehaired terrier.
  • One of film actor Charlton Heston's dogs.
  • A Tibetan spaniel of television actress June Lockhart (*Lassie*).
  • A dog owned by silent-screen star Mary Pickford (*Polyanna*).
  • The standard poodle of television actress Marj Dusay (Monica Warner on *Facts of Life*).

Tooshie • One of pro basketball player Karl Malone's Labrador retrievers.

Tooti • One of several Great Danes owned by actress

Meredith MacRae and husband, Greg Mullavey. See **Shinka** and **Tonka**.

Topper • A cocker spaniel owned by television and movie actor Tom Selleck (*Three Men and a Baby*).

Toro • A Doberman pinscher owned by Charo, the widow of bandleader Xavier Cugat. *Toro* means "bull" in Spanish.

Toto • The name of Dorothy's dog, a Boston terrier, in L. Frank Baum's *The Wonderful Wizard of Oz* (1900), which became a classic movie in 1939 starring Judy Garland. The movie star Toto, a cairn terrier, was paid $125 a week for his performance.
 • A cairn terrier of television actor David Hasselhoff (*Baywatch*).
 • A dog owned by actor Paul Muni (*The Story of Louis Pasteur*).

Tough • The giant schnauzer of film actress Bo Derek.

Towser • A science-fiction dog in writer Clifford Simak's 1944 story "Desertion." On the planet Jupiter, the dog is able to think and speak.

Toy • A poodle owned by opera diva Maria Callas.
 • A fox terrier of comedic actress-producer Lucille Ball.

Tracie • A spaniel owned by poet Robert Herrick.

Trader • Skipper's dog in the television series *Jungle Jim*.

Tramp • The ardent admirer of Lady in the Walt Disney animated feature film *Lady and the Tramp* (1956).
 • The family dog on television's *My Three Sons*.

• Another family dog on television's *Room for One More.*

Tramp, Jr. • The dog in the 1953 movie *Room for One More.*

Tray • A dog in Thomas Campbell's poem "The Harper."
• One of three dogs mentioned in Shakespeare's play *King Lear* (Act III, Scene 6). Lear thinks that his dogs, as well as his daughters, are turning against him ("The little dogs, and all . . . see, they bark at me.") See **Blanche** and **Sweetheart.**

Tramp • The ardent admirer of Lady in the Walt Disney animated feature film *Lady and the Tramp* (1956).

Treacle • Dame Agatha Christie's Manchester terrier. (Treacle is British for molasses.)

Trevor • An Irish setter of U.S. president William Howard Taft.

Trip • A dog owned by author Harriet Beecher Stowe (*Uncle Tom's Cabin*).

Tripoli • In the 1942 film *Air Force*, the dog saved by the crew of the B-17 *Mary Ann*.

Trixie • One of actress-singer Doris Day's many dogs.

Trouble • A bloodhound owned by writer F. Scott Fitzgerald and his wife, Zelda.

Trowneer • In T.H. White's *The Sword in the Stone*, one of King Arthur's many dogs.

Truelove • One of U.S. president George Washington's dogs.

Trump • English painter William Hogarth's pet pug. They both appear in at least one of Hogarth's paintings.

Tsar • The dog of British actor Christopher Lee (*The Curse of Frankenstein*).

Tuck • One of *Rebel without a Cause* actor James Dean's dogs.

Tulip • Writer J.R. Ackerley's Alsatian, about whom he wrote in "My Dog Tulip."

Tumber • See **Timber Doodle.**

Tumblebrutus • Growltiger's "bosun" in T.S. Eliot's "Growltiger's Last Stand."

Tundra • The dog in the 1977–86 television series *Love Boat.*

Tuppinsky • A Wheaton cairn terrier of film actress Shelley Duvall (*The Shining*).

Turi • A poodle of England's Queen Victoria.

Turk • One of the dogs in the novel *Swiss Family Robinson.*

Twinky • A dog owned by child actor (now grown up) Corey Feldman.

Tzutsee • A Pekingese owned by author Beatrix Potter.

U

Ubu • Television producer-writer Gary David Goldberg's pet dog who doubles as his production company's logo (with a Frisbee in its mouth!), with the voice-over, "Sit, Ubu, Sit."

Ulli • A German shepherd owned by Matthew Margolis, founder and president of the National Institute of Dog Training in Monterey Park, California.

Underdog • A caped superhound that appeared on television in the 1960s. (Like **Snoopy**, Underdog appears in the annual Macy's Thanksgiving Day parade.)

Uranis • One of Actaeon's hounds, meaning "heavenly one."

Useless • The dog of Sundance, played by actor Earl Holliman, in the television series *Hotel de Paree*.

V

Valentine • A Labrador retriever of mail-order entrepreneur Roger Horchow.

Vanilla • The name of the dog on the classic radio show *Amos 'n' Andy*.

Varmint • One of actress-singer Doris Day's many dogs.

Vera • A Rottweiler owned by cartoon-comic book publisher Stan Lee.

Veto • The name of U.S. president James Garfield's dog. Ironically, Garfield never vetoed any bills in office, possibly because he served in office only 199 days.

Vicky • A French poodle owned by Julie Nixon, daughter of U.S. president Richard M. Nixon.

Victory • A golden retriever of U.S. president Ronald W. Reagan.

Vigi • A dog owned by King Olaf of Norway.

Virgil Thomson • Producer-actor John Houseman's dachshund, whom he named after his composer and music-critic friend Virgil Thomson.

Vivien Leigh • A poodle named after the British actress (*Gone with the Wind*) by actress Jaclyn Smith (*Charlie's Angels*).

Vlad the Impaler • Another one of media vampire Elvira's Rottweilers, named after the prince of Walachia in the mid-fifteenth century, the source of the Dracula legend.

Vulcan • One of U.S. president George Washington's many dogs, named after the Roman god of fire and metalworking.

W

Waffles • Diane Keaton's brown dachshund in Woody Allen's 1979 film *Manhattan*.

Wags • A dog featured in Bill Marriner's comic strip *Wags, the Dog That Adopted a Man*, which debuted in 1905 but lasted only a few years.

• Another Wags surfaced in Milton Caniff's comic strip *Dickie Dare*, the dog owned by Dickie Dare.

• Also the shortened name of Admiral Wags, the black cocker spaniel owned by Rear Admiral Frederick Sherman on the carrier *U.S.S. Lexington* at the Battle of the Coral Sea in May of 1942.

Waldo • The sheepdog featured in the 1970–71 television series *Nanny and the Professor*.

Wally • One of several golden retrievers owned by television actress Staci Keanan (*Going Places* and *My Two Dads*).
• One of singer-actor Bobby Sherman's dogs.

Wang • The Shih Tzu of Happy Rockefeller, widow of U.S. vice president Nelson Rockefeller.

Wat • The terrier of Princess Beatrice of England.

Wawe • The toy terrier of singer Merle Haggard.

Wazzle • A yellow Labrador retriever that won a 1994 Delta Society award for providing help to her owner who has multiple sclerosis and automobile accident injuries. The dog even answers the phone!

Weejie • An elkhound dog owned by U.S. president Herbert Hoover. Sometimes spelled Wegie.

Weenie • In Kay Thompson's Eloise stories, the dog who lives at the Plaza Hotel in New York City. It wears sunglasses and resembles a cat.

Weiner • A miniature dachshund of television actor David Hasselhoff.

Weldemann • A dachshund owned by Queen Victoria.

Wendel • A dog of actor Brian Keith (*Nevada Smith*).

Wessex • A wirehaired terrier owned by writer Thomas Hardy. Wessex was "quarrelsome" and "ill-behaved." See Moss.

Whip • The Labrador retriever of film and television producer Barry Diller.

Whiskers • The West Highland white terrier of pro golfer Tom Weiskopf.

Whiskey • The terrier of U.S. senator Daniel P. Moynihan, who has occasionally been known to sip a bit of whiskey.
  • A pug owned by screen actor George Brent (*Forty-second Street*).
  • The name of dogs owned by actor Don Galloway (*Ironsides*) and by English actress Ann Todd (*The Paradine Case*).

White Angel • A Lhasa apso owned by heiress Peggy Guggenheim.

White Fang • On *The Soupy Sales Show*, one of Soupy's canine puppets—big and mean! See **Black Tooth**.

White King • The dog of film actress Thelma Todd (*Monkey Business*).

White Shadow • The white German shepherd in *Mickey Mouse Club's Corky and White Shadow* series. It was played by Chinook, which appeared in another series about a mountie and his dog from 1949 to 1954. See **Chinook**.

White Tips • A dog owned by Caroline Kennedy, daughter of U.S. president John F. Kennedy.

Whitey • On the television series *Boston Blackie*, the name of Boston Blackie's black terrier.

Whoopee • A fox terrier of comedic actress-producer

Lucille Ball, possibly named after a cushion, a song, or a sexual act.

Wickle • A dog of actress Lucie Arnaz, daughter of comedic actress Lucille Ball.

Wild Willie • One of rock singer Axl Rose's dogs.

Wildfire • The canine protagonist of the 1955 film *It's a Dog's Life*. It won the Patsy Award that year for best performance by an animal.

William • A Sealyham terrier owned by actor Rex Harrison and his wife, Lilli Palmer.

Willie • General George Patton's white English bull terrier. In the 1970 movie *Patton*, the dog was played by **Abraxas Aaran**.
   • Television actress Priscilla Presley's Doberman pinscher.
   • The name of the Hansen family dog in the television series *Mama*.
   • A poodle owned by actress Betty White and her husband, game-show host Allen Ludden.

Wimper • A Southern-accented bloodhound in Hanna-Barbera television cartoons.

Windsor Bob • King George VI's Labrador retriever.

Winkie • A miniature poodle of film actress Claudette Colbert (*It Happened One Night*).

Winks • The bacon-loving dog of U.S. president Franklin D. Roosevelt. He cleaned off breakfast plates with relish.

Winnie • One of several wirehaired terriers owned by 1920s comedic movie actor Edmund Lowe (*Flagg and Quirt*).

Winston • In cartoons, Hector Heathcoat's dog.

Wolf • The name of President John F. Kennedy's Irish wolfhound.
 • Writer Dorothy Parker's Bedlington terrier.
 • Lady and Lad's son in Albert Payson Terhune's *Lad: A Dog*. The real-life Wolf was run over by a train trying to save another dog.
 • Sigmund Freud's first dog, an Alsatian that he acquired for daughter, Anna.
 • One of Heathcliff's "hairy monster" dogs in Emily Brontë's *Wuthering Heights*.
 • According to Washington Irving's tale, the dog who slept alongside Rip Van Winkle.

Wolfie • The Keeshond of U.S. representative Pat Schroeder.

Wolverton Ben • A Labrador retriever of English King George V.

Wolverton Jet • Another Labrador retriever owned by King George V of England.

Woodrow Wilson • Writer Dorothy Parker's Boston terrier.

Woody • A poodle owned by actress Robin Riker (Bobbi Turner on *Thunder Alley*).

Woofer • Winky Dink's Southern-accented bloodhound in the Hanna-Barbera television cartoon series *Winky Dink and You*. It wore a deerstalker cap like the one worn by cinema's Sherlock Holmes and its voice was that of ventriloquist Paul Winchell.

Wotan • One of film actor Charlton Heston's dogs, named after the chief Germanic god.

Wrinkles • A Shar-pei owned by Liberace—a great name for the unusually wrinkled breed.

• One of television actor-producer Michael Landon's dogs.

X

Xenophon • A dachshund, named after the ancient Greek historian, belonging to French prime minister (1968–69) Maurice Couve de Murville.

Xerxes • A Pekingese, named after the Persian king, owned by Queen Alexandra of England, who was an animal lover.

Y

Yang • A Chow Chow of Beatle drummer Ringo Starr. See Ying.

Yankee Doodle • A dog owned by movie actress-dancer Ginger Rogers (*Top Hat*).

Yang • A Chow Chow of Beatle drummer Ringo Starr. See Ying.

Yap • The dog of Tom Tulliver in George Eliot's novel *Mill on the Floss*.

Yeller • The name of the star of the 1957 movie *Old Yeller*. Also see Spike.

Yonex • One of Czech-born tennis great Martina Navratilova's dogs, named after a brand of tennis racket.

You Know • A dog owned by author and humorist Mark Twain. Also see **Don't Know** and **I Know**.

Youki • One of French actress Brigitte Bardot's dogs.

Yuki • A white mongrel discovered by Luci Baines Johnson, daughter of U.S. president Lyndon B. Johnson, at a Texas gas station.

Yukon • An Alaskan malamute owned by U.S. president Herbert Hoover.

Yukon King • The Alaskan husky dog of Sergeant Preston of the Northwest Mounted Police on the radio series *Challenge of the Yukon* and, later, on a television series *Sergeant Preston of the Yukon*. The husky, according to the story, was raised by a wolf named Three Toes.

Z

Za • An Alsatian sheepdog that served France in the canine corps during World War I.

Zack • A dog owned by television interviewer Barbara Walters.
• The toy poodle of television actress Jennie Garth (Kelly Taylor on *Beverly Hills 90210*).

Zandra • A Dalmatian owned by chef-restaurateur Wolfgang Puck.

Zar • Another German shepherd owned by German tennis pro Steffi Graf. See **Max**.

Zargon • A Great Dane of English singer-actress Olivia Newton-John.

Zeach • One of U.S. president George Washington's hounds.

Zelda • One of Paul Revere and the Raiders' lead singer Mark Lindsay's Doberman pinschers. See **Rusty** and **Scott**, as in the F. Scott Fitzgerald family.
• One of two dogs owned by film actress Margot Kidder (*Superman*).

Zero • A mutt that appeared in the comic strip *Little Annie Rooney*.
• A dog of Bee Gee singer Barry Gibb.

Zeus • The Rottweiler of Debbi Fields of Mrs. Fields's Cookies fame, named after the chief god of the ancient Greeks..

Zinfandel • A schnauzer belonging to Heloise (*Hints from Heloise*). It comes from the name of a dark grape used in California wine making.

Zip • Paul Bunyan's terrier, according to American folklore.

Zoë • A miniature Pomeranian of movie actress Shelley Duvall (*The Shining*).

Zona • One of many King Charles spaniels owned by Gladys, Duchess of Marlborough.

Zora • The Afghan hound of screen legend Gary Cooper (*High Noon*).

Zorro • A terrier owned by acting legends Douglas Fairbanks and Mary Pickford. Fairbanks had starred in and written the screenplay of the 1920 movie *The Mark of Zorro*. (*Zorro* means "fox" in Spanish.)

Zozo • The German shepherd of socialite Betsy Bloomingdale.

Zsa Zsa Gabor • A dog owned by television talk-show host Ricki Lake, obviously named after the Hungarian-born actress.

Zurcha • A Saluki hound owned by Vita Sackville-West and husband, Harold Nicolson.

Zuzu • A Chow Chow owned by author-trendsetter Martha Stewart.

TOP 100 MALE DOG NAMES

1. Max
2. Rocky
3. Lucky
4. Duke
5. King
6. Rusty
7. Prince
8. Buddy
9. Buster
10. Blackie
11. Charlie
12. Sam
13. Bandit
14. Benji
15. Champ
16. Spike
17. Brandy
18. Sparky
19. Shadow
20. Rex
21. Rambo
22. Gizmo
23. Teddy
24. Jake
25. Smokey
26. Bear
27. Bruno
28. Butch
29. Mickey
30. Toby
31. Snoopy
32. Tiger
33. Coco
34. Barney
35. Fluffy
36. Samson
37. Pepper
38. Spanky
39. Brownie
40. Casey
41. Sandy
42. Brutus
43. Skippy
44. Sammy
45. Dusty
46. Scruffy
47. Jack
48. Pepe
49. Cody
50. Blacky
51. Baron
52. Midnight
53. Spunky
54. Bobby
55. Beau
56. Oliver
57. Tyson
58. Leo
59. Dino
60. Baby
61. Murphy
62. Snowball
63. Randy
64. Willie
65. Fred
66. Apollo
67. Boomer
68. Junior
69. Chico
70. Chester
71. Fritz
72. Pete
73. Buttons
74. Corky
75. Maxwell
76. Oscar
77. Winston

78. Bo
79. Ricky
80. Ben
81. Petey
82. Spot
83. George
84. Mikey
85. Ralph
86. Zeus
87. Bullet
88. Joey
89. Muffin
90. Lobo
91. Simba
92. Peppy
93. Major
94. Harry
95. Alex
96. Patches
97. Bingo
98. Macho
99. Tojo
100. Pee Wee

Source: New York City Department
of Health, 1996.

TOP 100 FEMALE
DOG NAMES

1. Princess
2. Lady
3. Sandy
4. Sheba
5. Ginger
6. Brandy

7. Samantha
8. Daisy
9. Missy
10. Misty
11. Lucky
12. Muffin
13. Pepper
14. Sasha
15. Candy
16. Cindy
17. Coco
18. Tiffany
19. Cookie
20. Baby
21. Penny
22. Maggie
23. Pebbles
24. Fluffy
25. Lucy
26. Queenie
27. Molly
28. Dutchess
29. Shadow
30. Casey
31. Tasha
32. Bambi
33. Heidi
34. Precious
35. Tara
36. Cleo
37. Kelly
38. Honey
39. Roxy
40. Susie
41. Beauty
42. Gigi
43. Crystal
44. Sheena
45. Bonnie
46. Chelsea

47. Nikki
48. Trixie
49. Holly
50. Jessie
51. Tina
52. Buffy
53. Blackie
54. Amber
55. Mandy
56. Peaches
57. Ebony
58. Gypsy
59. Katie
60. Linda
61. Sophie
62. Maxime
63. Goldie
64. Midnight
65. Sugar
66. Taffy
67. Fifi
68. Sheeba
69. Lulu
70. Duchess
71. Angel
72. Chloe
73. Buttons
74. Annie
75. Rosie
76. Tootsie
77. Patches
78. Foxy
79. Minny
80. Mindy
81. Tiny
82. Suzie
83. Dolly
84. Cleopatra
85. Lassie
86. Ruby

87. Mimi
88. Natasha
89. April
90. Brandi
91. Cuddles
92. Nina
93. Ashley
94. Bandit
95. Shannon
96. Cocoa
97. Suzy
98. Sadie
99. Murphy
100. Cinnamon

Source: New York City Department of Health, 1996.

RANK OF "ROYAL" NAMES FOR DOGS IN THE U.S.

Rank	Name
1	Lady
2	King
3	Duke
5	Prince
8	Princess
17	Duchess
20	Queenie
21	Rex
103	Baron
191	Queen

TOP 10 CAT NAMES IN U.S. AND U.K.

Female
1. Samantha
2. Misty
3. Patches
4. Cali/Calico
5. Muffin
6. Angel/Angela
7. Ginger
8. Tiger/Tigger
9. Princess
10. Punkin/Pumpkin

Male
1. Tiger/Tigger
2. Smokey
3. Pepper
4. Max/Maxwell
5. Simon
6. Snoopy
7. Morris
8. Mickey
9. Rusty/Rusti
10. Boots/Bootsie

TOP 10 DOG NAMES IN U.S. AND U.K.

In U.S.
1. Lady
2. King
3. Duke
4. Peppy
5. Prince
6. Pepper
7. Snoopy
8. Princess
9. Heidi
10. Sam
10. Coco

In U.K.
Female/Male
1. Sheba/Ben
2. Sam(antha)/Max
3. Bess/Sam
4. Gemma/Pip
5. Rosie/Duke
6. Megan/Prince
7. Lucky/Captain
8. Sandy/Tyson
9. Bonnie/Butch
10. Cindy/Oscar

89 POSSIBLE NAMES FOR BORZOIS (RUSSIAN WOLFHOUNDS) OR EASTERN EURO-PEAN BREEDS

Alex
Alexei
Alexandre
Anastasia
Anatoli
Andrei
Anna
Anton
Belinsky
Boris
Borodin
Chekhov
Czar
Czarina
Dostoyevsky
Dmitri
Elena
Evgeni
Feodor
Feodora
Galina
Georgei
Gogol
Gorbachev
Gorby
Gregor
Grischa
Igor
Ilya
Irina
Ivan
Ivana
Jascha
Karamazov
Katerina
Katrina
Katrinka
Katya
Leonid
Lenin
Lev
Luba
Ludmilla
Maria
Mayakovsky
Mikhail
Mischa
Nabokov
Natasha
Nekrasov
Nikolai
Nikita
Nina
Oblomov
Olga
Onegin
Ostrovsky
Pasternak
Pavel
Peshkov
Piotr
Pushkin
Raskolnikov
Rasputin
Sascha
Sergei
Sigmunt
Sobaka
Sofia
Sonia
Sonya

Tamara
Tania
Tanya
Tasha
Tatiana
Tolstoy
Turgenev
Vanya
Varvara
Vassili
Vassilia
Vera
Vladimir
Yeltsin
Yuri
Zamyatin
Zara
Zhivago

60 POSSIBLE NAMES FOR ORIENTAL BREEDS

Am
Anna
Bang
Bong
Chan
Chang
Charlie
Charlie Chan
Cholly
Chong
Chop Suey

Chow Mein
Dolly
Folly
Fong
Foo Yung
Fuji
Gai Pan
Genghis Khan
Gong
Hachiko
Kamikaze
Kannika
Kato
Kenzan Go
King Kong
Kubla Khan
Leechee
Luke
Lu-Lu
Lunyu
Manchu
Mao
Ming
Moo Goo
Ping
Pong
Pittipoo
Sashimi
Sayonara
Shan
Sing
Solly
Sookie
Suki
Sushi
Suzie Wong
Tanneko
Tao
Ting
Tse Tse

Tsing Tao
Wang
Wing
Wong
Wong Man
Xerxes
Yang
Ying
Ying Yang

60 POSSIBLE NAMES FOR DACHSHUNDS, GERMAN SHEPHERDS, SCHNAUZERS, ETC.

Adolf
Bernhard
Brown
Dieter
Dietrich
Elsa
Emil
Ernst
Franz
Frida
Frieda
Friedrich
Fritz
Gerhard
Gertrud
Gottfried
Greta
Gretchen
Gretel
Gustav

Hans
Heidi
Heinrich
Heinz
Hermann
Hildegard
Horst
Hummel
Ilsa
Johann
Johanna
Katharina
Katrinka
Kleine
Konrad
Kurt
Lieb
Liebc
Liesel
Ludwig
Mach
Magda
Marlene
Marta
Max
Maximilian
Otto
Rudolf
Schatzi
Siegfried
Stefan
Trinka
Ulrich
Ursula
Ulli
Werner
Wilhelm
Wilhelmina
Wolf
Wolfgang

106 POSSIBLE NAMES FOR MEXICAN CHIHUAHUAS

Adela
Adelina
Adelita
Alfonso
Amarillo
Amigo
Amor
Amparo
Anaz
Andres
Angel
Anita
Antonio
Beatriz
Blanco
Carlos
Carlota
Carmen
Catalina
Chico
Chito
Chiquito
Concepción
Concha
Conchita
Consuelo
Cuervo
Diablo
Diego
Dolores
Domingo
Don Quixote
Dulce
Enrique
Esteban

Federico
Felipe
Feliz
Feo
Fernando
Francesca
Francisco
Frijol
Garcia
Gomez
Gonzalez
Gris
Hernando
Hombre
Hondo
Ignacio
Ines
Isabel
Jaime
Jimenez
José
José Cuervo
Joaquín
Juan
Juana
Juanita
Linda
Lopez
Luis
Luisa
Luna
Lupe
Lupita
Luz
Manuel
Manuela
Margarita
Maria
Marta
Martin

Mercedes
Miguel
Moreno
Muñeca
Nieves
Ofelia
Oso
Pablo
Paco
Pancho
Pancho Villa
Pedro
Pepe
Perro
Perrito
Pilar
Poco
Poquito
Ramón
Rita
Rodrigo
Rojo
Rosa
Rosario
Sancho
Teresa
Tigre
Toro
Vicente
Victor
Zapato

66 POSSIBLE NAMES FOR FRENCH POODLES, BICHON FRISÉS, ETC.

Alsace
André
Antoine
Armand
Beau
Bébé
Belle
Bijou
Bleu
Bleue
Bordeaux
Brigitte
Burgundy
Chablis
Chardonnay
Charles
Chien
Claude
Colette
De Gaulle
Denise
Étienne
François
Françoise
Geneviève
Georges
Georgette
Gigi
Gilbert
Henri
Henriette
Jacqueline
Jacques
Jean

Jean-Claude
Jean-Pierre
Jeanne
Jules
Louis
Louise
Lucien
Lucienne
Madame
Madeleine
Madamoiselle
Marcelle
Marie
Michel
Michèle
Monique
Monsieur
Nicole
Odette
Pierre
Philippe
Raoul
René
Renée
Simone
Solange
Souris
Suzanne
Toutou
Yves
Yvette
Yvonne

64 POSSIBLE NAMES FOR IRISH WOLFHOUNDS, SETTERS, ETC.

Brendan
Brian
Casey
Colleen
Danny
Danny Boy
Dennis
Doherty
Donlevy
Feeney
Fitzgerald
Fitzpatrick
Flaherty
Flanigan
Hackett
Harris
Kavanaugh
Kelly
Kennedy
Kerry
Kevin
Kildare
Limerick
Magillacuddy
Malone
Maureen
McAllister
McAvoy
McCabe
McCafferty
McCann
McCarthy
McCartney
McClintock
McCormick

McCoy
McCrory
McDonald
McDougall
McElroy
McFarland
McGee
McGinnis
McMurphy
Murphy
O'Brien
O'Casey
O'Connor
O'Doherty
O'Donnell
O'Dwyer
O'Flaherty
O'Harris
O'Herlihy
O'Keefe
O'Malley
O'Neill
O'Shaughnessy
O'Shea
O'Sullivan
Patrick
Sean
Shaughnessy
Sullivan

136 POSSIBLE NAMES FOR SCOTTISH TERRIERS, CAIRN <u>TERRIERS, ETC.</u>

Aberdeen
Anderson
Armstrong
Ben Nevis
Brodie
Bruce
Buchan
Buchanan
Caledonia
Cameron
Campbell
Chisholm
Clyde
Coburn
Cockburn
Colleen
Craig
Crawford
Cumming
Cummings
Cunningham
Davidson
Douglas
Drummond
Dumfries
Dunbar
Duncan
Dundee
Elgin
Elliot
Erskine
Ferguson
Fleming
Forbes

Forsyth	MacFarlane
Fraser	MacGillivray
Frasier	MacGregor
Frazer	MacInnes
Galbraith	MacIntosh
Galbreath	MacIntyre
Galloway	MacKay
Gordon	MacKenzie
Graham	MacKintosh
Gunn	MacLachlan
Hamilton	MacLaren
Hamish	MacLean
Hay	MacLellan
Hebrides	MacLeod
Henderson	MacMillan
Hunter	MacNab
Innes	McNaughton
Johnston	MacNeil
Johnstone	MacPherson
Keith	MacRae
Kelso	MacTavish
Kennedy	Malarkey
Kerr	Mathieson
Laddie	Maxwell
Lamont	McCloud
Lindsay	McDuff
Lassie	Menzies
Leslie	Mitchell
Livingstone	Montgomery
Logan	Morrison
MacAllister	Munro
MacArthur	Murray
MacAuley	Napier
MacCallum	Nessie
MacCulloch	Ogilvie
MacDonald	Ogilvy
MacDougald	Orkney
MacDougall	Paterson
MacDuff	Paisley
MacEwan	Peebles

Pringle
Ramsay
Robert the Bruce
Robertson
Rose
Ross
Russell
Scotch
Scott
Scottie
Scotty
Shaw
Sinclair
Stewart
Strachan
Stuart
Sutherland
Tweed
Toto
Wallace
Whisky
Wilson

49 POSSIBLE NAMES FOR ITALIAN BREEDS

Amore
Benito
Bianca
Bianco
Brando
Bruno
Cara
Caro
Carlo

Carmine
Caruso
Dante
Diavolo
Don Corleone
Donna
Enrico
Felice
Flavo
Giancarlo
Giapetto
Gigio
Gina
Gino
Giordano
Giovanni
Giuseppe
Graceffo
Grigio
Gucci
Lasagna
Linguini
Luciano
Luigi
Marcello
Mario
Mastroianni
Nero
Orso
Pavarotti
Piccolo
Pinocchio
Pucci
Signor
Signora
Signorina
Stefano
Topo
Tosca
Vito

54 ROYAL, POLITICAL, AND MILITARY NAMES

Royal, Political

Ambassador
Baron
Baroness
Count
Countess
Czar
Czarina
Duchess
Duke
Earl
Emperor
Empress
Her Highness
Highness
His Highness
Kaiser
King
Lady
Lord
Majesty
Pasha
Pharaoh
Premier
President
Prime Minister
Prince
Princess
Queen
Queenie
Rex
Senator
Shar
Sheik
Shogun
Squire

Tsar
Tsarina
Your Highness
Your Majesty

Military

Admiral
Captain
Colonel
Commander
Corporal
Five Star
General
Lieutenant
Major
Officer
PFC
Plebe
Private
Sarge
Sergeant

32 POSSIBLE NAMES FOR BLACK AND DARK CATS OR DOGS

Anthracite
Black
Black Bear
Blackberry
Black Hawk
Blackie
Black Jack
Blacky

Charcoal
Coal Dust
Crow
Cuervo
Dusky
Ebon
Ebony
Inkster
Inky
Jaguar
Jet
Mandingo
Midnight
Old Crow
Olive
Oliver
Othello
Raven
Sable
Schwartz
Schwartzy
Schwartzkopf
Sooty
Umbra

Blanche du Bois
Blanco
Blondie
Buckra
Chalky
Frostie
Frosty
Hail
Hail Storm
Igloo
Ivory
Jack Frost
Lily
Marble
Paleface
Pearl
Pearly
Pearly Mae
Pearly White
Silver
Sleet
Snow
Snowdrop
Snow Flake
Snow Man
Snow White
Snowy
Vanilla
White Bread
White Cloud
Whitey

37 POSSIBLE NAMES FOR WHITE AND BLONDE CATS OR DOGS

Alabaster
Argentine
Belo
Bianca
Blanca
Blanche

15 POSSIBLE NAMES FOR GRAY CATS OR DOGS

Ash
Ashley
Ashy
Cinder
Cindie
Cindy
Dustin
Dusty
Greystone
Grigio
Lord Greystone
Mousey
Mousy
Smokey
Smoky

27 POSSIBLE NAMES FOR BROWN CATS OR DOGS

Auburn
Brownie
Bruno
Buster Brown
Café
Caffe
Chestnut
Coco
CoCo
Cocoa
Cocoanut
Coffee

Henna
Hershey
Koko
Ko Ko
Kokomo
Mahogany
Morena
Moreno
Olive
Oliver
Rusty
Sienna
Tawny
Topaz
Walnut

23 POSSIBLE NAMES FOR A "REDHEAD"

Burgundy
Cardinal
Carmine
Cerise
Cherry
Claret
Crimson
Henna
Magenta
Pinkie
Pinky
Red
Redd
Rose
Rosé
Rosey
Rosie
Rosy

Rouge
Ruby
Scarlet
Sherry
Vermillion

❧

13 POSSIBLE NAMES FOR A YELLOW CAT OR DOG

Amber
Apricot
Butter
Buttercup
Canary
Champagne
Dandelion
Goldenrod
Goldy
Lemon
Lemonade
Saffron
Sunflower

❧

REPETITIOUS NAMES MAKE THE HEART GROW FONDER

Pet Name	(Owners)
Baba	(Clark Gable, Sally Struthers)
Bee Bee	(Tanya Roberts)
Bobo	(Doris Day, Bruce Lee)
Boo Boo	(Daryl Anderson)
Ching-Ching	(Shirley Temple)
Cho Cho	(Billy Dee Williams)
Choo-Choo	(King George VI)
Chou-Chou	(Judy Garland)
Co-Co	(Bob Hope)
Coco	(Fredric March)
Didi	(Kathryn Grayson)
Dum Dum	(Hanna-Barbera)
Fat-Fat	(Louise Nevelson)
Fifi	(Robert Wagner and Jill St. John)
Gee Gee	(Elizabeth Taylor)
Gigi	(Jane Goodall, Beverly Sills, Tennessee Williams)
Gogo	(Greer Garson)
Goo Goo	(Dom DeLuise)
Gris-Gris	(Charles de Gaulle)
Jo-Jo	(Liberace)
Kiki	(Kathryn

Grayson,
Sugar Ray
Leonard,
Orson Welles)

Lulu (Orson Bean,
Sugar Ray
Leonard,
Kristy
McNichol, Ed
Norton,
Françoise
Sagan, Queen
Victoria)

Lu-Lu (Marty Ingels,
Shirley Jones)

Mei Mei (Robert
Mondavi)

Mini-Mini (Colette)

Moumou (Émile Zola)

Nana (Serge
Gainsbourg)

Nini (Brigitte
Bardot)

Pepe (Robert
Wagner)

Tchu-Tchu (Albert
Schweitzer)

Toto (David
Hasselhoff)

Vic Vic (Ray
Bradbury)

Win Win (Ray
Bradbury)

ZoZo (Betsy
Bloomingdale)

Zsa Zsa (Eva Gabor)

Zizi (Theophile
Gautier)

ZuZu (Martha
Stewart)

NAMED AFTER THEATRICAL OR POLITICAL ROLES

Pet Name
(Owner and Pet's Breed)

Thomas à Becket
(Richard Burton's
Yorkshire terrier; Burton
played the role of Becket in
the movies)

Chrissy
(Suzanne Sommers' cat;
Sommers' role on *Three's
Company* was Chrissy)

Cleo
(Elizabeth Taylor's Siamese
cat, short for Cleopatra,
one of Taylor's major roles
in the movies)

Kirk
(William Shatner's
Doberman pinscher;
Shatner was Captain Kirk
on *Star Trek*)

Lance
(Robert Goulet's German
shepherd, short for Sir
Lancelot, Goulet's role in
the Broadway musical
Camelot)

Leader
(U.S. senator Robert Dole's
miniature schnauzer; Dole
was the Senate Republican
leader)

Matt
(James Arness's Bichon
frisé; Arness was Matt

Dillon on television's popular *Gunsmoke* series)

Max
(Don Adams's miniature poodle; Adams played Maxwell Smart on his television show *Get Smart*)

Miss Kitty
(James Arness's Bichon frisé; the major female role on *Gunsmoke*)

President
(Franklin D. Roosevelt's Great Dane; FDR was president of the U.S. longer than any other man)

Zorro
(Douglas Fairbanks's terrier; Fairbanks starred in the movie *The Mark of Zorro*)

❖

PAIRS OF NAMES: GOOD THINGS COME IN PAIRS

<u>Names</u> of <u>Pets</u>	<u>(Owner)</u>
Ashley and **Scarlet**	(Regis Philbin)
Bonnie and **Clyde**	(Tiffani-Amber Thiessen)
Byron and **Shelley**	(Sean Astin)
Chin and **Chilla**	(Paul Gallico)
Ethel and **Lucy**	(Ronnie Schell)
Kit and **Caboodle**	(Kenny Rogers)
Laddie and **Lassie**	(Lou Costello)
Laverne and **Shirley**	(Michael Landon)
Matt and **Miss Kitty**	(James Arness)
Joan Pawford and **Kittie Dearest**	(Sally Struthers)
Scotch and **Soda**	(Jane Wyman)
Scott and **Zelda**	(Mark Lindsay)
Mark Spitz and **Lickety Spitz**	(Dolly Parton)
Teeney and **Weeney**	(Martha Stewart)
Vivian and **Vance**	(Colleen Dewhurst)
Ying and **Yang**	(Ringo Starr)

NAMES IN GROUPS

<u>Group</u>	<u>Names</u> (Owners)
Cheeses—Brie, Camembert, Gouda, Muenster, and Velveeta	(Bill Beyers)

Cleansers—Ajax, (Nanette
Borax, Brillo, Fabray)
and Spic & Span

Drinks—Gin, (Richard
Martini, and Lockridge
Sherry and wife)

Gone with (Richard
the Wind— Simmons)
Ashley, Melanie,
Prissy, Rhett Butler,
and Scarlett

Knowledge— (Mark
Don't Know, Twain)
I Know, and
You Know

Leaders— (Florence
Bismarck, Nightingale)
Disraeli, and
Gladstone

Spices— (Della
Allspice, Cajun, Reese)
Cinnamon, Nutmeg,
Spice and Sugar

Wines— (Heloise)
Sauvignon and
Zinfandel

Wines— (Frank
Chardonnay and
and Chablis Kathie
Lee
Gifford

ALCOHOLIC BEVERAGES AS AN INSPIRATION FOR THE NAMING OF PETS

Bourbon
(a dog in Jack London's
Call of the Wild)

Brandy
(Don Adams's miniature
poodle)

Chablis
(Frank and Kathie Lee
Gifford's Bichon frisé)

Chardonnay
(Frank and Kathie Lee
Gifford's Bichon frisé)

Clicquot
(Joan Crawford's white
French poodle)

Gin
(Brigitte Bardot's dog)

Gin
(Richard and Frances
Lockridge's Siamese cat)

Heineken
(Doris Day's dog)

Martini
(Richard and Frances
Lockridge's Siamese cat)

Martini
(Cheryl Tiegs's wirehaired
fox terrier)

Pilsner
(Linda Blair's terrier)

Sauvignon
(Heloise's schnauzer)

Scotch and Soda
(Ronald Reagan and Jane

Wyman's Scottish terriers)
Sherry
(Richard and Frances
Lockridge's Siamese cat)
Whiskey
(George Brent's pug)
Whiskey
(Don Galloway's dog)
Whiskey
(Daniel Moynihan's terrier)
Whiskey
(Ann Todd's dog)
Zinfandel
(Heloise's schnauzer)

107 FAMOUS CAT LOVERS

(More Names to Give Your Cat?)

St. Agatha
Loni Anderson
Charles Baudelaire
Orson Bean
Jeremy Bentham
Bismarck
Amanda Black
Ray Bradbury
Anne Brontë
Charlotte Brontë
Emily Brontë
Samuel Butler
Lord Byron
Karel Capek
Roger Caras
Claudia Cardinale

Thomas Carlyle
Raymond Chandler
Chateaubriand
Lord Chesterfield
Sir Winston Churchill
Georges Clemenceau
Jean Cocteau
Colette
Confucius
Robin Cook
Calvin Coolidge
Countee Cullen
Sandy Dennis
Bo Derek
Benjamin Disraeli
Albert Einstein
T.S. Eliot
Nanette Fabray
Anatole France
Benjamin Franklin
Eva Gabor
Paul Gallico
Théophile Gautier
Gladstone
Edward Gorey
Francisco Goya
Pope Gregory the Great
Pope Gregory III
Peggy Guggenheim
Thomas Hardy
Ernest Hemingway
Victor Hugo
Henry James
Jean-Auguste-
    Dominique Ingres
Thomas Jefferson
Samuel Johnson
B. Kliban
Edward Lear
Robert E. Lee

Vladimir Lenin
Pope Leo XII
Abraham Lincoln
Sophia Loren
Louis XV of France
Martin Luther
Sir Compton Mackenzie
Anna Magnani
Stephane Mallarmé
Edouard Manet
Marie Antoinette
James Mason
Guy de Maupassant
Mohammed
Michel Eyquem
  Montaigne
Sir Philip Neri
Sir Isaac Newton
Florence Nightingale
Peter O'Toole
Louis Pasteur
General George S. Patton
St. Patrick
Jane Pauley
Petrarch
Pablo Picasso
Pope Pius VII
Edgar Allan Poe
Mme. Récamier
Rembrandt
Cardinal Richelieu
Tanya Roberts
Franklin D. Roosevelt
Teddy Roosevelt
Jean-Jacques Rousseau
May Sarton
Albert Schweitzer
George Bernard Shaw
Robert Southey
Mme. de Staël

Théophile-Alexandre
  Steinlen
Algernon Charles
  Swinburne
Elizabeth Taylor
James Taylor
Ellen Terry
Gary Trudeau
Mark Twain
Queen Victoria
Horace Walpole
H.G. Wells
Jessamyn West
Cardinal Wolsey
Émile Zola

14 FAMOUS CAT HATERS

(Names Not to Give Your Cat but Maybe Give Your Dog?)

Alexander the Great
Hilaire Belloc
James Boswell
Johannes Brahms
Julius Caesar
Pierre de Ronsard
Dwight D. Eisenhower
Genghis Khan
Henry III
Pope Innocent VIII
Benito Mussolini
Napoleon Bonaparte
Percy Bysshe Shelley
Noah Webster

56 FAMOUS DOG <u>LOVERS</u>

(More <u>Names</u> <u>to</u> <u>Give</u> Your <u>Dog</u>?)

King Arthur
Lucille Ball
Brigitte Bardot
Bob Barker
David Cassidy
Calvin Coolidge
A.J. Cronin
Doris Day
Bo Derek
Charles Dickens
Shannen Doherty
Edward VII of England
Corey Feldman
Mrs. Fields
Eva Gabor
Zsa Zsa Gabor
George V
George VI
Gladys, Duchess of
  Marlborough
Kathryn Grayson
Peggy Guggenheim
Warren G. Harding
Rex Harrison
David Hasselhoff
Charlton Heston
Earl Holliman
Lyndon B. Johnson
Michael Landon
Liberace
Greg Louganis
Demi Moore
Anaïs Nin
Dorothy Parker
Brad Pitt

Vincent Price
Ronald W. Reagan
Della Reese
Franklin D. Roosevelt
Theodore Roosevelt
Axl Rose
Maurice Sendak
William Shatner
Richard Simmons
Aaron Spelling
Elizabeth Taylor
Albert Payson Terhune
James Thurber
Rudolph Valentino
Queen Victoria
George Washington
Betty White
Tennessee Williams
Bruce Willis
Woodrow Wilson
Duke of Windsor
William Wordsworth

MAJOR CAT BREEDS OR TYPES AND THEIR CELEBRATED OWNERS

Abyssinian
Tomie de Paola
Gladys Taber
Liz Smith
Nancy Walker
Christopher Walken

Angora
Honoré de Balzac
Karel Capek
Théophile Gautier
Whitney Houston
William McKinley

Black (various breeds)
Roger Caras
Thomas Carlyle
John Spencer Churchill
Winston S. Churchill
Calvin Coolidge
Lou Costello
Elvira
Théophile Gautier
Deirdre Hall
Harry Hamlin
P.D. James
Andrew Lang
Gertrude Lawrence
Alicia Markova
Yoko Ono
Robert Southey
Elizabeth Taylor
Joan Van Ark
Betty White

Burmese
Valerie Bertinelli
Victoria Principal
Eddie Van Halen

Ginger
Edward Gorey

Himalayan
Loni Anderson
Morgan Fairchild
Donna Mills
Regis Philbin

Maine Coon
Roger Caras
Bo Derek
James Gunn

Manx
Bill Beyers
Gladys Taber

Ocicat
Tomie de Paola

Persian
Willie Aames
Loni Anderson
Matthew Arnold
Ed Asner
Catherine Bach
Mariah Carey
Raymond Chandler
Richard Crenna
Erasmus Darwin
Bo Derek
Erik Estrada
Morgan Fairchild

F. Scott Fitzgerald
Zelda Fitzgerald
Fannie Flagg
Joan Fontaine
Tony Geary
Peggy Guggenheim
Lisa Hartman
Whitney Houston
Marty Ingels
Shirley Jones
Marilyn Monroe
Clayton Moore
Aaron Neville
Florence Nightingale
Yoko Ono
Albert Payson Terhune
Jonathan Taylor Thomas
Mark Twain
Frankie Valli

James Gunn
Rutherford B. Hayes
Luci Baines Johnson
Michael Joseph
Gertrude Lawrence
Vivien Leigh
Frances Lockridge
Richard Lockridge
James Mason
Pamela Mason
Christopher Norris
Vincent Price
Miranda Richardson
Tanya Roberts
Shelley Smith
Cybill Shepherd
Gladys Taber
Elizabeth Taylor
Harold Wilson

Russian Blue
Edith Head

Siamese
Jack Albertson
Ed Asner
Tallulah Bankhead
Jamie Lyn Bauer
Richard Burton
Roger Caras
Amy Carter
Kim Cattrall
James Dean
Linda Evans
Roberta Flack
Errol Flynn
Gerald R. Ford
Eva Gabor
Paul Gallico
Greer Garson

Tabby
Roger Caras
John Spencer Churchill
Whitney Houston
Michael Joseph
Louise Nevelson
Horace Walpole

Tortoiseshell
Lafcadio Hearn
Michael Joseph
Edgar Allan Poe

MAJOR DOG BREEDS AND THEIR CELEBRATED OWNERS

Airedale terrier

Edgar Rice Burroughs
Richard Condon
Calvin Coolidge
A.J. Cronin
Olivia de Havilland
Tomie de Paola
Bo Derek
Stephen Dorff
Warren G. Harding
Paul Muni
Mary Robson
Ronnie Schell
James Thurber
John Wayne
Woodrow Wilson

Akita

Amanda Bearse
Helen Keller
Sean Lennon
Osmond Brothers
Byron Scott
Nicole Brown Simpson
Hal Williams
Pia Zadora

Alaskan malamute

Cheryl Ladd

Australian shepherd

Demi Moore
Bruce Willis
Flip Wilson

Basset hound

Harry Anderson
Dinglehoofer
Clint Eastwood
Rex Harrison
Bob Hope
Socrates Miller
Marilyn Monroe
Queen Alexandra
Cokie Roberts
Anson Williams

Beagle

Eva Gabor
Sara Gilbert
Charles James
Luci Baines Johnson
Lyndon B. Johnson
Barry Manilow
Roger Staubach

Bichon frisé

James Arness
Barbara Taylor Bradford
Mary Frann
John Gavin
Frank Gifford
Kathie Lee Gifford
Chick Hearn
Aaron Spelling
Tanya Tucker

Boston terrier

Warren G. Harding
Dorothy Parker
Yves St. Laurent

Boxer

Lauren Bacall
Humphrey Bogart

Dian Fossey
Steffi Graf
John Larroquette
David Niven
Dorothy Parker
Pablo Picasso
Sylveter Stallone

Britanny

Susan Dey

Bulldog

Colette
Calvin Coolidge
Frances Day
Olivia de Havilland
Edward VII of England
Linda Evangelista
Warren G. Harding
Prince Henry
Ice-T
Stan Lee
Beryl Markham
Nancy Mitford
Dorothy Parker
Ann Pavlova
Vincent Price
Wallis Warfield
 Simpson
Betty White
Tennessee Williams

Cairn terrier

Joy Adamson
A.J. Cronin
Shelley Duvall
Prince Edward
King Geroge V
J. Edgar Hoover
Bert Lahr

Mary Kate McGeehan
Liza Minnelli

Chesapeake Bay retriever

Theodore Roosevelt

Chihuahua

Xavier Cugat
Sylvia Fairbanks
Sugar Ray Leonard
Gertrude Stein

Chinese Shar-pei

Liberace
Robin Wright

Chow Chow

Bijan
Tisha Campbell
Calvin Coolidge
Walt Disney
Sigmund Freud
David Lloyd George
James Hampton
Liberace
Merle Oberon
Martha Stewart
Sally Struthers
Uma Thurman

Cockapoo

Dom DeLuise
Sandy Duncan
Gene Kelly
Jennifer Jason Leigh
Ronald W. Reagan

Cocker spaniel

June Allyson
Lauren Bacall

Brigitte Bardot
Humphrey Bogart
Elizabeth Barrett
   Browning
George Bush
Leslie Charleson
A.J. Cronin
Edward VII
Lesley Gore
Katharine Hepburn
Arte Johnson
John F. Kennedy
Sugar Ray Leonard
Liberace
Harold Lloyd
Fredric March
Garry Marshall
Richard M. Nixon
Vita Sackville-West
Lawrence Sanders
Tom Selleck
Fredrick Sherman
Kate Smith
Elizabeth Taylor
Harry S Truman
Brenda Vaccaro
Virginia Woolf

Collie

Pat Boone
Edgar Rice Burroughs
Calvin Coolidge
Doris Day
Bo Derek
Judy Garland
Mark Harmon
Tom Hayden
Herbert Hoover
John James
Lyndon B. Johnson

Michael Keaton
Walter Mondale
Marilyn Monroe
Paul Newman
Nicholas II
Jack Pickford
Beatrix Potter
Randolph Scott
Sir Walter Scott
Susan Strasberg
Albert Payson Terhune

Dachshund

Matthew Arnold
Claire Chennault
Charlie Chaplin
Couve De Murville
Marion Davies
Doris Day
James Dean
David Hasselhoff
Rita Hayworth
William Randolph
   Hearst
John Houseman
Dorothy Parker
Pablo Picasso
Vincent Price
Liz Smith
Adlai Stevenson
Liv Ullmann
Queen Victoria
E.B. White
Fay Wray

Dalmatian

Dick Clark
Michael J. Fox
Gina Gallego
Eugene O'Neill

Wolfgang Puck
Connie Selleca
Bobby Short
Richard Simmons
Adlai Stevenson
John Tesh

Doberman pinscher
Willie Aames
Bea Arthur
Mariah Carey
Charo
John F. Kennedy
Mark Lindsay
Bela Lugosi
Priscilla Presley
Tanya Roberts
William Shatner
Rudolph Valentino

English springer spaniel
Steve Allen
David Bates
George Bush
Jayne Meadows

German shepherd
Bea Arthur
Laurie Burton
Catherine Bach
Lucille Ball
Betsy Bloomingdale
Isak Dinesen
Yvonne De Carlo
Bo Derek
Shannen Doherty
Michael Douglas
Irene Dunne
Patricia Ellis
Joan Fontaine

Eva Gabor
Zsa Zsa Gabor
Devon Gummersall
Ron Goulart
Robert Goulet
Steffi Graf
Linda Gray
Rutherford B. Hayes
Charlton Heston
Herbert Hoover
John F. Kennedy
Carol Lawrence
Robert Ludlum
Bela Lugosi
Norman Mailer
Ken Norton
Donny Osmond
Matthew Margolis
Maureen McGovern
Jack Paar
Tyrone Power
Ronald W. Reagan
Gene Roddenberry
Princess Stephanie
Stefanie Powers
Maurice Sendak
Roy Rogers
Sydney Sheldon
Blair Underwood
Rudolph Valentino
Debra Winger

Golden retriever
Pamela Anderson
Lauren Bacall
Bill Blass
Shannen Doherty
Gerald R. Ford
Bob Goen
Deirdre Hall

Mariette Hartley
Bo Hopkins
Staci Keanan
John Larroquette
Joey Lawrence
Mary Tyler Moore
Bill Murray
Paul Newman
Arnold Palmer
Michael Paré
Dennis Quaid
Dan Reeves
Ronald W. Reagan
Robin Riker
Maurice Sendak
David Soul
James Stewart
Tiffani-Amber Thiessen
Jack Wagner
Betty White
Oprah Winfrey
David Wolper

Great Dane

Clara Bow
Sid Caesar
Mike Douglas
Wallace Ford
Bruce Lee
Ruta Lee
Greg Louganis
Meredith MacRae
Greg Mullavey
Unity Mitford
Olivia Newton-John
Valerie Perrine
Alexander Pope
Franklin D. Roosevelt

Labrador retriever

Karen Black
Bill Blass
Barbara Cartland
Martin Charnin
Gary Collins
Kevin Costner
Tom Cruise
Armand Deutsch
Barry Diller
Shannen Doherty
Duke of York
Earl of Mountbatten
Eddie Furlong
Deirdre Hall
Bill Harris
Tom Hayden
James Herriot
Bo Hopkins
Roger Horchow
King George V
King George VI
Vivien Leigh
Stephen Macht
Karl Malone
Barbara Mandrell
Mary Ann Mobley
Prince Charles
Princess Anne
Richard Pryor
Wolfgang Puck
Ronald Reagan
Paul Reiser
Diana Rigg
Arnold Schwarzenegger
Frank Sinatra
Rex Stout
Queen Victoria

Lhasa apso
Burt Bacharach
Richard Burton
Phyllis Diller
Eva Gabor
Peggy Guggenheim
Bob Hope
Michael Learned
Liberace
Bob Mackie
Carole Bayer Sager
Elizabeth Taylor
Jonathan Taylor Thomas

Maltese
Ann-Margret
Halle Berry
Phil Donahue
Bob Hope
Elvis Presley
Harriet Beecher Stowe
Henry David Thoreau

Mastiff
Kirstie Alley
Dirk Bogarde
Marlon Brando
Laraine Day
George Di Cenzo
Douglas Fairbanks
Rutherford B. Hayes
Sherman Hemsley
Elliott Roosevelt
George C. Scott

Pekingese
Queen Alexandra
Richard Burton
Dorothy Gish
Carole Lombard

Duke of Marlborough
Beatrix Potter
Alice Roosevelt
Elizabeth Taylor
Edith Wharton
Betty White

Poodle
Don Adams
Tammy Faye Bakker
Lucille Ball
Kay Ballard
Tallulah Bankhead
Ingmar Bergman
Erma Bombeck
Pat Boone
Omar Bradley
Carol Burnett
Red Buttons
Maria Callas
Winston S. Churchill
Claudette Colbert
Miriam Cooper
Joan Crawford
George Cukor
Sammy Davis, Jr.
Doris Day
Bo Derek
Joyce De Witt
Walt Disney
Kirk Douglas
Betsy Drake
Marj Dusay
Barbara Eden
Jane Fontaine
John Forsythe
Jenny Garth
Dr. Jane Goodall
Ruth Gordon
Cary Grant

Michael Gray
June Havoc
Helen Hayes
Katherine Hepburn
Patricia Highsmith
Marty Ingels
Shirley Jones
Grace Kelly
Karen Kelly
Georgette Klinger
Gypsy Rose Lee
John Lehmann
Vivien Leigh
Liberace
Allen Ludden
John Mitchell
Marilyn Monroe
Mary Tyler Moore
Anaïs Nin
Julie Nixon
Richard M. Nixon
Dorothy Parker
Eleanore Patterson
Minnie Pearl
Vincent Price
Debbie Reynolds
Don Rickles
Robin Riker
Elke Sommer
Aaron Spelling
Gertrude Stein
John Steinbeck
Alison Steele
Barbra Streisand
Jacqueline Susann
Patrick Swayze
Elizabeth Taylor
James Thurber
Ivana Trump
Janine Turner

Robert Vaughn
Albertina Walker
Barbara Walters
Betty White
Tennessee Williams

Pomeranian

Fran Drescher
Shelley Duvall
King Edward VII
David Hasselhoff
Walter Savage Landor
Constance Talmadge
Queen Victoria
Tammy Wynette

Pug

George Brent
Winston S. Churchill
William Hogarth
Stan Lee
Sally Jessy Raphael
Sylvia Sidney
James Thurber
Queen Victoria
Duke & Duchess of
  Windsor

Rottweiler

Sid Caesar
Leonardo Di Caprio
Shannen Doherty
Elvira
Mrs. Fields
Carrie Fisher
Brian Austin Green
John Larroquette
Tommy Lee
Craig T. Nelson
Jack Scalia

Carrie Snodgress
Malcolm-Jamal Warner

Saint Bernard
Lucius Beebe
Dick Clark
Charlton Heston
Karl Lewis Miller
Marge Schott
Betty White

Samoyed
Martin Charnin
Jimmy McNichol
Julie Parrish
Ann Sten
Patrick Wayne

Schnauzer
Bo Derek
Robert Dole
Errol Flynn
Heloise
Tommy Lasorda
Liberace
Bruce Lee
Sugar Ray Leonard
Bob Waterfield

Scottish terrier
Lionel Barrymore
Eva Braun
Humphrey Bogart
Bette Davis
Isak Dinesen
Elinor Donahue
Sheena Easton
Zsa Zsa Gabor
Herbert Hoover
Bert Lahr

Jean Muir
John Muir
Dorothy Parker
Ronald W. Reagan
Franklin D. Roosevelt
Theodore Roosevelt
James Thurber
Queen Victoria

Sheepdog
Bea Arthur (Belgian)
Tallulah Bankhead
    (English)
Linda Gray
Colette (Belgian)
Calvin Coolidge
    (Shetland)
Jimmy Cannon
James Monroe
Ronald Reagan
    (Belgian)
Jeanette MacDonald
    (English)
Rod McKuen
Franklin D. Roosevelt
    (English)
Gardner McKay
Beatrix Potter
Katharine Ross
    (English)
Brenda Vaccaro
    (Belgian)
Joan Van Ark
    (English)
Natalie Wood
Tennessee Williams
    (Belgian)

Shih Tzu
Wallis Annenberg

Marisa Berenson
Zachary Ty Bryan
Susan Clark
Zsa Zsa Gabor
David Hasselhoff
Marty Ingels
Shirley Jones
Alex Karras
Jerry Lewis
Happy Rockefeller
Elizabeth Taylor
Michael York

Siberian husky
Sean Astin
Sid Caesar
King Edward VII
Kate Jackson
Ronald W. Reagan
Eddie Velez

Weimaraner
Dean Cain
Dick Clark
Dwight D. Eisenhower

Welsh corgi
Dirk Bogarde
Prince Charles
Queen Elizabeth II
King George VI
David Lloyd George
Beverly Sills

West Highland white terrier
Bo Derek
Joan Fontaine
Cornelia Guest
Alfred Hitchcock
Henry Kravis

Liberace
Katie Wagner
Tom Weiskopf

Wolfhound
Princess Alexandra
  (Russian)
Jane Ardmore
  (Russian)
Theda Bara (Russian)
Bo Derek (Russian)
Herbert Hoover (Irish)
John F. Kennedy (Irish)
Ruta Lee (Russian)
Princess Mary (Irish)
John Tyler (Italian)
Rudolph Valentino
  (Irish)
Mai Zetterling (Irish)

Yorkshire terrier
Tammy Faye Bakker
Richard Basehart
Richard Burton
Johnny Carson
Eva Gabor
John Gardner
George Hamilton
Julie Harris
Alex Haley
Audrey Hepburn
Carol Lawrence
Barbara Mandrell
Maureen McGovern
Demi Moore
Tricia Nixon
Joan Rivers
Marcia Rodd
Monica Seles
Marina Sirtis

Elizabeth Taylor
Arthur Treacher
Bruce Willis
Darryl F. Zanuck

THE FAMOUS FELINES OF T.S. ELIOT

(from T. S. Eliot's *Old Possum's Book of Practical Cats* or other writings of Eliot)

Admetus
Alonzo
Asparagus
Augustus
Bill Bailey
Bombalurina
Bustopher Jones
Carbucketty
Cassandra
Coricopat
Demeter
Electra
Etcetera
George
Griddlebone
Grizabella
Growltiger
Grumbuskin
James
Jennyanydots
Jerrylorum
Jonathan
Macavity
Mr. Mistoffelees
Morgan
Mungojerrie
Munkustrap
Old Deuteronomy
Peter
Plato
Pouncival
Quaxo
Rumpleteazer
Great Rumpus Cat
Rum Tum Tugger
Sillabub
Skimbleshanks
Tantomile
Tumblebrutus
Victor/Victoria

ABOUT THE AUTHOR

Ed Lucaire, a longtime animal lover and celebrity watcher, is coauthor of *Joan Embery's Amazing Animal Facts* and author of *Fascinating Facts about Felines*.

He is also the author of seven other books, including *The Celebrity Almanac*, *Celebrity Setbacks*, and *Phobophobia*. His articles, reviews, and excerpts have appeared in *New York* magazine, *Spy*, *The Wall Street Journal*, *The New York Times*, *Reader's Digest*, *Daily News*, *Games* magazine, and others. He is a graduate of Amherst College.

Through the years, he and his family have owned cats and dogs with names such as Lucy, Inky, Wolfgang, Teddy, Schatzie, Alex, Max, Slats, and Smokey.